The Practical Decision Maker

Second Edition

Introduction

Setting the Direction

So much time spent and so little accomplished. This is the headshaking feeling of frustration with which most of us approach modern decision making (DM). In this resource-scarce, decentralized, diversified, turbulent world of management, we seldom feel the excitement and joy of deciding and implementing. Rather, we decide and duck. Occasionally, on the little issues, we receive only a little negative feedback and are relieved that the decision worked. This recurrent frustration with the process and results of DM is sapping the capacity for leaders to lead. They feel unsure and doubtful about their decisions about the future and, as a result, invite second-guessing and disregard.

It is not that leaders do not want to decide. Rather, they do not know how. First of all, they lack a knowledge base about the fundamentals of decision-making steps and crucial elements of problem solving. Second, they do not have confidence that their decision will be correct. In this rapidly changing world about them, they look to make a perfect choice when there is no such choice to be made. They seek to optimize when it is no longer possible. Third, they do not go about DM in a manner that inspires confidence from their followers or colleagues. They are often vague and inept in structuring their decision-making process. Great DM takes practice. This practice requires a certain level of comfort with discomfort. For all these, and other reasons, DM can be frustrating.

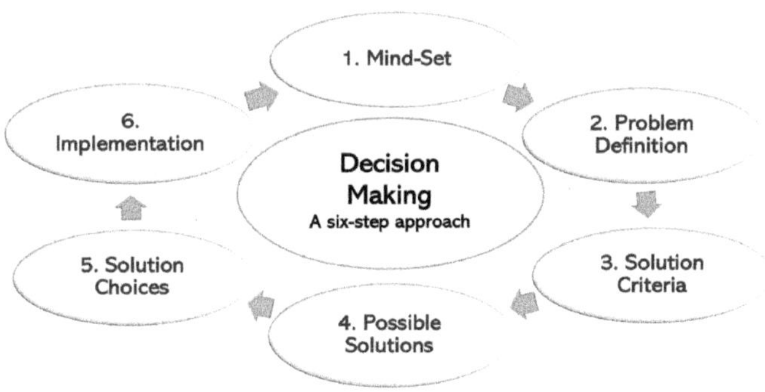

Figure I.0. Decision Making: A Six-Step Approach.
Author created (updated from 1st edition)

It is to this purpose that we write this book. In fact, we wish to argue that DM is as easy as 1-2-3:

1. DM must be menu driven. Rather than making the DM process complex, it is important to make it user friendly and simple. We propose that DM can be described as a series of six core steps, to which may be added elements that describe particular intents or conditions. It is for the leader to answer eight simple questions to determine the entire decision-making process. We provide the menu; you choose.
2. It depends. How you decide depends on what you want to accomplish. Is it DM for planning? Priority setting? Is this an issue that addresses organizational toxicity? Are there long-term and short-term consequences? All these are "it depends" questions. You need to be strategic and know what you want to accomplish with your decision-making process. When you ask, "how should I decide?," we respond, "it depends." You choose the answers to the eight questions and then adapt your process accordingly.
3. You need structuring devices. The term *structuring device* may be an unfamiliar concept for you. In theoretical terms, a structuring device is a normative tool that provides a set of rules and allows users to approach choice behavior in a cognitive manner (P. Hill, 1986; Hill et al., 1979; Thompson, 2017; Vroom & Jago, 1988; Vroom & Yetton, 2010). In other words, it is a technique for how people come to a decision. We would describe a

structuring device more simply. It is a technique for ordering how people decide about things. When I was a child learning how to spell, my teacher taught me the structuring phrase "*i* before *e* except after *c*." Later, I learned mnemonic devices to remember key issues or information, and I learned how to structure critical information into tables and charts. When I became principal of a multi-track year-round school, the color-coded Action Plans were invaluable since everything had to be done twice! Developing mind maps assist in writing School Plans for Student Achievement and have ensured that all elements are represented. Similarly, without the dreaded Gantt chart, I daresay none of us would have completed our dissertations in a timely manner.

Structuring devices are seemingly simple, understandable tools that order our way of thinking and moving to decisions. When you choose the right device for the right situations, you can save a great deal of time. I worked with an international board of a major service organization that had to set priorities across nineteen possible program areas. All were wonderful projects, and the board felt the task was impossible. By using a precedence chart, we got a decision in ninety minutes. They already knew what had to be done, but they needed a device to order their thought process and move them forward. Which structuring devices you use is determined by the conditions in your organization and decision-making setting.

FORMAT OF THE BOOK

It is with these three considerations in mind that we have written this handbook. Chapter 1 describes key issues in DM and problem solving. It lays out what has to be done and why. Chapter 2 then follows with a description of the six core steps in DM and how each operates. Chapter 3 is the "it depends" chapter. It describes eight questions you must answer to adopt the decision-making process in order to meet your intents and conditions. The conditions that are identified by your answers will demonstrate additional elements that need to be added to the core model. When you have finished these chapters, you will have determined your decision-making process. You will have completed your decision-making menu.

Chapters 4, 5, and 6 provide a new menu—a catalog of fifty-three structuring devices that you may use at various points in the decision-making process. These chapters describe 1) each device, 2) what it is used for, 3) how it operates, and 4) any cautions or variations of use, including technology applications. These chapters constitute the bulk of the book and should be read once for understanding and then used later as a reference section as decision-making needs arise. Chapter 7 provides four case illustrations using the decision-making process. In chapters 8 and 9, we offer some tips to those facilitating the decision-making process and identify some potholes that are inherent in using structuring devices.

We wish you joy in the chapters ahead.

Contents

The Practical Decision Maker

A Handbook for Decision Making and Problem Solving

Second Edition

Thomas R. Harvey, Sharon M. Corkrum, Shari L. Fox,
David C. Gustafson, and Deanna K. Keuilian

ROWMAN & LITTLEFIELD
Lanham • Boulder • New York • London

Published by Rowman & Littlefield
An imprint of The Rowman & Littlefield Publishing Group, Inc.
4501 Forbes Boulevard, Suite 200, Lanham, Maryland 20706
www.rowman.com

86-90 Paul Street, London EC2A 4NE, United Kingdom

British Library Cataloguing in Publication Information Available

Library of Congress Cataloging-in-Publication Data Available

ISBN 9781475863185 | ISBN 9781475863192 (epub)

Preface

This is a book about decision making. When we first began talking about revising this book, never in our wildest dreams could we have imagined the decisions leaders would be faced with at this moment in time. Leaders have always had to make challenging decisions—what direction to move their company, whether to keep an employee or let them go, whether to share bad news with their board of directors, and a plethora of other challenges. Never in modern times have they been faced with the decision-making challenges COVID-19 has provided. Making good decisions in these challenging times has been no small feat. These types of decisions have involved change, uncertainty, anxiety, stress, and the unfavorable reactions of others. When we think of what makes someone a great leader, decisiveness is one characteristic that comes to mind. Why, then, is it so difficult for some leaders to make decisions? For some, it is the uncertainty, and this uncertainty creates discomfort and, in some cases, paralysis through analysis. These efforts often prove futile and waste valuable time in the face of uncertainty.

With the onset of the pandemic, expectations of leaders to create change is far greater; the consequences for failure are far more severe. Leaders today are called on to create consensus out of *discensus*, to build a common movement toward the future. These leaders need help. They need strategies that address their real, practical needs in a complex world. It is to this end that we have written this book. Our hope is that it provides skills and insights for those who have the courage to lead.

We have not done this without help, however. We want to thank the students at the University of La Verne who test-drove our ideas, and we want to thank our families who have supported and loved us throughout the years as we have tried out ideas on them and who have been honest cauldrons for our notions.

"I" STATEMENT

We sometimes use stories that one of us has personally experienced. In these cases, we use the first person "I." "I" may mean Tom, Deanna, Dave, Sharon, or Shari. We have not attempted to differentiate. "I" may mean any one of us.

FINAL NOTE

The five of us have either taught or studied at the University of La Verne in the last forty or so years. During this time, La Verne has been one of the best kept secrets in academia. For us it has been a wondrous place of intellect, challenge, and collegial support. It is a place where the study of management and leadership has been provocative and advanced. Our greatest thanks go to a university that has survived more than a century by doing the simple things well. We hope this book does it some humble honor.

Chapter One

Decision Making Defined

Making decisions and leadership have a symbiotic relationship. If there were no choices to be made by anyone anytime, there would be no need for a leader. Accordingly, it is the role of leadership to make tough decisions and to set the context within which others decide. Great leaders understand the profound impact that making decisions can have on their organization. The way in which leaders approach decision making (DM) can be as important as the decision itself. As the world has become more complex and fraught with difficult choices, the need for strong, visionary leadership has increased and, hence, the need for more skilled decision makers.

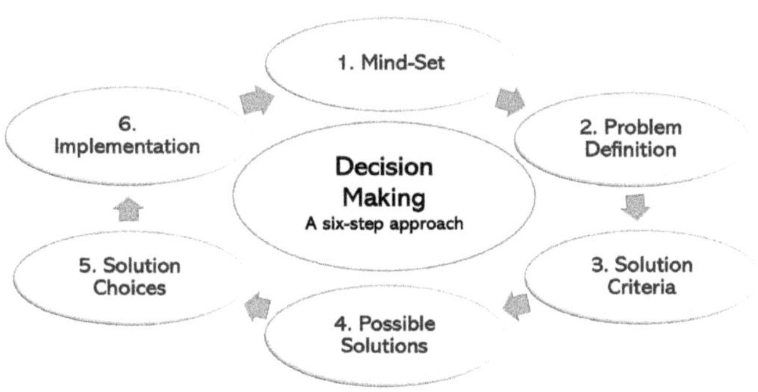

Figure 1.0. Decision Making: A Six-Step Approach.
Author created (updated from 1st edition)

DECISION MAKING DEFINED

DM is the act of choosing and implementing a solution to an identified problem or situation. Simon (2012) expands on this definition by suggesting there are four features to the generic process of decision making:

1. Identifying the problem
2. Searching for alternatives
3. Choosing a course of action
4. Evaluating past choices

Cohen, March, and Olsen (1972) have a slightly different rendition of the elements of DM:

1. Participants and their various agendas
2. Problems to be solved
3. Solutions to be selected and implemented
4. Decision opportunities
5. Timing

Klein, Orasanu, Calderwood, and Zsambok (1993) identify the four key features of DM:

1. Dynamic and continually changing conditions
2. Real-time reactions to these changes
3. Ill-defined goals and ill-structured tasks
4. Knowledgeable people

Other theorists would add different layers of abstraction. For us, we want to return to the most basic and clearest of definitions. DM is the act of choosing and implementing a solution to an identifiable problem or situation.

DECISION MAKING AND PROBLEM SOLVING

You may be asking yourself, "How is decision making different from problem solving?" Throughout the years, we have sought to make the distinction between these two conceptual areas. From our experiences as an elected city official, a superintendent of schools, higher education professors, a school district administrator, and a high school principal, one indelible impression remains: There is no fundamental difference between DM and problem solving, other than nomenclature. The essential steps for each are the same. The need to manage each is the same. The fundamental result of each is the same. As Gertrude Stein would say, "a rose is a rose is a rose." So rather than creating arcane academic distinctions, we have surrendered to the reality that DM and problem solving are not different. Throughout this book, we will use the terms interchangeably. The decision-making process pertains to all decision situations, whether individual or group. We encourage you to understand the essence of DM and problem solving.

DM is the act of choosing and implementing a solution to an identifiable problem or situation.

Implication of Definition

DM is an action; it is something one does. It is choosing from among an array of options, A, B, or C. It requires leaders who are willing to be held accountable and who, despite all the ambiguities and confusions, are willing to say, "let's go with 'N.'" Peters and Waterman (2006) talk about great leaders having a bias for action and having the will to act. Action is easy when time is slow and information is limited; however, we do not live in such a time. Allow us to illustrate this reality:

If you take man's existence on this earth, at least to the degree we know it, and divide it into lifetimes according to actuarial tables, we have had 800 lifetimes on this earth. Of these 800 lifetimes, 650 have been spent in caves. It has only been in the last 70 lifetimes that we have any experience with the written word; the last 6 lifetimes we have the printed word; the last 4 lifetimes we could tell accurate time; the last 2 lifetimes we have had the electrical motor. Most everything you have experienced in the last week, month, or year has not been a function of previous lifetimes but the most recent lifetime (see table 1.1).

Table 1.1. Change in Technology.
Author created (1st edition)

800 Lifetimes	
650 in Caves	
Last 70:	writing
Last 6:	printed word
Last 4:	tell accurate time
Last 2:	electrical motor

Consider technology. From the Sumerian invention of the plow around 3500 BCE to advancements in metallurgy by the Hittite and Shang around 1500 BCE, each of these early technologies slowly, but surely, set a foundation for future invention. Similarly, the invention of the slide rule in 1622 eventually paved a new path to an explosion of innovative technologies during the Industrial Revolution (1760–1840)—a time in which the photograph, the telegraph, and the typewriter emerged. Fast forward to 1944 with IBM's unveiling of the massive electromechanical computer known as the Harvard Mark 1 to IBM's groundbreaking debut of the personal computer in 1981. From the iPhone in 2007 to today, sleek, wearable technologies allow users to not only stay connected with others but also monitor their personal finances, health, and overall wellness.

Then there is the example of speed. In 3000 BCE, the camel was first domesticated near modern-day Somalia. This provided humankind a means of accelerated and extended travel as the camel could go eight miles per hour. A thousand years later, we had the spoke-wheeled chariot. Over short distances, the chariot could go as fast as twenty miles per hour. In 1784 CE, we had the Royal English mail coach; it could go ten miles per hour. By 1825, the steam locomotive had reached a speed of twelve miles per hour. In nearly six thousand years, we did not fundamentally change our capacity for speed; however, just fifty-five years later the steam locomotive could go one hundred miles per hour, and the capacity for speed grew rapidly from there. Today, civilian access to spaceflight is quickly becoming a reality.

Technology and speed are not a function of past lifetimes but the most recent one or two lifetimes. A variety of other examples could be used, but they all point to the same reality—most of history has experienced stability with explosions of growth. In the last two lifetimes, the speed of change has so accelerated that it's formed into a concept known as the J curve (see figure 1.1).

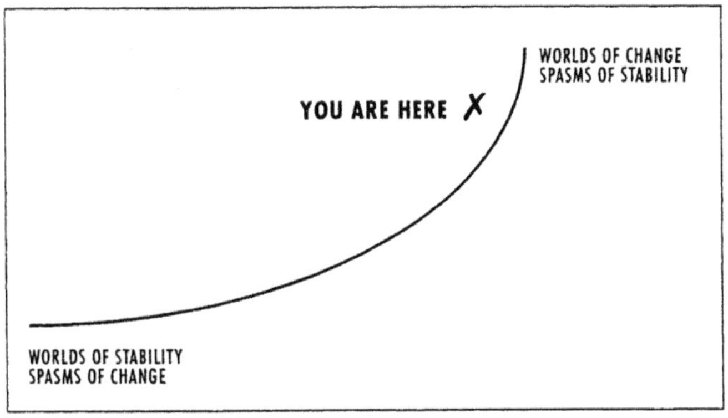

Figure 1.1. J Curve. ***Author created (1st edition)***

Simply put, the J curve is a trend line that illustrates how stable times, when presented in an intervention (or invention), can lead to dramatic growth. We are now the first generation to fully live and work beyond the J curve, a world filled with steadiness followed by increasingly rapid change. In our current world, information expands exponentially thanks to news media, social media, and the internet.

Because we live in a world beyond the J curve, a world of accelerating change, and as such, there is a tendency to delay action. We look for the perfect decision, which classic theorists called *decision optimization*. We look to examine all the alternatives with all the information and then choose the best alternative. In a stable environment, it is indeed possible to know all the alternatives and have all the information; however, in the turbulent world beyond the J curve, whenever we think we have all the alternatives, a new one pops up.

When we think we have all the information, new information emerges. If we wait for maximization in such a fast-changing world, we may never act. When we wait for more information or for more alternatives, we can actually experience paralysis by analysis. Simon (2012) describes the need to replace the term *optimization* with *satisficing*. In satisficing, one picks an alternative based on a thorough display of alternatives and information but never on a complete display. Ultimately, one must act in the face of an ever-changing reality. There are no perfect choices but only sound processes performed in a complex time and setting. A retired superintendent, who continues to mentor up-and-coming administrators, once said, "You can only make the best decision with the information you have at that moment."

Decision Making Is an Act of Choosing

Choice is the defining element of DM. That choice is complicated by three characteristics: uncertainty, ambiguity, and conflict (Nutt, 1989). Let's take the first of these characteristics, uncertainty. When we are certain about the consequences of alternatives, the choice becomes easier. "If we do A, then B will follow"—this is a peaceful place to be as the outcome is very predictable. If we change it a little and say, "If we do A, then B will likely follow," then the known consequence becomes not as comfortable. If we take it a little further and say, "If we do A, then B might follow, but C, D, and E might also happen," discomfort begins to set in. Finally, if we say, "If we do A, then who knows what happens," leaders become paralyzed by the lack of consequence. Uncertainty makes decision choice significantly more difficult.

Likewise, ambiguity complicates choice. When my spouse asks me what food I want for dinner and I say, "Italian and not too far from here," choice is simplified. On the other hand, if I reply, "Anything will do, I guess, but I had Mexican food for lunch," the ambiguity about my preference complicates the decision choice. When I know that my needs or the needs of the decision are set, then the choice is greatly facilitated.

The third condition that complicates choice is conflict. When my needs or wants are incompatible with others, the choice of alternatives becomes more complicated. In the face of conflict, we may need to seek other positions or alternatives that can meet multiple sets of needs. Too often, we allow conflict to harden positions and limit our exploration of alternatives. Conflict can bring emotion and adversarial partisanship into DM.

In making decision choices, if we had 1) certainty of consequences, 2) clearly articulated needs, and 3) no conflict over needs or alternatives, then the choice process would be simple. In fact, we would not need leadership because the choice could already be determined. The reality is that uncertainty, ambiguity, and conflict do exist and do confuse DM. It is the role of the efficient choice maker to generate and examine adequate information and reduce these three confounding characteristics to ensure a quality decision. One consequence of these characteristics is the tendency in a world beyond the J curve to make temporary solutions, ones with shorter time durations. As decisions become more complex, the permanence of solutions lessens. This is not a sign of decision inadequacy but simply the realities of DM in such a fast-paced world (Tosi, Mero, & Rizzo, 2000). In this case, we make a series of incremental decisions.

Decision Making Involves Implementation

It is not enough to make a decision; one must also follow through on implementation. When you ask employees what frustrates them most about DM, they immediately point to the failure of implementation. Think about strategic planning. How many organizations do you know that have elaborate strategic plans, but nothing ever happens? Plans are memorialized on a framed poster and hang in a conference room or, even worse, sit on a bookshelf collecting dust. These types of organizations plan for future actions; they just don't follow through on them.

The other pitfall of implementation is creating of "doables" (Weeks, 1994). Too often implementing strategies are simply not doable because they are either too vague or unattainable. It is important in DM to create action plans that specify concrete actions that stand a good chance of success. This is referred to as the "theory of small wins" (Harvey, 1995). You cannot have good DM without realistic, doable implementation.

Decision Making Involves Identifiable Problems or Situations

DM is not an abstract exercise; it is a concrete process that requires detail and specifics. One of the clear failures of problem solving is problem definition. Too often decision makers only deal with symptoms instead of real problems. The keystone here is providing sufficient and sound data to identify real problems. Impressions, prejudgment, guesswork, and assumptions are insufficient to true problem identification. This is not to say that qualitative data are inappropriate but, instead, to insist that the gathering of data should be rigorous and thorough.

Information and People

As we explore the definition of the term *decision making*, there are two words that undergird everything: *information* and *people*. In an increasingly complex, J-curve world, information serves a vital role:

- It clarifies uncertainty, ambiguity, and conflict.
- It informs and energizes implementation.
- It defines true problems.
- It confounds action.

Whether good or bad, the world of DM continues to change at an increasingly rapid pace—and it is not slowing down anytime soon. The sheer amount of available information can be especially overwhelming. Even with the seemingly endless amount of information at our fingertips, it can often be ambiguous or incomplete. Rarely is information neatly packaged for leaders. More often than not, information is disjointed and appears only as a bunch of factoids, numbers, ideas, or images. Processing this information and giving direction can be unnerving, but it is necessary.

In addition to information, people who are involved in decisions can make the process decidedly more complex. With a range of opinions, personal agendas, perspectives, and collective experiences, making sense of information and working with people to reach a decision can seem like a daunting task. It takes leaders equipped with better skills and better tools to succeed.

Now more than ever, leaders of today's organizations must be aware of the contributions that diverse working populations can bring to an organization. Those voices that once sat silently must be heard while decisions are being considered. Leading a group with diverse opinions and experiences can seem overwhelming, but in today's modern world, it is a necessary skill that all leaders need to refine. Though beyond the scope of this book, there are many great resources emerging from research on the concept of inclusive practices, managing one's blind spots, recognizing bias, and understanding the impact of privilege and power. Today's leaders are strongly encouraged to read, listen, and reflect on their own personal practice. With a deeper awareness of oneself, an understanding of DM, and a quicker field of different structuring devices, you will be well equipped to be a good decision maker in a world beyond the J curve.

Decision-Making Models

The literature is replete with various decision-making models and problem-solving approaches. There are political models, economic models, game theory, bureaucratic models, rational models, linear models, quality models, and the like (Murray, 1986). The trouble for most of us is that these models do not seem to help much. Too often, they are simply abstract battles over nomenclature, or differences about what is viable information, or academic turf wars. Existing decision models are not meant for leaders—they are meant for theorists. This conclusion may not make us particularly popular with our academic colleagues, but the reality is that leaders need help immediately in making decisions—there is just not the time to dive into elegant abstractions. It is for these leaders who sense this need that we write this book. It is a book that serves to bridge the arcane distinctions and bring order and simplicity to the complexity of deciding.

Who Decides?

One prominent element of the research on DM is "who decides?" There are some decisions that are appropriately the province of individuals. They require expertise and simple rationality. Other decisions require majority rule and formal decision processes. While yet others require long-term commitment and, hence, need to be decided by consensus—the widespread, conscious commitment to a solution choice and the willingness to make it work.

In their seminal work, Thompson and Tudor (1959) suggest a way to view who decides. They pose the question as a two-by-two matrix controlled by two variables: 1) consequences of alternatives and (2) preference about desirable outcomes.

In cell 1, consequences are known, and there is no conflict over preferences. The decision is almost a non-decision. Rational models and computers can decide. In cell 2, consequences are unknown but agreement is high; here majority rule can work and multiple insights are needed. In cell 3, consequences are known but agreement is low (see table 1.2).

Table 1.2. Structure of Organizational Decisions.
Author created (1st edition)

Consequences of Alternatives	*Preferences about Known Desirable Outcomes*		
		Agreement	*Disagreement*
	Known	1. Computation	3. Consensus or compromise
	Unknown	2. Judgment of group	4. Inspiration

The problem, hence, becomes one of gaining commitment. Here, consensus is needed or sabotage will ensue the decision choice. Compromise acts as a backup process to consensus. In cell 4 is inspiration. Consequences are unknown and agreement is low. This is a poor decision setting and calls on the leader to decide and inspire others to follow. There is much danger in cell 4 because information is so low and insights/needs are not shared. In fact, Nutt and Wilson (2010) agree that the further one moves away from cell 1 decision settings the tougher decisions are and the more decision makers need to a) collect more information, b) garner greater participation, and c) use greater caution and care.

Jones and Bearley (1994) provide yet another way to look at who decides. They classify decisions in four approaches: consultation, command, consensus, and convenience.

Consultation means talking with individuals and/or the entire work group and then making the decision yourself. While this approach may often take the leader a little more time, the benefits of this approach include being able to gather information to make a high-quality decision and maintaining efficiency in the decision-making process. Only people who have relevant information participate, and you make the decision on your own. It is crucial in this method to make the rules clear. They give information, not advice, and you make the decision.

Command means making the decision yourself, without prior discussions with subordinates. This method is quick and requires minimal time from the leader. It capitalizes on the manager being informed, and the responsibility for the decision is clear.

Consensus means getting the group together and working toward substantial agreement. Unanimity, of course, is not often achieved, so the rule is to reach a level of agreement without serious disagreement. Assets of this approach are the following: 1) it generates high acceptance of the decision, 2) it produces problem solutions and plans, and 3) it increases teamwork and a sense of community. Consensus can make people feel valued when they have been given the opportunity to be consulted.

Convenience means making the decision in whatever manner seems to be the easiest. That may be through delegation, asking for volunteers, or appointing someone to make the decision. In other words, you ensure that no one makes a federal case over how the decision is made. Convenience methods are good for relatively unimportant decisions, such as where to place the new microwave in the staff lounge. This approach avoids time-consuming participation and can often be seen as a reward by the person(s) selected to make decisions.

The level of participation depends on the kind of decision to be made. Choosing the wrong method for a decision setting makes either inefficiency and wasted time or poor quality in decision choice.

Accordion Process

Another consideration in choosing participants for a decision process is the problem of representation. It is common to form a task force of representatives of various constituency (e.g., two administrators, two teachers, two classified staff, two parents, and two community members). Those not included, however, often feel slighted and uninvolved. To rectify this potential problem, we propose the use of the Accordion Process device. It is called "accordion" because of an in-and-out process. The process goes as follows: 1) the decision team meets and works through the early steps of the decision; 2) the team then disperses to discuss ideas with the broader mass of constituents; 3) team members then recommend, discuss results of considerations, and proceed to next steps; 4) as the decision-making progresses, team members then go out again and consult with a broad base of constituents; 5) the team reconvenes and discusses constituents' concerns and moves to tentative decision choice; and 6) once again, team members consult with a broad mass of constituents. This process can go on as long as necessary or useful. The point is that a lot of constituents can be involved without being part of the decision team. This expands investment and ownership in the decision outcome. A pictorial version of this process can be seen in figure 1.2.

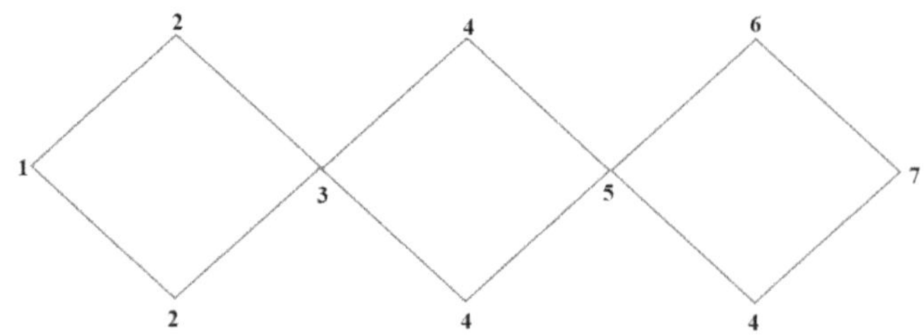

Figure 1.2. Accordion Process. ***Author created (1st edition)***

The Accordion Process is appropriate whenever the decision process involves a team of representatives, individuals who act as stand-ins for wider constituent groups.

A FINAL NOTE

Much could be written about decision theory, but we wish to leave you with simply the essence of what you need to know. Once again, we argue that DM is as easy as 1-2-3.

1. DM is the act of choosing and implementing a solution to an identifiable problem or situation. Today's leaders face two primary challenges in DM: information and people. Making sense of information and understanding people can be overwhelming and frustrating, but it is essential.
2. Leading teams of people with diverse backgrounds, experiences, and opinions can make an organization stronger. It can also present some challenges when trying to reach a decision. When making decisions, leaders must be rooted in an awareness of oneself and others, have an understanding of DM, and be able to respond with an appropriate structuring device(s).
3. Including people in the decision-making process increases the quality and efficiency of decisions. Knowing when and how to involve people in the decision-making process is a major element of successful DM.

With these elements of theory in mind, you are now ready to explore the essential steps in DM and problem solving.

Chapter Two

Core Steps in Decision Making

Leaders spend much of their time making decisions or facilitating others in solving problems. At the end of a week, some leaders feel drained by having to react to problem after problem each day. They often see these problems as barriers and feel that they get in the way of attaining their goals. Others, however, seem to draw energy from dealing with decisions and are invigorated by working on problems. They seem to have a systematic approach that allows them to effectively involve stakeholders in resolving problems and making decisions that work in their organization.

This chapter presents an approach to decision making (DM) and problem solving that, when applied consistently, can enroll those affected by a problem in a systematic resolution. Although problems will never go away, the use of this approach can remove the feeling of endlessness—one problem after another.

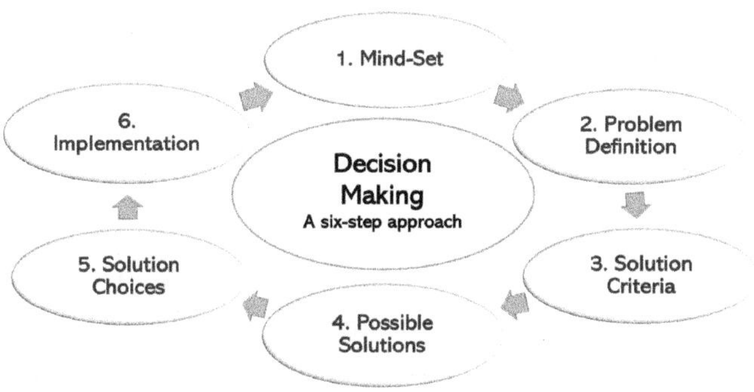

Figure 2.0. Decision Making: A Six-Step Approach.
Author created (updated from 1st edition)

DECISION MAKING/PROBLEM SOLVING

Throughout the years, we have reviewed hundreds of problem-solving/decision-making approaches—each with its subtle nuances or its focus on a certain type of problem or decision. Many organizations will tell you that they have their own unique problem-solving model, and some consulting organizations have made fortunes selling their models. All of these renditions of problem solving share several common elements. These elements, although they may appear across several steps, include the following:

- Identifying the problem
- Developing possible solutions
- Choosing a course of action

Problem identification, although it may vary depending on the type of problem or decision, ultimately comes down to a clear statement of the problem to be solved or the decision to be made. It may include causes, conditions, goals, or other components, but its intent is to give decision makers a clear understanding of what, specifically, they are to decide or resolve.

All approaches have some step, or set of steps, that generate a variety of possible solutions. These are often called alternatives. We tend to avoid the term *alternative* because, to some language purists, the term means the choice between two mutually exclusive possibilities. Also, it implies that you must choose one of the alternatives. Since we do not live in a dichotomous, right-or-wrong world but, rather, in one of a variety of shades, the best resolutions are often combinations of parts of several possibilities. In reality, to build the consensus necessary for effective long-term implementation of a solution, we must develop solutions that go beyond any one alternative and build on several possibilities.

At some point, you must act. You must make the decision. All problem-solving models include a step, or steps, intended to make a choice of a solution to the problem. This may include what sounds like a sophisticated methodology to come to a decision, or it may be simply "choose an alternative."

Many problem-solving models stop at this point. They tend to imply that once the decision is made the game is over; however, most of us know that implementing a decision is often more difficult than deciding what to do. Implementation can generate resistance in an organization and often creates more problems. Therefore, we believe that any approach to DM and problem solving must address implementation. This is the make-or-break point where the organization either grows from the situation or is thrown back into more chaos and more problems.

The decision-making/problem-solving approach presented in this book is a synthesis from our study and work with many models. The basic six-step approach is presented in this chapter. The next chapter presents the adaptation of the basic model to different types of problem situations.

THE SIX-STEP APPROACH

The six-step approach to DM and problem solving depicted herein includes, in order of use, mind-set, problem definition, solution criteria, possible solutions, solution choices, and implementation. Although we have a tendency to want to jump immediately to developing solutions, the real payoff to lasting decisions is in spending time in the first four steps: setting the mind-set, defining and understanding the problem or decision situation, determining what it should look like when you are done (solution criteria), and exploring possible solutions. Pareto's 80/20 rule tells us that 80 percent of the time and payoff in reaching good solutions is in the first four steps.

Mind-Set

We are used to diving into a problem or decision so that we can get on with the next decision. In reality, the most satisfying resolutions to problems occur when all involved feel good about the outcome and when the participants can say that they found the process energizing. To do this consistently, you must start the process by focusing on the approach to the problem and the environment or context in which it exists. In the mindset step, you do not deal with the problem or decision itself. Rather, you concern yourself with how you think about the decision/problem and with the context of the problem or decision situation (see figure 2.1).

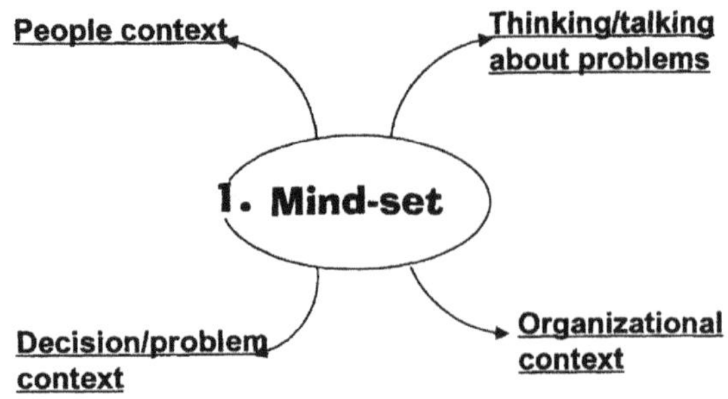

Figure 2.1. Mind-Set. *Author created (1st edition)*

Thinking about Problems

To some, the word *problem* has a negative connotation. It implies that something bad has happened and we are now faced with yet another tough decision to make. Successful leaders, entrepreneurs, and inventors view problems as opportunities for action. These creative minds do not run from problems—they welcome problems. Their mind-set stresses the positive. Confucius once said, "If you are positive, you'll see opportunities instead of obstacles." Having a positive mind-set has medical evidence to support it. Recent brain research has consistently demonstrated that when we think about a situation negatively our bodies generate chemicals that shut down the part of the brain that relates to creativity. This change in brain chemistry can also cause anxiety and anger and have a negative impact on the immune system.

How, then, can you think about decisions or problems in a way that supports creative problem solving? Start by changing your language and the language of the problem-solving team to that which supports creativity. Entrepreneurs often call problems opportunities or challenges. This simple shift in vernacular allows the mind to see problems as an opportunity to innovate. Einstein once famously remarked, "In the middle of difficulty lies opportunity." John Jones coined the term "situation that needs attention," or SiTNA. Reframing a problem as a "situation that needs attention" removes the negative focus and allows you to deal effectively with what you are concerned about, then engage in action planning (Jones &

Bearley, 2002). This approach refocuses your attention on the action necessary to achieve an outcome rather than taking Eeyore's approach, "If I close my eyes, will this mess disappear?"

When we view problems as issues, it can lead to distrust—people taking sides or looking at a problem as an "us versus them" issue—and foster a win-lose mentality. In DM and problem solving, you want to move away from either-or-thinking and toward a win-win consensus approach where everyone supports the outcome.

Organizational Context

All organizations face problems that require DM. Context refers to the circumstances and setting of the decision or problem. This may be a formal organization like a company, school, hospital, or church; it may be a group that is brought together such as a family, committee, club, or association; or it may be simply within the context of an individual. In any case, it is important to understand the context and what is currently happening within that context.

One concern in DM is the sense of direction of the organization. If there is a clear sense of vision and mission, then there is a foundation on which to make decisions. If the organization is in chaos, then the environment is reactive and decision makers are on their own to solve problems.

Another concern is the state of the organizational environment and culture. An environment that is trusting and supportive is more conducive to group problem solving than one that is toxic. Since teams within an organization tend to reflect the internal conditions of the organization, these are brought into the decision-making process. Often, you must deal with concerns about conflict, openness, trust, and communication as part of establishing a mind-set that is supportive of problem solving.

Decision-Making Context

Most decisions and problems have parameters. These parameters are things such as resources (people, money, facilities, and time) and legal requirements. These givens must be clear up front so as not to waste the energy of the problem-solving team.

It is important to deal with these concerns directly. Since good problem solving requires open and honest communication, these givens are things brought to the table. The decision-making team should be told specifically what the givens are including any time or resource constraints. If there are legal or governmental regulations, these must be known at the beginning. These then become part of the solution criteria for later consideration.

One useful way to set the decision-making context is to establish a charge, charter, or mission for the group that contains the givens. This should be clear and specific and should contain all necessary data to guide the process.

People Context

Most decisions involve more than one person either directly or indirectly. These stakeholders make up the people context of any decision or problem. They determine who should be involved. Their prior experience with each other will influence the process and must be clear up front. If they become directly involved on the decision-making team, they bring with them needs and constraints that must be addressed. If the members of the team represent a number of different stakeholder groups, you must set up processes to keep these groups informed and to solicit their input. Use the Accordion Process device, as presented in chapter 1, to use these groups in the DM.

Just like any neighborhood, school, or workplace, a group can vary in both their similarities and differences. Demographic changes, coupled with advances in technology, have brought a wide variety of people together. These exciting changes make it more likely that we will be interacting in more and more heterogeneous groups (Allen, 2011). In fact, wise leaders purposely create diverse teams with the goal being to leverage that diversity to create an inclusive environment. They look to create teams that represent a mixture of age, gender, and cultural backgrounds. In addition, they look to create teams that have a high level of cognitive diversity, mixing people together who have different thinking styles, habits, and perspectives. When these team characteristics exist, research has shown that DM is accelerated, collaboration is reinforced, and thinking outside the box becomes the norm

(Sakpal, 2019). Additionally, when group members have time to get to know one another and learn about their differences, better DM is made due to different perspectives (Thomas, 1999). Larson (2017) asserts that inclusive teams make better decisions 87 percent of the time, that they make decisions two times faster with one-half the number of meetings, and deliver 60 percent better results.

Leaders know all too well that people bring with them their individual attitudes, biases, skills, and experiences. It is important to understand how these factors can both support and hinder the decision-making process. Some of these attitudes may limit what they see as possible in deciding. "They won't let us do that" can stifle the process from the beginning. You have to be both positive and realistic. You have to deal directly with some of the more obvious constraints such as time demands and scheduling. In addition, it may be useful to establish mechanisms to manage other potential people problems such as conflict and communication in the beginning. This way, when they occur, there is an established agreement on how to manage the situation. When you are proactive in managing the limitations, you create a positive sense of potential.

The mind-set step sets the tone for DM and problem solving (see figure 2.1). Do it well, and the remainder of the process will be more profitable and enjoyable. You may be surprised at the synergy that can be generated when this step is done well and when people agree to focus their collective energy on resolving a problem.

Problem Definition

John Maxwell said, "Positive thinking must be followed by positive doing." Once the mind-set is established, you are ready to address the decision or the SiTNA. The outcome of the problem-definition step is a clear, specific statement of the problem with which everyone involved agrees. In other words, there is a clear understanding of the problem by all stakeholders. Again, there is a tendency to want to move quickly through this step so that you can move forward toward a solution. Avoid this urge as it leads to having to do it over again or to solving symptoms rather than the real problem.

To some extent, how you approach this step depends on the type of problem you are trying to solve. For purposes of this discussion, we will focus on four categories of problems (see figure 2.2).

1. *Shortfall*: In this type of a problem, something is out of whack or is not up to your expectations. In most cases, you are "reacting" to a situation. Some type of corrective action is required to reestablish some previous condition.
2. *Opportunity*: Here something has occurred that gives you or the organization an opportunity for growth and change if only you can take advantage of the situation.
3. *Improvement*: In this case, you simply want to improve what you are doing or to reengineer the way the organization is doing something. There is no immediate need—rather, simply a desire to improve.
4. *New venture*: In this case, you want to move into the unknown. This is a new venture for the organization—one that it has never encountered before.

Each of these four categories requires different information and strategies to define the problem. If there is a *shortfall*, then the SiTNA relates to meeting predefined expectations. To define this type of problem, you need to determine the gap or discrepancy between the desired condition (expectation) and what is actually occurring (existing condition). This gap (or discrepancy), then, is the problem. In situations involving quality, you need to look at why the gap occurs. These causes then determine what you must fix to eliminate the gap. One error that is often made is to focus on a symptom rather than pushing to discover the real problem.

Opportunity usually occurs because of some change in either the internal or external environment, for example, changes in the law, new resource availability, and new niches to market. Here, there is no gap or discrepancy because there are no prior standards or expectations. In this case, you must clearly define the opportunity. The problem, then, usually becomes whether or how to take advantage of the opportunity once it is clearly defined.

Improvement is a proactive approach to getting better and staying ahead. As a world-class athlete trains for an upcoming competition, so must the leader continually examine ways to improve the organization to maintain peak performance levels. This will require some definition and quantification of the new, improved level. Rather than trying to "tinker" with their current way of doing business (the status quo), organizations focus on outcomes.

A *new venture* takes us to places we have never been before. Visionary leaders such as Elon Musk embrace bold new ventures. Whether it be semiautonomous navigation in Tesla automobiles or the successful launch of the reusable SpaceX Falcon rockets, Musk is never one to back down from an opportunity. With each successful Falcon launch, Musk's vision of humans colonizing Mars by 2024 becomes one step closer to reality (SpaceX, 2021).

With this type of problem, you must start with a clear and compelling vision. Part of problem definition, then, is to set clear, incremental goals that move you toward the vision. In today's rapidly changing world, organizations must constantly do this type of problem solving in order to remain viable for the future. This proactive approach focuses on where we want to be at some point in the future. It involves inventing and planning to achieve some new and exciting future.

In all four categories of problems, the outcome of the problem-definition step is to arrive at a concise definition of the problem with which all stakeholders agree. Depending on the type of problem or decision, this may take the form of a question, a statement of a discrepancy, a new desired state, or a set of goals. Do not move on to the next step until you have consensus on the problem, and it is clearly stated in precise terms.

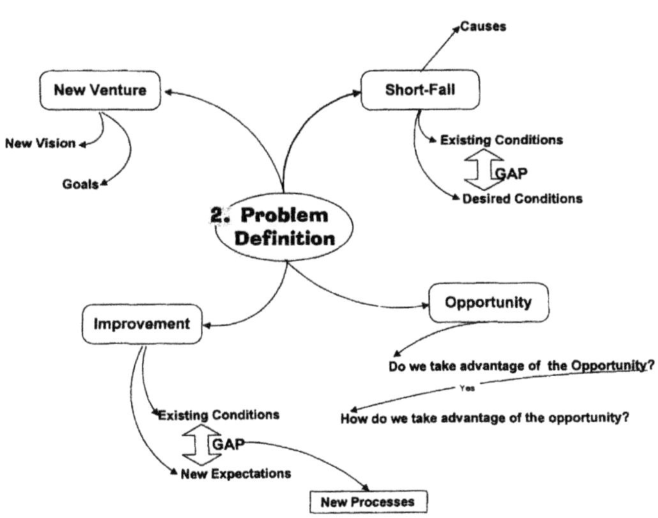

Figure 2.2. Problem Definition. ***Author created (1st edition)***

Solution Criteria

Once the problem is defined, people are ready to tell you *their* solution. If you move directly to generating solutions, it often becomes a battle of *my* versus *your* solution. To avoid this and to make the solution process more analytic rather than emotional, you need to focus your attention on the solution criteria (see figure 2.3). This defines the parameters of what you want any solution to look like, and how you will know that you have a good solution. This provides a vehicle to evaluate and combine possible solutions and helps you prevent the "hardening-of-positions."

Depending on the type of problem, these criteria may be general and may be written in the form of outcomes. For problems that are more quantifiable the criteria will have specific, quantified indicants. Certain types of decisions demand quantification. These include most problems related to quality and other decisions where measurement is possible or is traditionally used. The following list offers a few examples of solution criteria for different decision situations.

- Purchase a car that has a one-hundred-thousand-mile warranty, has a five-star safety rating, and gets at least thirty miles to the gallon
- Hire an administrative assistant who speaks Spanish, has G Suite certification, and has been commended for excellent customer service
- Reduce student absences by 15 percent next semester

Needs versus Wants

When you begin this process, people usually come up with a list of criteria and then decide that any solution must meet all of them. This may be the optimal solution but may not be practical. You must work at this until you have a satisfying set of criteria that is within both the resources of the organization and the context of the decision. Therefore, you often divide the criteria into at least two categories: needs and wants. A need is a criterion that the solution *must* meet. Without it, the solution simply does not resolve the problem. A want is a criterion that the solution *should* meet, but it is not required. Sometimes it is useful to have a third category, *nice-toos*. These *nice-toos* are things that, if the solution could meet, it would be nice or serendipitous, but they have little impact on choosing the final solution. They are often used as tiebreakers or as guides to combining parts of possible solutions to get the biggest payoff.

Use a process to develop your solution criteria and indicants that brings the group together in consensus. If you can bring the members of the problem-solving team together, it will be easier to reach consensus on the final solution to the problem.

Document the criteria so that they are clear and the measures are specific. Do this in a form that you can use in the solution-choice step.

Figure 2.3. Solution Criteria.
Author created (1st edition)

Possible Solutions

Now, at last, it is time to get out our ideas on how the decision or problem can be resolved. The point in this step is to generate as many possible solutions as you can. Be creative. Often that creative idea, which initially was considered outrageous, is the one that either leads to an innovative solution or that triggers other creative solutions. Remember, the more the merrier! In this complex world of rapid change, good solutions emerge by combining parts of a number of ideas and by building on them.

Remember to use techniques that fit the group. If, during mind-set, you discover that there is some conflict or cliques that could form around possible solutions, use techniques that allow for individual participation. If, however, the problem-solving team is working well together, use techniques that will encourage maximum creativity and interaction.

Once you have generated a variety of possible solutions, you must clarify, combine, and document them (see figure 2.4). During the clarification process, make sure that everyone understands exactly what is being proposed in each possible solution. This is not a time for judgment or discussion, only for understanding.

If there are a large number of possible solutions, you will want to try to combine some that appear to have the same elements. Combine only with the agreement of the contributors of those that are similar. If they do not agree that they are the same, do not force the issue. Again, *don't* allow judgment or analysis. This is an idea-generating step, not a focusing one.

If you are dealing with a complex problem that other organizations have resolved, you may want to do some research on their solutions; however, do not be quick to borrow or adopt someone else's idea. Your organization may have a very different structure or political environment that would make the other's solutions unworkable in your organizational context. Use what you learn to build your own unique solution that fits your unique situation. A general rule is to adapt, not adopt.

If your problem or solutions have a high risk for the organization, you will want to determine the consequences of each possible solution. There are two types of consequences, those caused by the implementation and those caused if the solutions fail. Impact on the organization might mean a large drain on available cash or a major psychological toll on personnel. One recommended step to deal with a high-risk problem is to document the probability of success/failure for each solution along with the consequences of failure. Be sure to include information on risk and consequences of each possible solution. This information may be used during the solution-choice step to develop a risk-management strategy for each of the options under consideration.

Let us add a caveat here. Do not reserve this step only for complex or risky decisions. It is equally important to take simple issues and think of an array of solution possibilities. In 2015, Jeep released the new Cherokee Trailhawk. After months of anticipation, I went to the dealership and made my purchase. Several family members and friends have owned and loved several Jeeps over the years. In my first seven months of ownership, the Jeep spent the better part of three months in the service department at the dealership. Each time it was "fixed," the dealer assured me that the issue had been resolved. Days would pass, and the service light would inevitably illuminate. After multiple trips to the service department and hours on the phone with Jeep trying to come up with a solution, I was ready to give up.

Jeep stuck with their one solution alternative. In the process, they alienated me and put a severe dent in their supposed service orientation. I had spoken to the dealer, countless customer service representatives, and even corporate. No one wanted to examine the solution possibilities. When you treat small problems in the same way as you treat large ones, small problems eventually become large ones. The message of service experience ultimately becomes one of "don't buy a Jeep."

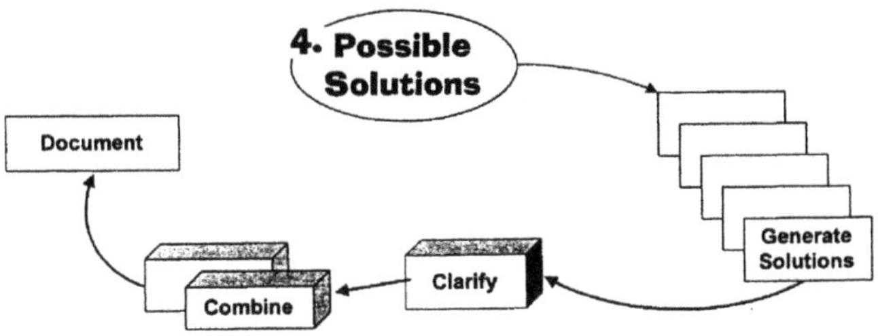

Figure 2.4. Possible Solutions. ***Author created (1st edition)***

Solution Choice

This step brings together your solution criteria and your documented list of possible solutions so that you can choose from among them or build a new solution by combining elements of several (see figure 2.5). When working with a decision-making team, *don't* vote! Work at it until you have consensus. Remember, if 51 percent vote for it, that leaves 49 percent who will try to sabotage your solution.

Consensus

Some people believe that consensus means that everyone agrees completely with the solution. In reality, consensus is a way of making decisions in a group where everyone is involved and must substantially consent to the final outcome (Seeds for Change, 2018). More specifically, it means the following:

- Everyone understands the problem and why this needs to be addressed.
- Everyone acknowledges being given the opportunity to be heard and to discuss and clarify concerns they may have.
- Everyone agrees to support the solution whether they agree fully with it or not. Occasionally this means that everyone agrees not to undercut the solution. In some cases, this may require that a solution include incremental, periodic reviews.

Consensus can be hard work. Depending on the size of the group, leaders need to be sure that the voice of less assertive team members are also afforded opportunities for airtime. To accomplish this, the leader must ensure respectful exchanges, active listening, and (in many cases) self-restraint as the group works toward their common goal. Leaders should not be afraid of disagreements or conflict during the consensus-building process—they should embrace it. A pilot test may be useful in arriving at consensus. Even reluctant participants will be open to see how a solution works on a small scale. You should agree to evaluate the pilot implementation before implementing the solution across the entire system. If you use a pilot this way, be sure to get agreement on the evaluation criteria and agree that full implementation will proceed only if the pilot meets the agreed-upon standards. Always keep in mind that consensus can lead to a big payoff that builds a broad base of support and minimizes covert resistance.

Deciding

Depending on the type of problem and on the kinds of solutions proposed, you may need to start by prioritizing the choices. Prioritization may be done for two reasons. First, the decision situation demands it; for example, the problem may be to develop a prioritized list of items for cutting the budget. The second reason for prioritizing is to help winnow down a large list of possible solutions to a more manageable one. This can help you eliminate some low-priority options.

Evaluate each of your possible choices using your solution criteria. If you developed consequences for each choice, use these consequences along with the solution criteria. Your best solutions satisfy all of your *needs*, meet the most *wants*, and have the least consequences. If you developed *nice-toos*, then add those to your consideration. A common error in DM is to develop solution criteria and then never use them as part of the solution-choice step.

Spend some time reviewing what the data show. You may be able to combine elements from two or more of your possible solutions to build one that satisfies more of your conditions and, therefore, meets more stakeholder needs.

No Viable Solution

What if none of your solutions meets your *needs*? Start by reviewing those that "fit" best. You may be able to build a new solution that meets all of your *needs* by combining parts of several possible solutions. If this is impossible, start by reviewing your solution criteria to make sure that you have not created an impossible set of conditions. *Don't* fall into the trap of changing your criteria to fit the solutions. Do the review without considering the solutions.

If the criteria are valid and cannot be altered within the context of the organization and decision situation, then return to the step of generating possible choices and push for creativity in meeting the demands of your solution criteria. Every problem has an acceptable solution; however, beware that you do not get caught in a dilemma. A dilemma is a situation with *no* acceptable solution. In this case, your problem becomes "How do we manage this dilemma?" Some laws and government regulations become dilemmas over which we have no control.

Once the group reaches a decision, be sure that the documentation of the selected choice is complete. This is especially true if the decision is passed along to another team for implementation. In this case, make sure that there is representation from the problem-solving team on the implementation team to properly communicate the solution.

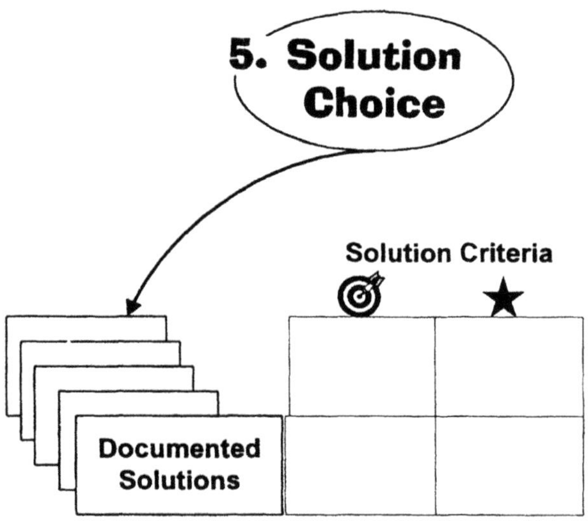

Figure 2.5. Solution Choice. ***Author created (1st edition)***

Implementation

Implementation requires purposeful, advanced planning and should not be neglected. This step is often taken for granted and is not well planned. Many well-thought-out solutions never get fully implemented or are rejected by the organization due to poor implementation strategies.

Implementation has three distinct steps: planning, doing, and inspecting (see figure 2.6). Planning usually involves action planning. This includes identifying the tasks or steps required to implement the solutions, determining responsibilities and resource needs, and setting of checkpoints and measures for progress.

Doing and inspecting are the carrying out of the action plan. Here you manage the plan and monitor the implementation process. The implementation plan should always include checkpoints. Checkpoints are closely monitored and measured. Inspection is simply the evaluation of the implementation of the problem definition, solution criteria, and any additional summative measures defined in the implementation plan.

In some cases, organizations are able to run a computer simulation to "check out" the solution virtually before implementing it in the entire organization. A virtual simulation or even a small-scale pilot test may facilitate consensus in the choice step. Although some solutions can be implemented immediately, new ventures may take weeks, months, or even years to be fully realized. New ventures often require incremental implementation. In our earlier example, Musk and the team at SpaceX set incremental goals to accomplish their ultimate goal of colonizing Mars. This includes being the first private company to successfully launch, orbit, and recover a spacecraft; the first private company to launch an object (Musk's personal Tesla Roadster) into orbit around the sun; and the first private company to send astronauts to orbit and to the International Space Station (SpaceX, 2021). Each of these steps propel toward overcoming the problem. Incremental implementation is often used where there is high risk and lack of experience.

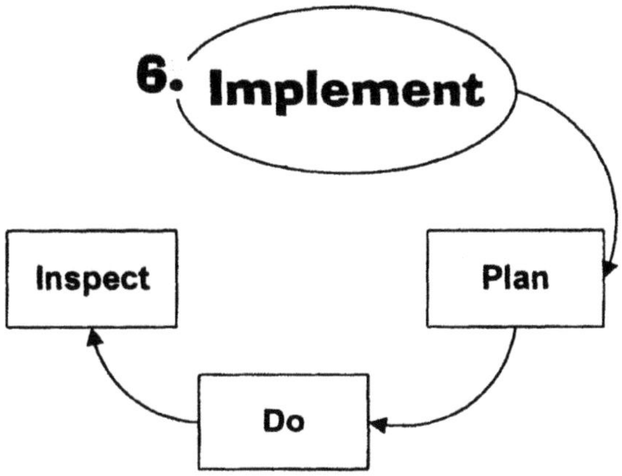

Figure 2.6. Implement. *Author created (1st edition)*

Evaluation, Revision, and Renewal

Although not a formal part of our six-step decision-making approach, these three processes are important for the successful implementation of the solution and for learning from the process so that the organization can do a better job on the next SiTNA.

There are two aspects to evaluation. First, you must evaluate the solution itself to determine if it solves the problem to the specification defined by the solution criteria and to see how it is working in its actual implementation. This process starts as part of the summative measures that are part of the inspection process during implementation; however, it is important to continue to monitor the solution for a period of time to find out if it continues to meet the needs of the stakeholders. You may need to do some adjusting so that it better fits the realities of the organization.

Second, you should evaluate the problem-solving process itself. Organizational learning can be as important as profits and loss. By evaluating the process, the organization can become better at DM and move toward a proactive, rather than reactive, approach to dealing with opportunities and SiTNAs.

Revision to the solution may be necessary to better fit the solution to the "real world" application. Likewise, the solution may need some revision over time to keep the solution viable in the future.

The concept of renewal indicates that, to remain viable in a complex and ever-changing environment, organizations must remain flexible and constantly renew themselves. Therefore, solutions should be monitored over time to assure that they still work under the current conditions. Then they should be renewed as required. This idea tends to be counter to our feeling that when it is fixed, it is fixed. Now we can forget about it.

The mind map shown in figure 2.7 depicts our six-step approach to solving problems. Use this map to learn the process so that it becomes second nature to you.

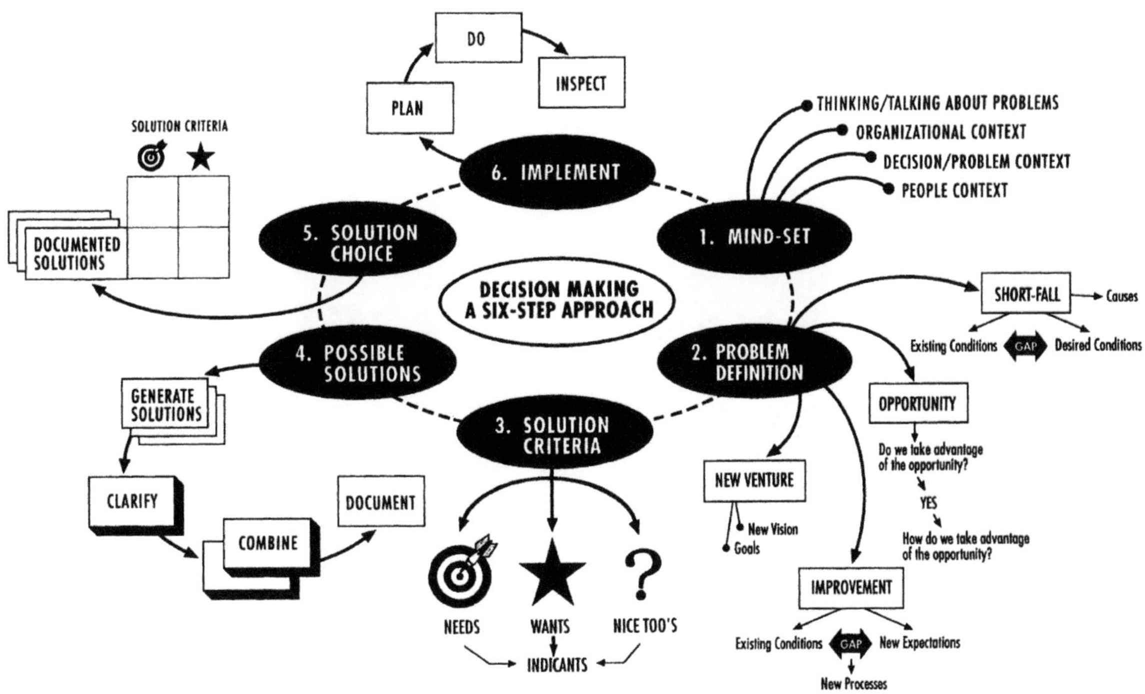

Figure 2.7. Decision Making: A Six-Step Approach (Mind Map). *Author created (1st edition)*

Chapter Three

Adapting the Core Steps

One of the reasons that there is a plethora of decision-making models is that many of them focus on a particular type of problem, or on a class of problems unique to a particular type of organization. In the previous chapter, we presented our six-step approach to decision making (DM). While we understand that "one size does not fit all" situations, we do suggest that you can take the basic six-step approach and, with some minor additions and variations, apply it successfully in a variety of organizational and decision settings. It is the discipline and ordered-thought processes imposed by the approach that aid you in DM, not the approach itself.

We discussed a few variations in the previous chapter, especially in the problem-definition step. This chapter presents specific questions that you can use to adapt the approach. Also, we include specific suggestions on how to adapt the six-step approach to different settings.

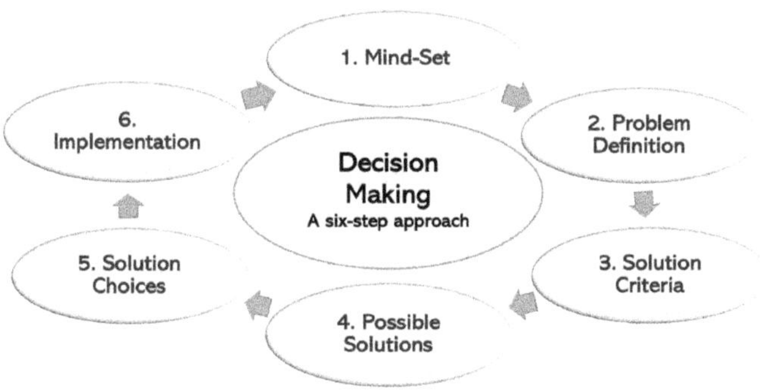

Figure 3.0. Decision Making: A Six-Step Approach.
Author created (updated from 1st edition)

STEP 1: MIND-SET

Is There a History of Toxicity in the Organization?

This question relates specifically to how people work with each other, communicate with each other, and relate to each other. If there is a "negative tone" or toxic quality in the organization, time must be spent confronting these behaviors, then establishing a new set of beliefs, behaviors, and expectations. People bring to the situation that needs attention (SiTNA) all the baggage of the organization.

Unless they establish new patterns of behavior for the decision-making team, the same toxicity will be manifested in the team.

Successful DM is based on cooperation and trust. If these are not present in the organization, you must establish an atmosphere within the problem-solving team that is conducive to these attitudes and behaviors. The conditions that exist between the parties involved do affect the reasoning processes and emotions of everyone involved. The conditions should be objectively identified and discussed without judgment to clear the air so that productive problem-solving behaviors can take place. The seminal work of Filley (1975) suggests three steps to help overcome the toxic baggage that people bring to the problem-solving situation:

1. Review and adjust the relational conditions.
2. Review and adjust perceptions.
3. Review and adjust attitudes.

Relational Conditions

Relational conditions are concerned with establishing a physical and emotional environment in which productive problem solving can take place. Such things as the size of the group, spatial arrangements, and time constraints must be considered. Mechanisms for communication and managing conflict must be established. If the number of stakeholders is large this may require setting up an Accordion Process (see chapter 1) for communication. This should include a process for sharing information with all parties involved. The primary decision-making process of consensus (win-win) should be understood and agreed upon with the possibility of a backup strategy.

Perceptions

Perceptions relate to individuals and how they view the situation. We often fail to notice that our perceptions exist. Our tendency to overlook them may affect our mind-set when working in problem-solving teams. We must bring our perceptions forward to move forward. Up-front reality testing of these perceptions should take place so that the members of the team are seeing the behavior of others as it actually exists rather than how they assume it is. McGowan (2016) suggests four ways to do this:

1. Set our egos aside as we consider the overall relationship.
2. Reflect on the positive qualities of others and what they bring to the table.
3. Keep an open mind. Listen for a moment before making assumptions.
4. Imagine yourself in your team member's space.

The PITS approach to running meetings (Jones & Bearley, 1994) suggests that the team must deal with the personal (P) and interpersonal (I) conditions of the group before moving to the task (T) of the group and, finally, summary (S). This process should be carried into the regular meetings of the team so that you can keep the perceptions clear.

Attitudes

Attitudes and feelings of the individual members of the decision-making team are other "screens" that affect how they work together. For example, if there is a prevalent attitude that "they won't cooperate," then it will be difficult to develop long-term cooperation in the group.

Stark (2013) suggests that conflict resolution can occur through adjusting attitudes and recommends the following strategies:

1. Know the importance of attitude—display confidence and lean into conflict.
2. Assume positive intent—assume the best of people.
3. Do not complain, act—focus on what you can control.
4. Quickly apologize when you are wrong.
5. Be quick to forgive—there is great healing in letting go of anger.
6. Listen—use your ears more than your mouth.
7. Stay calm and focused.

Filley (1975) suggests a set of beliefs that, when consciously accepted and practiced by the members of the team, support the win-win approach required for productive problem solving and organizational change. In toxic environments, we suggest that you work with the team to get acceptance of these (or similar) beliefs. If you form positive beliefs, you change behaviors.

- Belief in the availability of a mutually acceptable solution
- Belief in the desirability of a mutually acceptable solution
- Belief in cooperation rather than competition
- Belief that everyone contributes to the success of the team
- Belief in the views of others as legitimate statements of their positions
- Belief that differences in opinion are crucial
- Belief in the trustworthiness of other members
- Belief that the other party can compete but chooses to cooperate

As the PITS approach suggests, these agreed-upon beliefs should be posted and reviewed at each meeting of the team. Also, using and posting these beliefs with teams in organizations that are not toxic is very effective in focusing the members on the win-win behaviors required for productive DM. Remember, if there is toxicity in the organization or subgroup, you must attend to this issue at the mind-set stage. Otherwise,

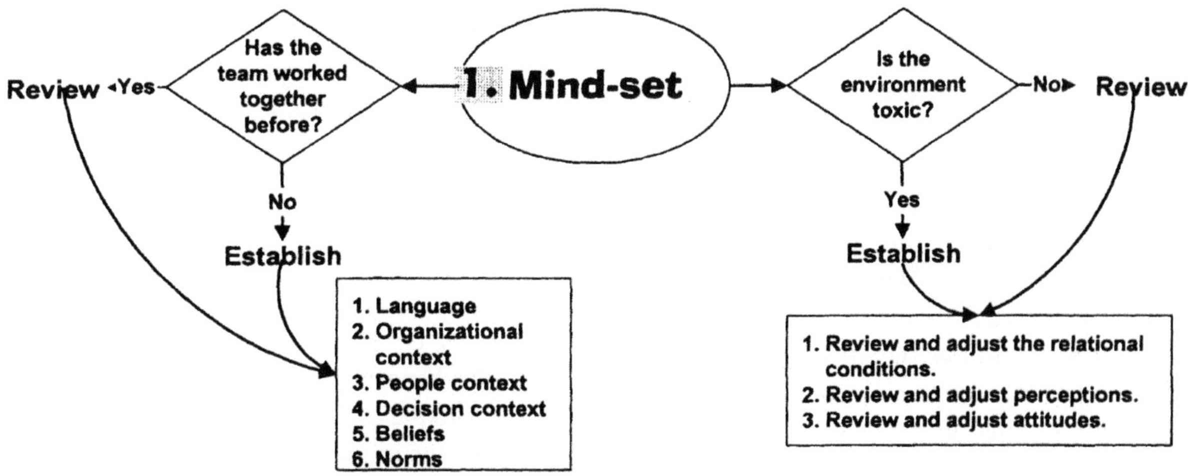

Figure 3.1. Mind-Set. *Author created (1st edition)*

it will choke you later at the problem-definition and solution-choice steps.

Have the Members of the Problem-Solving Team Worked Together Before?

If this is a new team, you must spend time working on the mind-set components of how you think, talk, and feel about the decision as well as the context of the decision. We suggest that you spend time on the recommendations in the previous question and that you establish a set of positive norms for the group. Some sample norms are the following:

- We will think, talk, and act positively about the SiTNA.
- All of us will participate 100 percent at all times.
- We will allow others to be different.
- Each of us will take complete responsibility for our own feelings.
- Each of us will speak only for ourselves.
- Each of us will take 100 percent responsibility for our own communications.
- We will share what we know, think, and feel.
- We will push ourselves for cooperation.

If the group has worked well together before, then review the components of mind-set and establish and post norms for the group. At each meeting of the team, we suggest that you do a quick review of the agreements from the mind-set step and that the norms be reviewed and posted. Also, follow the PITS approach at every meeting and deal with personal and interpersonal concerns before moving to the task elements of the decision process.

Figure 3.1 maps out specific questions that you can use to adapt the mind-set step.

STEP 2: PROBLEM DEFINITION

What Type of Problem Are You Dealing With?

In chapter 2, we described four different types of problems: shortfall, opportunity, improvement, and new venture. Each of these types requires different processes to determine the detail needed to properly define the problem. Some of the needs for each type are presented in the following sections.

The Shortfall

Here the concern is that something is not meeting predefined expectations. Use a discrepancy approach to begin to define this type of a problem. Identify exactly what the predefined expectations are. These are the desired conditions that you want your solution to achieve. In many cases, the desired conditions are quantifiable, especially in cases involving concerns related to quality. In other cases, the desired conditions may be covered by policy or law. In some problems involving a shortfall, the expectation may not be clear. Examples might include a product that is not meeting customer expectations, parents who are unhappy with the way discipline is being managed, or a bad back necessitating a change in form when golfing. In these cases, part of the process is to determine exactly what the expectations (desired conditions) are.

Once you know—and have documented—the desired conditions, determine what actually exists (the existing conditions). Again, the existing conditions may be quantifiable, or they may have to be defined descriptively. For example, customers may expect that orders are delivered on time. The existing condition is that, on the average, orders are five days late.

Now you can determine the discrepancy or the difference between the existing conditions and the desired conditions. This tells you what the shortfall is; however, it does not tell you why. At this point, look at the conditions that cause the shortfall. For the late orders, it may be that the people in sales are not following the guidelines on lead time; or there is a vendor who is often late with needed materials; or there is a bottleneck in manufacturing; or there is some combination of causes. If you were able to quantify the "gap," try to quantify the conditions so that you know how much of the gap is caused by each condition.

Once you have identified what you believe to be all of the conditions, take a hard look at them, and ask, "Are these symptoms of another, perhaps bigger, problem?" or "Is one or more of these the root cause of the shortfall?"

If the answer is "we have a bigger problem," then refocus your effort on identifying the primary or root cause of the problem. A major error at this point is to jump to the wrong conclusion about the real problem.

Armed with this information and the supporting data, you are ready to write a clear, and if possible, quantified statement of the problem. For problems involving a shortfall, it is often useful to state the problem as a question.

Remember, a shortfall decision is one that requires your attention. Opportunity decisions or new venture dreaming, for instance, can be put off because they do not pose immediate threats to the organization. Shortfall decisions do. There is something wrong in the organization, and you have to fix it. There are occasions when you excuse the problem and find it trivial and of no immediate consequence. Be careful: while some of these may be ignored, they often turn into much larger problems later. For the most part, if it is a situation that you have to fix now and cannot be avoided, you have a shortfall decision.

Opportunity

The problem associated with an opportunity is how to take advantage of a possibility in the organization's environment. Most opportunities have a limited window of opportunity. This window is most often related to time but may involve other resources. Also, creativity and innovation are usually required to exploit many opportunities.

Start by defining exactly what the opportunity is, what the benefits are to the organization, what the costs are to the organization, and what the constraint or requirements of the opportunity are. Use this information to determine whether or not to take advantage of the opportunity.

If you decide to proceed, you must take an inventory of the resources in the organization to determine the scope of the problem. Once this is done, write a clear definition of the problem. This often takes the form of a clear statement of the opportunity and some targets or goals for taking advantage of the opportunity.

Note that with the opportunity, you often do a double cycle of problem solving. In the first cycle, the problem is "Do we take advantage of this opportunity?" If the answer is "yes," then the second cycle becomes "How do we take advantage of this opportunity?" Although some opportunities are considered mandates, a common error that organizations make involving opportunities is that they do not include feasibility in the solution criteria. They simply jump in and expend resources and then later abandon the process.

Improvement

Given the chance, most organizations or people want to improve. The question here, then, is "How can we do things better?" Beware of this question. Often, we try to get more mileage out of tired, outmoded, processes or policies. Reengineering asks the question in a slightly different manner: "How can we reinvent what we do so that we can do it better?" In either case, the intent is to be proactive and to improve what we do, how we do it.

Start by defining specifically what the improvement is. If possible, quantify it in some measurable way. Beware of statements about feeling better about something. Also, you may want to make the improvement stretch the organization, but make sure that this stretch is realistic. Once this is done, the improvement becomes the desired condition.

Next, determine the existing condition or current state in the organization in relationship to the proposed improvement. If you quantified the improvement, quantify the existing conditions in a similar manner. Now determine the discrepancy, or gap, between the existing and desired conditions. This gap becomes your problem. Improvements require the commitment of resources. Inventory your resources in relationship to the improvement. Use this information to help you with the final decision on the problem.

Write a concise statement of the problem. As with the shortfall, it may be useful to state the problem as a question. Before you proceed you may want to do a strength, weaknesses, opportunities, and threats (SWOT) analysis. This will give you data to determine if the organization will survive the improvement.

New Venture

The gurus of the world advise organizations that they must invent their future or reengineer radical improvements if they are to survive in the complex, rapidly changing world of the future. Here the problem becomes "How do we carry out this new venture? This is essentially a planning problem.

To define this type of a problem, you must know what the new venture is. Therefore, you usually start with a clear, specific, and compelling vision of the future state. Once the vision is known, you can further define the problem by setting incremental goals to achieve the vision. You will now want to concentrate on planning how to accomplish the goals.

Since you are going into the great unknown, at least as far at the organization is concerned, you will want to analyze the risks and opportunities to the organization to help you make the go, no go decision.

Is the Problem Clear, and Do We Have High Agreement on the Problem Definition and Desirable Outcomes?

The final test of the problem-definition step is to make sure that the problem is clear and that there is agreement on the problem. Make sure that the statement of the problem includes the appropriate quantification so that you will clearly know when the problem is solved.

We strongly suggest that you have consensus on the problem and that everyone agrees on the statement of the problem and on the outcomes. If there is the slightest hint of disagreement, follow up on it so that all of the team members are comfortable with the definition. A useful technique is to have each member of the team write a definition of the problem, then post and compare these definitions.

Figure 3.2 maps out specific questions that you can use to adapt the problem-definition step.

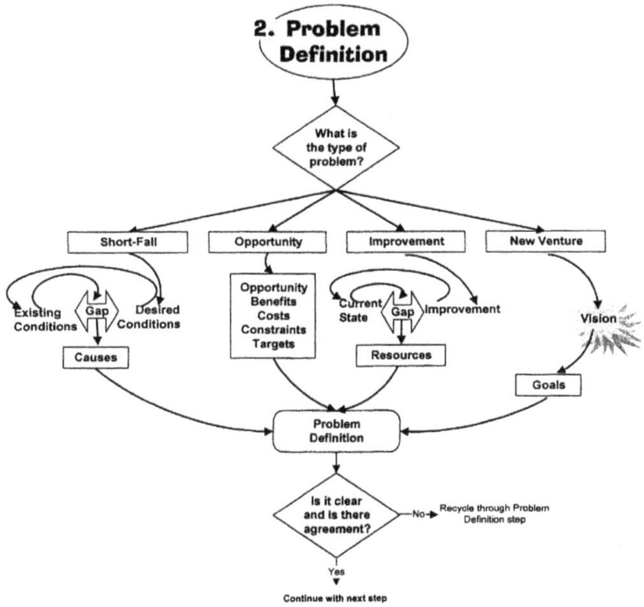

Figure 3.2. Problem Definition. *Author created (1st edition)*

STEP 3: SOLUTION CRITERIA

Does the Organizational or Problem Context Require That the Solution Criteria Be Quantified?

All problems require solution criteria. The rule is quite simple: *Do not move on to identifying possible solutions until you agree on the solution criteria.* This is typically the step deleted in other problem-solving models and is the one most frequently skipped by those using this model. See figure 3.3.

We implore you, *do not skip this step.* When used correctly, you and your team will discover that the fatigue associated with making decisions is reduced, the trap of falling into subjectivity is less likely, and options become clearer as well as easier to prioritize.

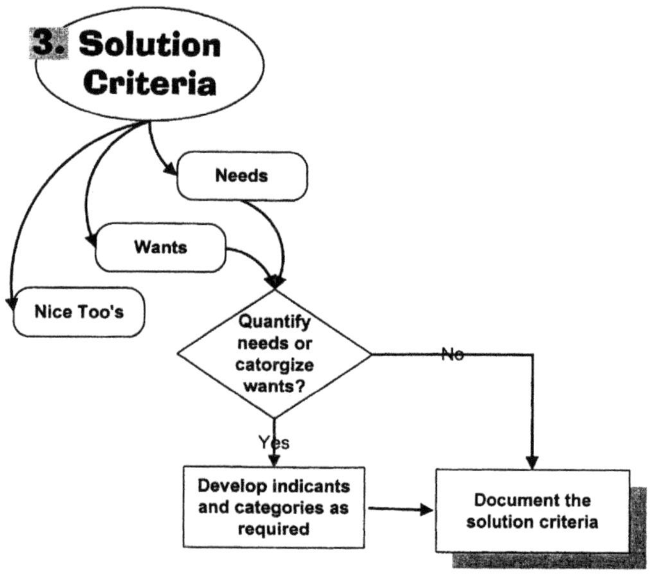

Figure 3.3. **Solution Criteria.** *Author created (1st edition)*

The process for developing solution criteria is similar for all types of problems. Typical decision criteria might include ease of implementation, cost, risk levels, cost savings, return on investment, and increase in customer satisfaction. Once the criteria are established, the team determines *needs* and *wants*, then, if necessary, *nice-toos* and consequences. The only question is, do you need quantification? This is determined by the context of the problem situation. Problems involving shortfall or improvement usually require some quantification. Problems related to quality concerns almost always include quantification because the quality process is based on measurement. For some problems, quantification is not a good idea because it is too limiting.

In addition to the quantification of needs, you may find it useful to categorize or assign weights to the wants. This gives you better data for making choices that meet most of the wants in the situation. If you use categories for wants, the three categories high, medium, and low are sufficient. If you have more than three categories, people spend too much time splitting hairs between the categories. For weights, we have found it easiest to assign a number from 1 to 10 to each want. When comparing possible solutions during the choice step, you can simply add up the weights of the wants to get a quick comparison.

Because our students and those teams we have consulted with throughout the years have struggled with this step in the decision-making model, let us look at some scenarios and provide some examples of solution criteria for each.

1. A team has been tasked with developing a new lawn edger. The criteria that viable solutions must meet include the following:

   a. Must be safe to operate
   b. Must be economical
   c. Must be portable
   d. Must be easily serviceable
   e. Must be aesthetically pleasing

   To make this even clearer, the team prioritizes and provides even stricter guidelines (see table 3.1).

   Once solution choices have been generated in step 5, then the team returns to step 3 and uses these criteria to determine the best solution.
2. A school district is considering selling their current district office building that is fifty years old to a commercial developer and relocating to a new building in the community. Their stakeholder team develops the following criteria that any possible solution must meet:

   a. The cost of relocation must cost less than the cost of repairs to the current building.
   b. The relocation must be acceptable to those affected by the move.
   c. The relocation must be accessible to the community.
   d. The relocation must meet appropriate environmental regulations and not cause any adverse effects.
   e. The sale of the current building must generate more dollars than the cost of the new building.

Table 3.1. Criteria Prioritization.
Author created (updated from 1st edition)

Criteria	*Priority*	*Description*
1. Safety	NEED	Meets industry regulations for safety
2. Economical	NEED	Maximum unit cost of $50, maximum development cost of $50
3. Portable	WANT	10 pounds or less
4. Easily serviced	NEED	Should be serviceable with screwdrivers and wrenches; should be performed by the untrained user in 15 minutes or less
5. Aesthetically pleasing	NICE-TOO	Customer surveys have reported users want something attractive

The team identifies each criterion as a *need*, a *want*, or a *nice-too*. Once solution choices have been generated in step 5, then the team returns to step 3 and uses these criteria to determine the best solution.

3. A special education teacher determines that her students will conduct banking transactions including making deposits, withdrawals, or cashing checks at a bank. She asks herself, "What would good performance of this task look like?" She came up with the following criteria for successful completion of the task:

    a. Student selects needed form (deposit, withdrawal)
    b. Student fills in form with necessary information
    c. Student endorses check
    d. Student locates teller
    e. Student states type of transaction
    f. Student counts money to be deposited to teller
    g. Student puts received money in wallet

    The teacher determined that all of these criteria are *needs* in order for the student to perform the task well.

4. And one final example: You want to take your team out to a restaurant to celebrate a victory. Where will you go? Criteria might include the following:

    a. Cost—not to exceed $50 per person (*need*)
    b. Food allergy accommodations—must have options for those attending (*need*)
    c. Entertainment—would be nice but not required (*nice-too*)
    d. Distance from the office—not to exceed ten miles from office (*want*)

You would look at all your options in step 5 and make your choice based on which restaurant best meets these criteria.

STEP 4: POSSIBLE SOLUTIONS

Is There Prior Experience with This Problem?

Most problem situations are not new to either the organization itself or to the world. While you want to be careful not to adopt a solution that will not work in your environment, you do want to collect information before you complete the process of generating possible solutions. If you are having trouble thinking of solutions, do your investigation before you start this step. This will help prime the pump with ideas. If members of the team have a variety of creative solution possibilities, then carry out the investigation at the end to see if you have missed some useful ideas. See figure 3.4.

Carry out your investigation in three areas: internally, externally, and in the literature. You may find applications internally in unrelated areas that can be applied to the current situation. Other organizations or individuals may have valuable experience that can be applied to your SiTNA. Often, there are useful approaches in the literature, and the literature may have ideas that you think are good but that have proven to be unworkable. Online services are good places to start your search of the literature. They provide access to a variety of databases and repositories of information.

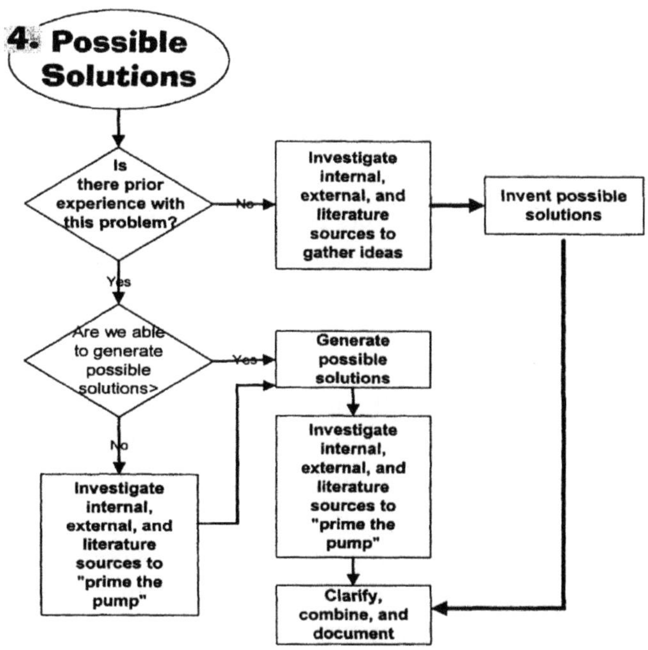

Figure 3.4. Possible Solutions. *Author created (1st edition)*

STEP 5: SOLUTION CHOICE

Before we discuss the questions relevant to this step, we want to stress the need for agreement on the solution that is ultimately implemented. You must push for consensus or win-win agreement on your final choice. To understand this in more detail, we will briefly discuss other forms of agreement.

Consensus is a win-win agreement that focuses initially on goals and needs rather than solutions. It is based on a belief that there is an acceptable and agreeable solution and on the law of plenty rather than scarcity. In essence, the final solution meets goals for all of the stakeholder groups involved and is acceptable to all parties. Win-win strategies imply that everyone will be open and honest with information, feelings, facts, and opinions and that all parties have had input on the content of the decision.

Voting is a win-lose agreement that almost always ends up with some losers, especially if the situation is of any consequence. These losers will get even later. In the best case, they will quietly go along with the solution, or the worst case, they will covertly sabotage the solution. There is always some resistance, even if it is silent non-support.

Compromise is a lose-lose agreement that forces both parties to give up something. It is based on the principle of half a loaf. That may be true if you are hungry, but half a baby does not work. Nobody feels good after a compromise. Although everyone will go along with the solution, much of the energy for long-term implementation has been sapped from the organization. Congress is very sophisticated in their use of lose-lose strategies. These include side deals, giving in on one issue to collect their pound of flesh later, and resorting to rules.

It is during the solution choice step that people may get hooked emotionally into a compromise game. We all come with our pet solution to the problem. Sometimes it is hard to work for the good of the whole rather than a quick personal gain.

Therefore, it is in the solution-choice step that the facilitator needs the most skill and bag of tools to propel the team through to win-win agreement. The questions related to this step serve as aids to the facilitator in the consensus process. See figure 3.5.

Is There a Need to Prioritize the Possible Choices Rather Than Choose from among Them?

Certain types of problems require prioritization. Sometimes when you have a large number of possible solutions you may find it useful to prioritize them so that you can eliminate those with low priority. Also, prioritization can get a decision-making team to work on combining parts of high-priority solutions to meet the most needs of the stakeholders. There are some problems that require prioritization. For example, the problem might require you to develop a list of possible capital expenditures that might be made depending on how much money becomes available at the end of the budget year. Here your outcome is a prioritized list.

Do your prioritization before you apply the solution criteria. This will focus the team's energy on the possible solutions with the highest payoff. Once you complete this process, continue the choice process by applying your solution criteria.

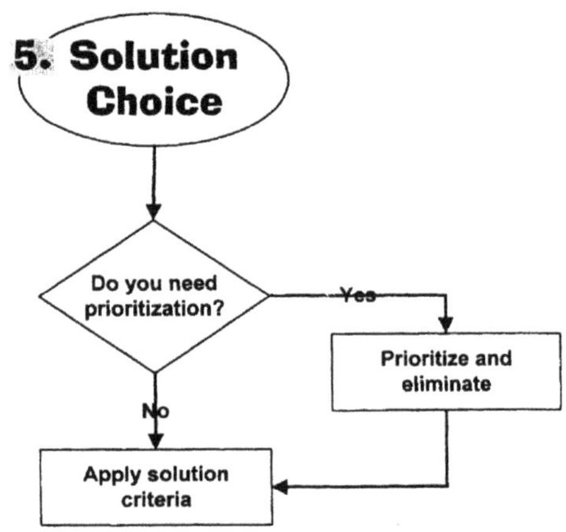

Figure 3.5. Solution Choice. *Author created (1st edition)*

STEP 6: IMPLEMENTATION

Is There a Time Crunch, or Is There High Risk Due to the Consequences or Cost?

If the answer to this question is yes, you may want to consider an incremental implementation or a multiphase implementation (see figure 3.6). Incremental implementation breaks the implementation into a number of smaller projects. This gives you better control and provides early mileposts to reevaluate. A multiphase implementation allows you to overlap several steps at a time and condenses the implementation. Some solutions do not lend themselves to incremental or multiphase implementation; however, where these types of implementations are possible,

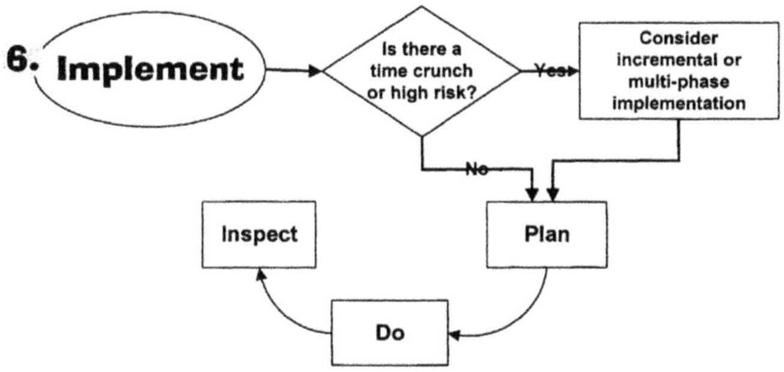

Figure 3.6. Implement. *Author created (1st edition)*

they can reduce risk, increase control, and provide for better management of time.

Once this question is answered, you are ready to proceed with implementation. Remember, implementation begins with action planning. In a way, implementation creates a new problem to solve—How do we implement the solution to meet the specifications, within the constraints provided? For complex situations, you will want to have the team continue to monitor, manage, and evaluate the implementation process.

CONCLUDING NOTE

In this chapter, we presented eight questions to help you adapt the six-step problem-solving approach to a variety of problem and decision situations. Also, we discussed some strategies that you can use in your adaptation. For convenience, we grouped all of the questions together in table 3.2. Figure 3.7 follows with a mind map that provides an overview of this chapter. Use it along with the one from chapter 2 to master this six-step problem-solving model.

The next chapter introduces you to the concept of structuring devices. Once you understand the use of these devices, chapter 6 shows you how to link the eight questions presented in this chapter with the adaptation of the six-step approach along with suggested devices.

Table 3.2. The Eight Questions of Adaptation. ***Author created (1st edition)***

1. Is there a history of toxicity in the organization?
2. Have the members of the problem-solving team worked together before?
3. What type of problem are you dealing with?
4. Is the problem clear, and do we have high agreement on the problem definition and desirable outcomes?
5. Does the organizational or problem context require that the solution criteria be qualified?
6. Is there prior experience with this problem?
7. Is there a need to prioritize the possible choices rather than choose from among them?
8. Is there a time crunch, or is there high risk due to the consequences or cost?

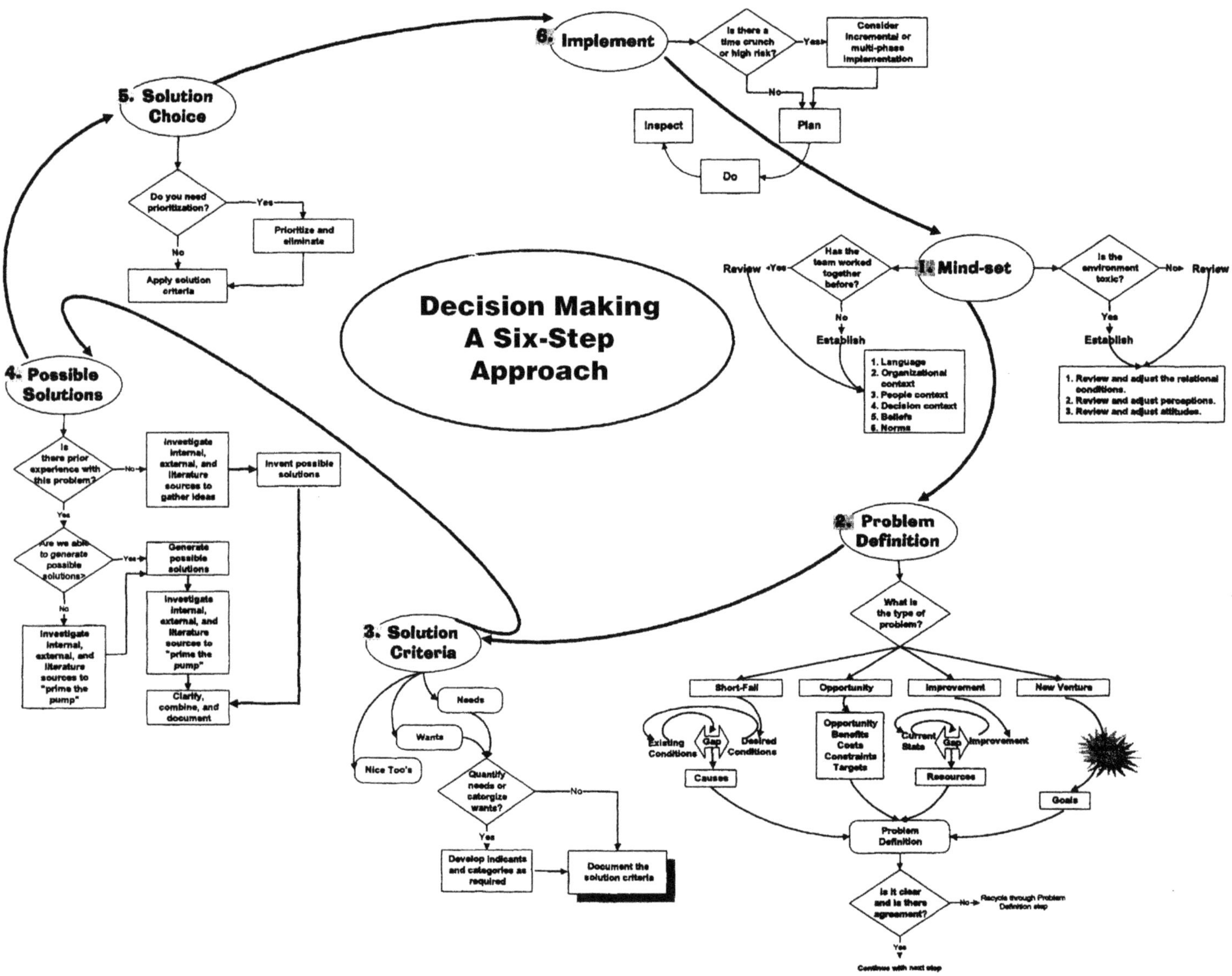

Figure 3.7. Decision Making: A Six-Step Approach (Mind Map). *Author created (1st edition)*

Chapter Four

Use of Structuring Devices

Decision making (DM) is as easy as 1-2-3. You have already learned about parts 1 and 2: the core steps in DM and the questions of adaptation. Part 3 goes into detail on how to use structuring devices properly.

ERRORS IN THE DECISION-MAKING PROCESS

There are two classic errors that decision makers commit when working through the decision process. The first is to assume that DM can be completed without the aid of structuring devices. The second is to use such devices too much or inappropriately. As Martin Luther King Jr. reminds us, "A genuine leader is not a searcher for consensus but a molder of consensus" (Martin Luther King Jr., Founders Day Address at the Sisters Chapel, Spelman College, April 11, 1960). Using resources such as structuring devices help bring individuals and teams to DM.

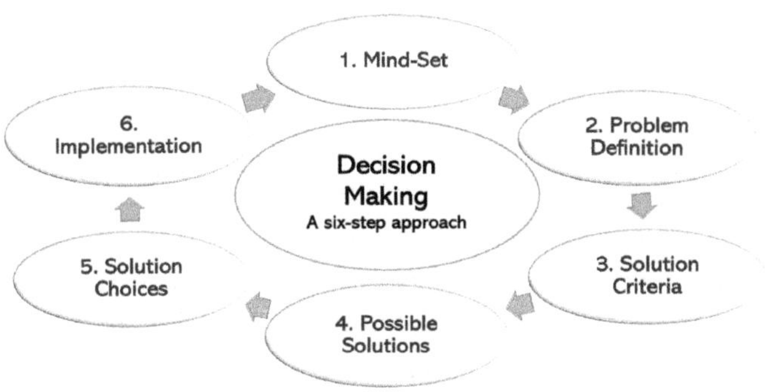

Figure 4.0. Decision Making: A Six-Step Approach.
Author created (updated from 1st edition)

Non-Use

As noted earlier, DM is easier when information is complete, conflicts are absent, and everyone agrees. Unfortunately, this is often not the case. As leaders, we are working with information that tends to be wild and incomplete; individuals have widely different needs and demands; and each situation varies in its context and consequences. In these cases, simply discussing the issue does not reasonably bring resolutions. We need help in focusing the decision process and organizing the complex array of possibilities. Great leaders are not any more ingenious than the rest of us; they are simply more pragmatic in knowing and using tools that get the job done (Yukl, 2012).

It is the role of structuring devices to give you the tools to proceed through the decision process. Let us pose an analogy. You can build a shed with your bare hands; it probably is easier to do with some rudimentary tools but not necessary. A skyscraper, however, is a different situation. You cannot build a high-rise building without an array of simple and complex tools, everything from hammers to cranes. There once was a world where decisions were like sheds, but that is no longer so. Decisions are far more complex, demanding, and imposing, and they require more sophisticated devices.

Inappropriate Use

The second error is using the structuring device too much. There are those "leaders" who only know one or two approaches to DM and use the same approaches for everything. As leaders, many of us want to elicit input, and we have our favorite one or two ways to do this. One such colleague of mine was no different. This person used the Snow Card device allowing for a variety of quick responses. Regardless of the composition of the group, the situation at hand, and/or the decision to be made, she facilitated a Snow Card activity. It is like a carpenter who is very handy at using a hammer and so he uses it for everything. When he needs to put a nail in place, it is a wonderful tool. But when he needs to smooth and level a piece of wood, it is decidedly clumsy. A plane would work much better.

A good carpenter has an array of tools and uses them appropriately. The premise here is that structuring devices are useful when used at the right time and for the right reason. Probably the most overrated technique in DM is brainstorming. Groups use it when they cannot determine what else to do. It becomes the all-purpose "hammer!" This is inappropriate. As noted earlier, there are different steps in DM and different contexts. Finding the right structuring device—or tool for the job—is essential. In chapter 6, we will illustrate the importance of choosing a structuring device that is congruent with the step and conditions that fit your decision needs. The rest of this chapter will attempt to set the fifty-three structuring devices in context.

MIND-SET

The mind-set phase is one in which individuals consider and focus the decision-making environment at hand. It has three areas of focus: 1) organizational context, 2) decision-making context, and 3) people/participant context (see table 4.1).

Organizational Context

In situations where group members are divided, come from different divisions or departments in an organization, and/or may be fairly new to the organization, there often is a need to get people together in identifying the central purpose and context of the organization. The three devices noted in table 4.1 (Boundary-Setting Mission Statement, Personal Power Grid, and SWOT) help establish the environment within which the decision will operate and help focus team members to a common purpose.

Decision-Making Context

Another constraint may be the toxicity the group members may bring to the decision-making setting. If there is some suspicion or distrust in the group, then we propose using Positive Context, Scenarios, or Anecdotes (table 4.1). These will not change the past; however, they will help describe the behavior you want to have in the future as you proceed through DM.

People/Participant Context

The third area of mind-set involves identifying appropriate people to be involved in the process and how they should be involved. The appropriate devices here would be Accordion Process, Participation Tree, and Stakeholder Analysis (table 4.1).

Table 4.1. Structuring Devices for Mind-Set. ***Author created (1st edition)***

Structuring Devices for Mind-Set	*Organizational Context Devices*
	Boundary-Setting Mission Statement
	Personal Power Grid
	SWOT
	Decision-Making Context Devices
	Scenario
	Anecdote
	Positive Context
	People/Participation Context Devices
	Accordion Process
	Participation Tree
	Stakeholder Analysis

PROBLEM DEFINITION

As noted in chapter 3, there are four categories of problems: shortfall situations that need attention (SiTNAs), opportunities, improvement issues, and new ventures. While these operate differently, they share common structuring devices. What differentiates between them is 1) the need for creative approaches to the problem definition, 2) the demand for clarification where the problem is muddled, 3) the necessity to uncover root causes, and/or 4) the need for a planning perspective. These are not mutually exclusive imperatives. They are a variety of ways to define accurately and clearly the exact nature of the decision or problem.

Creative Devices

There are times when the group is mentally blocked and needs a device that will open their thought processes. I remember working with a group that had worked together for fifteen years and had achieved a high level of "group think." They couldn't see beyond surface issues and symptoms. They needed creative approaches to reach beyond the obvious.

Brainstorming is probably the best-known device of all fifty-three and is very useful here. Nominal Group Technique, Mind Map, Metaphors, and SWOT can also be useful here (see table 4.2). These options allow for a group to identify problems by doing a "brain dump." These devices are helpful in list making; other devices bring focus and clarification.

Clarification and Grouping

The heart of problem definition is in clarifying and focusing issues and problems. Probably the simplest, most useful device here is Discrepancy Analysis (table 4.2). While there are a variety of other choices, we have a bias toward Discrepancy Analysis because it is so precise in identifying gaps between where we want to be and where we are. Three other devices are T Chart, Cost Iceberg, and Paper Plate Exchange.

Sometimes the problem is dispersed into a variety of subissues and needs focus and grouping. We ran into this need, for example, when working with a business on Total Qualitative Management problems. The problem revolved around decreasing customer satisfaction. The reasons for this decline were multiple and overlapping. We had a high need to deal with a wide array of problems and then group them for consideration. In such cases, we recommend Snow Cards, Affinity Diagram, or Interrelationship Digraph (table 4.2). These examine the connections between problems so that the decision process can address the broad issue rather than a myriad of subparts.

Cause/Effect

Sometimes the problem is clear, but the causes are not (total quality management is particularly concerned with cause analysis). Because cause analysis tends to be an analytical, quantitative process, Cause/Effect Diagrams and Pareto Diagrams are appropriate because the process tends to be more systematic and analytical than the others identified in table 4.2. Contingency Analysis, Flowcharts, and Tree Diagrams are more visually oriented approaches and, hence, appeal to the more creative side of participants. The Why Cycle is a strong, verbally analytic tool and requires tough-minded questioning. All devices help group members explore root causes.

Planning Decisions

Unlike the preceding issues, which involve definition of existing problems and causes, there is a set of decisions that involves planning toward the future and examining future issues and possibilities. Where some of the previous devices may be helpful in planning decisions, there is an array of devices particularly oriented toward planning: Vision Setting, Goal Setting, Cross-Impact Matrix, Competitor Mapping, and SWOT. All five of these structuring devices explore the future but in different ways. For example, one establishes a

Table 4.2. Structuring Devices for Problem Definition.
Author created (updated from 1st edition)

Structuring Devices for Problem Definition	*Creative Devices for Identifying Problems*
	Brainstorming
	Nominal Group Technique
	Metaphors
	SWOT
	Mind Map
	Clarification and Grouping Devices
	Discrepancy Analysis
	Cost Iceberg
	Paper Plate Exchange
	Snow Cards
	Affinity Diagram
	Interrelationship Digraph
	T Chart
	Cause/Effect Devices
	Cause/Effect Diagram
	Contingency Analysis
	Flowchart
	Pareto Diagram
	Tree Diagram
	Why Cycle
	Planning Decision Devices
	Vision Setting
	Goal Setting
	Cross-Impact Matrix
	Competitor Mapping
	SWOT

vision for the organization, which subsequently identifies new programs and processes. Another sets goals for the future. Cross-Impact Matrix looks at the effect one future event has on others and, therefore, identifies key actors (variables) in the future. The fourth, Competitor Mapping, uses an analysis of what others are doing to set standards or benchmarks for people to work toward. The last, SWOT, helps identify the strengths, weaknesses, opportunities, and threats.

SOLUTION CRITERIA

This is probably the simplest but most overlooked step in DM. As one pundit put it, "We have solutions in search of a rationale to fit them." We fasten onto a solution and then backload reasons why it works. This is a poor approach to DM because it introduces both politics and emotion into decision choice. You never wipe emotion and politics from DM, but you can reduce and control them. The key is to identify solution criteria in advance (as discussed in chapter 3). There are generally two classes of approach to doing this: creative and analytical.

Creative Approaches

The creative approaches involve opening up the right side of the brain and generating lists of potential criteria (table 4.3). With Brainstorming, Nominal Group Technique, Anecdotes, and Snow Cards, the group expands its vision of possible criteria by listing and storytelling. These devices do not define the criteria or create specificity; rather, it is the discussions that follow that will provide definition.

Analytical Approaches

Many leaders lean toward the analytical approaches because they are more precise and provide a helpful connection with the solution choice phase. The three approaches identified in table 4.3 are Criteria Development, Cause/Effect Diagram, and Criteria Standards. Each of these requires a clear definition of solution criteria, which will be used to systematically rate the adequacy of each solution alternative. Some of these do so with a simple check-off approach; others use quantified weights and ratings. The choice between these depends on the specificity that the organization or issue calls for and the capacity of the issue to be quantified. For example, if we want to measure knowledge acquisition, we can quantify that more easily than if we want to measure interest in lifelong learning. Additionally, if we are comparing a larger array of alternative solutions, we may need quantification more than if we had only five to eight alternatives. The decision conditions will affect which approach is used.

Table 4.3. Structuring Devices for Solution Criteria. ***Author created (updated from 1st edition)***

Structuring Devices for Solution Criteria	*Creative Devices*
	Brainstorm
	Nominal Group Technique
	Anecdotes
	Snow Cards
	Analytical Devices
	Criteria Development
	Cause/Effect Diagram
	Criteria Standards

POSSIBLE SOLUTIONS

Often, statements such as "There's only two choices here" or "Well, we can do it your way or my way" or "We have two or three choices" are common when searching for possible solutions. These are all statements that suggest that alternatives are either limited or known. For most decision situations, neither of these conditions is true. There are always more alternatives in a world beyond the J curve than we readily imagine, and most of these escape our easy examination. Structuring devices are useful in generating and focusing possible solutions.

Creative Approaches

One of the challenges of this step is simply to generate as many alternatives as possible. This is not a natural step for most leaders, as we tend to want to quickly find a solution. The wider the array of alternatives, the higher quality the choice. If you think there are only two alternatives, then you need to imagine at least twelve. If you think there's only five possibilities, then you need to generate a list of twenty-five alternatives. The creative approaches open up the mind to rapidly imagining possibilities. Once again, Brainstorming and Nominal Group Technique provide strategies for creating long lists of alternatives. Anecdotes, Analogies, and Mind Maps provide image-creating devices that spark creative thinking about alternatives and uses storytelling to generate possibilities (table 4.4).

Solution Expansion

A couple of devices that further expand solutions are Morphological Analysis and Competitor Mapping (table 4.4). The latter generates alternatives by examining what other effective organizations are doing. What can you learn about possibilities from your competitors? Morphological Analysis, on the other hand, expands alternatives by dissecting the decision issues into their component parts. On the surface, it appears complex; however, in practice, it is quite simple and usable, and it generates a very broad array of alternatives.

Focusing and Grouping

Sometimes the problem with brainstorming alternatives is that a lot of possibilities are overlapping, and the list is too long to consider in a systematic manner. It can be overwhelming. In these cases, the use of Snow Cards and Affinity Diagrams can help create groups of alternatives that clarify and combine possibilities (table 4.4). This brings focus and order to a mélange of alternatives.

Table 4.4. Structuring Devices for Possible Solutions. ***Author created (updated from 1st edition)***

Structuring Devices for Possible Solutions	*Creative Devices*
	Brainstorming
	Nominal Group Technique
	Anecdotes
	Analogies
	Mind Map
	Solution Expansion Devices
	Morphological Analysis
	Competitor Mapping
	Focusing and Grouping Devices
	Affinity Diagram
	Snow Cards

SOLUTION CHOICE

This step has the most structuring devices associated with it. Forty percent of the devices included in chapter 6 address the issue of solution choice. This is so because several critical dilemmas emerge during this phase:

- Sometimes the verbiage of discussion disguises the degree of consensus that already exists; there is a need to focus on areas of consensus and disagreement.
- Sometimes we cannot choose because we do not know the consequences of each alternative, or the information on consequences is unfocused and in disarray. As you remember from chapter 2, understanding consequences is essential to quality-choice behavior.
- Sometimes we need to be more systematic in considering each alternative; we tend to jump to conclusions, and more often than not, emotion drives us to premature choice. As leaders, we need to look at all alternatives analytically.
- Finally, there are times when it is not a choice between possibilities but, rather, ranking the relative choice among them. Priority setting is more needed than single choice selection.

It is to address these circumstances that these twenty-two devices are proposed (see table 4.5).

Focusing Choice

There is an array of very interesting structuring devices that can be used to focus the group's choice behavior. The word *interesting* is used because these devices are useful in catching the interest of participants. For example, Bean Count or Spend-a-Dot are fun activities that force choice. Advocacy Teams is an intriguing way to understand pros and cons of dichotomous alternatives (table 4.5). These devices use movement, artifacts, or role play to focus discussion and bring groups to choice.

Clarifying Consequences

As noted earlier, clarifying consequences is crucial to choice. For example, if we knew that buying more inventory would yield us a greater profit, we would definitely buy more stock. If we have no idea what the consequences would be of increasing our inventory, we would be at a loss to decide. Devices that clarify consequences of alternatives increase the quality of decisions. Included in chapter 6 are four devices that systematically examine consequences: Decision Tree Analysis, Risk Analysis, Payoff Matrix, and Cross-Impact Matrix (see table 4.5). Another device uses a visual display to explore consequences (T Chart). Finally, Scenarios uses a storytelling approach to understand potential, future consequences, and appeals to imaginative exploration.

Applying Analysis

Probably the most useful device for choosing among alternatives is Trade-Off Analysis. It is an eminently workable and understandable way to compare alternatives against solution criteria. It allows simple quantification to judge between alternatives. Criteria Development, Needs/Wants Matrix, and Multi-Attribute Analysis (a form of cost-benefit analysis) are forms of Trade-Off Analysis and provide different advantages. Pareto Diagram and Payoff Matrix can also be useful and are recommended (see table 4.5).

Prioritization

A very different problem is priority setting. The assumption of the other devices in this phase is that the group needs to choose one alternative and proceed with it. There are, however, times when weighing the relative importance of alternatives is called for. For example, when developing and reviewing department, site, district, or even your own personal budget, you need to know what your top priorities are and determine if you can afford it given your budget. If given a choice, of course it would be nice to budget everything you need or want, but you have to set priorities in order of need or preference. There are three excellent devices for priority setting: Precedence Chart, Priority Matrix, and Magnitude Estimation Analysis (table 4.5).

The Precedence Chart forces a spread of alternative projects. The second device, Priority Matrix, displays alternatives in these basic categories—high priority, medium priority, and low priority—and is particularly useful in planning decisions. The third device, Magnitude Estimation Analysis, is useful in survey feedback approaches to priority setting. These usually involve large groups of people who do not usually meet face to face.

Remember, use the right device for the right need.

Table 4.5. Structuring Devices for Solution Choice.
Author created (updated from 1st edition)

Structuring Devices for Solution Choice	*Focusing Choice Devices*
	Advocacy Teams
	Bean Count
	Multi-Voting
	Stack the Deck
	Straw Polling
	Human Sociogram
	Spend-a-Dot
	Anecdote
	Clarifying Consequences Devices
	Decision Tree Analysis
	Risk Analysis
	Payoff Matrix
	Cross-Impact Matrix
	T Chart
	Scenarios
	Analytical Devices
	Trade-Off Analysis
	Needs/Wants Matrix
	Pareto Diagram
	Payoff Matrix
	Multi-Attribute Analysis
	Priority-Setting Devices
	Precedence Chart
	Priority Matrix
	Magnitude Estimation Analysis

IMPLEMENTATION

The final step in the decision-making process is decision implementation. Once a decision is made, implementing the decision is next; otherwise, the whole process becomes suspect. This is the recurrent problem with strategic planning in many organizations. Implementation includes three elements: plan, do, and inspect. Even when we do implement, we fail to check, or inspect. To do this effectively, you need to craft implementation strategies that are specific and, at times, contingent.

Action Steps

Clearly the most important device in this step is Action Planning because it clearly specifies action steps, participants, resources, and time line. Related to Action Planning is the need to monitor the implementation process. Remember monitoring is critical to the implementation process. Gantt Charts can aid monitoring (table 4.6).

Alternative Pathways

At times, there is no one pathway to implementation but, instead, alternative pathways. By exploring alternative pathways, the decision group can establish contingencies. Things seldom go as expected, and contingencies allow mid-course correction. There are four devices useful for this purpose: Flowchart, Decision Trees, Gantt Chart, and Mind Map (see table 4.6). All four tend to be highly visual, and some can yield quantitative pathways (e.g., Decision Trees).

Implementation Strategies

Some devices are useful for crafting implementation strategies by sparking discussion of risk and resistance (table 4.6). Force Field Analysis is a classic change strategy approach that has been adapted to DM and deals with understanding resistance.

Risk Analysis and Contingency Analysis help a group understand the pros and cons of strategies and discuss ways to overcome resistance. Scenarios is a storytelling device for imagining future states and helping groups build back the future in developing strategies.

Table 4.6. Structuring Devices for Implementation.
Author created (updated from 1st edition)

Structuring Devices for Implementation	*Devices for Establishing Action Steps*
	Action Plans
	Gantt Chart
	Devices for Examining Alternative Pathways
	Flow Chart
	Decision Trees
	Gantt Chart
	Mind Map
	Devices for Developing Implementation Strategies
	Force Field Analysis
	Contingency Analysis
	Risk Analysis
	Scenarios

A FINAL NOTE

In chapter 6, we present fifty-three structuring devices for your potential use. Regardless of how complex your decision situation, you will only use a fraction of them at any one time. Earlier we used the analogy of a carpenter. A skilled carpenter needs a full toolbox, not because he will use all his tools on each job but, rather, because he can use the right tool for the right situation. Having a full repertoire of tools provides leaders with the capacity for choice and effective leadership. When structuring devices are needed, use them. Be judicious and use them only when they will move the decision-making process forward. Focus on the need, then pick the device.

A final caution is that we have included in this book only devices that can be used by the typical leader. We have not included highly mathematical game theory approaches or highly quantitative decision models. These have a role but not for everyday managers. Rather, we have focused our attention on improving the quality of DM in practical settings and for the practical decision maker.

Chapter Five

Designing Your Own Road Map for Decision Making

In the introduction, we said that decision making (DM) is as easy as 1-2-3. You now have all of the pieces to get started. It simply involves

1. knowing the six core steps of DM,
2. answering the eight basic questions of adaptation and adapting the core steps to fit your situation, and
3. selecting and applying appropriate structuring devices.

In this chapter, we put these steps together to show how you design a road map for your decision-making situation. A chart is included for each of the six core steps that presents some possible adaptations, tasks, and suggested structuring devices based on the answers to the eight basic questions of adaptation. Of course, you must consider the context of your particular problem and make the adaptations based on your needs, then choose structuring devices that fit your decision and your problem-solving team.

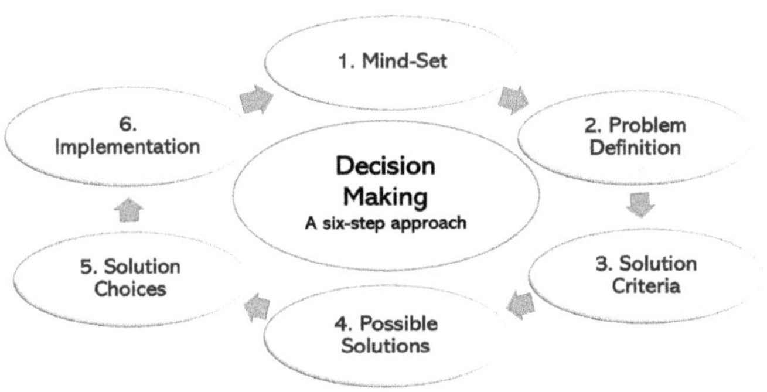

Figure 5.0. Decision Making: A Six-Step Approach.
Author created (updated from 1st edition)

CAUTIONS IN DESIGNING YOUR MAP

Mind-Set

No matter how you answer the two questions related to this step, there are some basic processes that you carry out during this step. You must always

- deal with your problem-solving language,
- review or establish the organizational context,
- set the context for DM,
- review or establish norms for the team, and
- determine the relational conditions (times, locations, etc.).

Never fall into the trap of ignoring this step. Even if you are working with a team that has a history of working together to solve problems, remember that each decision is a new situation, and the context, resources, and abilities of the members change as the decision-making environment changes. Also, if this is an ongoing team, there may be relationship issues that are carried over from prior experiences that may impact the new decision if they are not confronted and resolved.

Problem Definition

The adaptations and devices used in this step depend on the type of problem: shortfall, improvement, opportunity, or new venture. It further depends on the complexity of the decision and the degree of quantification needed to properly define the problem.

For the *shortfall* you always identify the existing and desired conditions or outcomes, then you look at the gap or discrepancy between them. Often you must determine the causes of the shortfall. In problems involving quality, you may need to identify the root cause so that you can "fix" the cause of the discrepancy. Select processes and structuring devices that yield the level of detail and quantification you need for your decision.

The *improvement* requires that you determine some new, improved state or condition. Also, you must precisely define the current state so that you can identify the amount of the improvement by looking at the gap between the current and improved, desired state. Sometimes it is useful to determine the conditions that contribute to the current state. You can use the same structuring devices that you use in the shortfall to determine the cause; however, with an improvement, you focus on the conditions that contributed to the current state, not the conditions that make up the cause of the gap as in the shortfall. With an improvement decision, it is often necessary to quantify the improvement so that you can determine the resources required to reach the desired level of improvement. Select processes and structuring devices that allow you to focus on the improved and current state and that help you clearly describe the gap (improvement).

Not all *opportunities* are worthwhile. Therefore, you must understand the opportunity and identify the costs, benefits, and constraints associated with the opportunity so that you can make an informed decision as to whether or not to take advantage of the opportunity. If you decide to proceed, you must set specific targets. Select processes and structuring devices that lead to a clear understanding of the opportunity and that help you set specific goals so that you benefit from the opportunity.

The *new venture* takes you to new places where you or your organization have never been before. While this is exciting, it can lead to disaster if not done in a systematic manner. Select processes and structuring devices that help you plan the new venture by setting a clear vision and defining specific targets and goals.

Solution Criteria

This step is frequently left out of other models and is the step frequently skipped by the novice user of this model. Never skip this step, and always use your criteria to help you select an appropriate solution. The processes and structuring devices you choose should lead to specific criteria, and if required, indicants that are quantified to the appropriate level. Always identify your *needs*, and if appropriate, include *wants* and *nice-toos*.

Remember, the real payoff for this step is to help you move beyond the usually mundane and preconceived solutions that people bring with them in the beginning to new levels of creativity and cooperation.

Possible Solutions

Identifying possible solutions is a creative process that requires that you push for new levels of creativity. Avoid yet another lifeless brainstorming session. Select processes and structuring devices that foster creativity and that generate excitement. Even with shortfall decisions that require a fix, you can discover creative possibilities that move you beyond the problem and that create new commitments and energy in the organization.

Solution Choice

Always use your solution criteria to help you focus your solution. If there are many possibilities, select processes and devices that help you winnow and combine the possibilities. Often, you can create solutions that gain broad support by combining all or part of several possibilities into a new solution. If the solution requires prioritization, select structuring devices that lead to a prioritized list. Otherwise, use processes and structuring devices that build a consensus around a solution.

Implementation

The final step in the decision-making process is decision implementation. You can make a decision but if you do not implement it, then the whole process becomes suspect. This is the recurrent problem with strategic planning. We talk a lot but do little. Implementation includes three elements: plan, do, and inspect. Even when we do implement, we fail to inspect. In order to do these three elements effectively, you need to craft implementation that is specific and, at times, has a contingency.

THE 1-2-3 OF DECISION MAKING

There are six charts that follow, one for each of the core steps (see figures 5.1–5.6). These are designed to help you carry out the 1-2-3 of DM. Use them to help you adapt the core steps and to help you select processes and structuring devices that are appropriate. Not all of the structuring devices are included. Some of the devices are designed to fit a particular set of conditions. We have selected some of the more common ones. We leave it to you to fill your tool chest by learning all of the devices so that you have the proper tools for a variety of decision situations.

How to Use the Charts

The six charts that follow, one for each of the problem-solving steps, show some typical adaptations based on the answers to each question and some of the more common structuring devices that you might use. Remember, your specific decision, your organization, and your team also play an important part in your choice of processes and structuring devices.

In the last column, "Task or Common Structuring Devices," an asterisk by a structuring device indicates that we strongly suggest that this structuring device is appropriate unless there is some compelling reason not to use it.

We did not include all of the structuring devices. Some of them have special applications or have a high degree of quantification that is only needed for complex or quantifiable decisions. We suggest, however, that you consider all of the devices appropriate for a step to determine those that best support your decision-making needs, the context of your organization, and the specific needs of your problem-solving team.

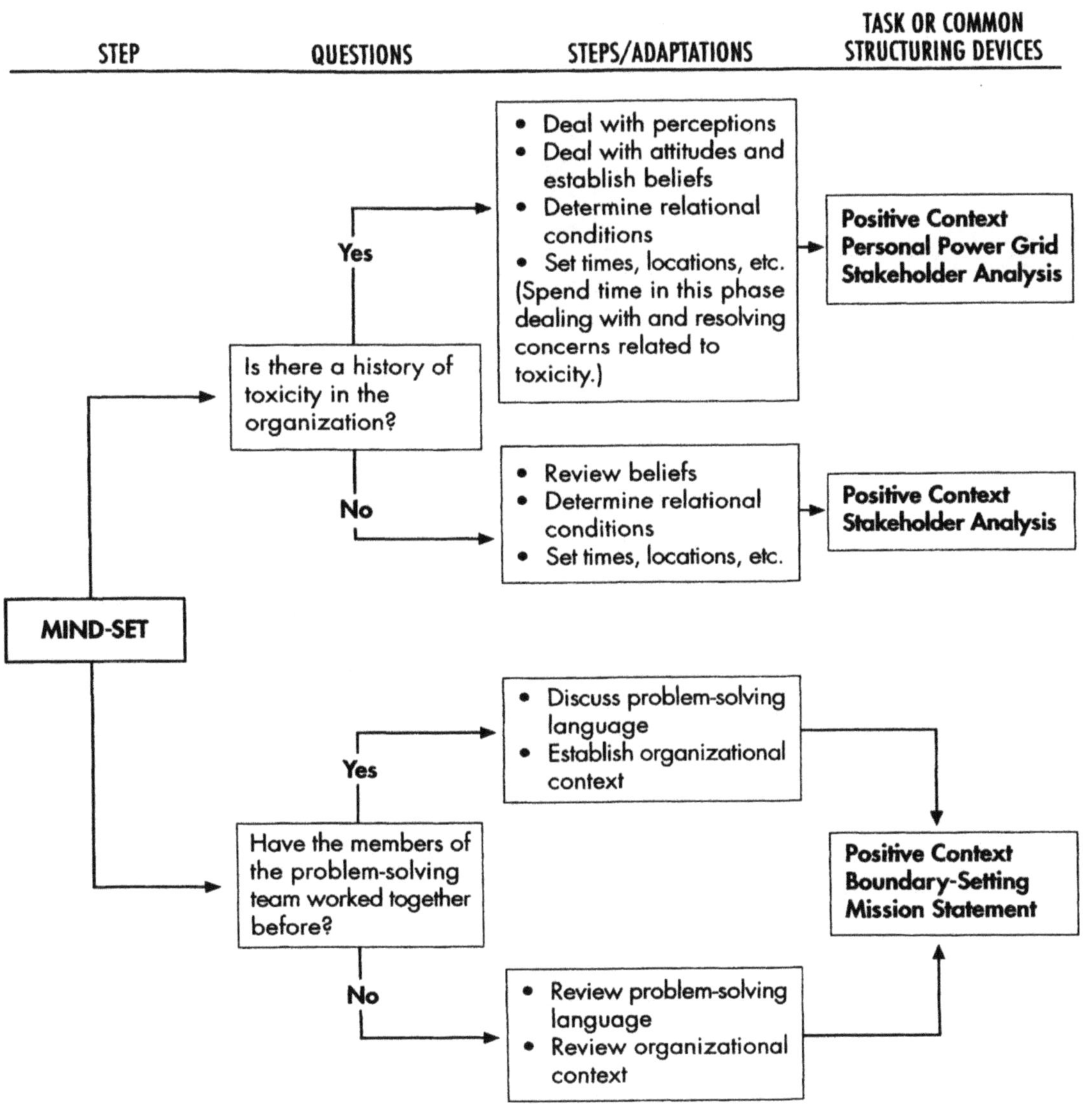

Figure 5.1. Mind-Set. *Author created (1st edition)*

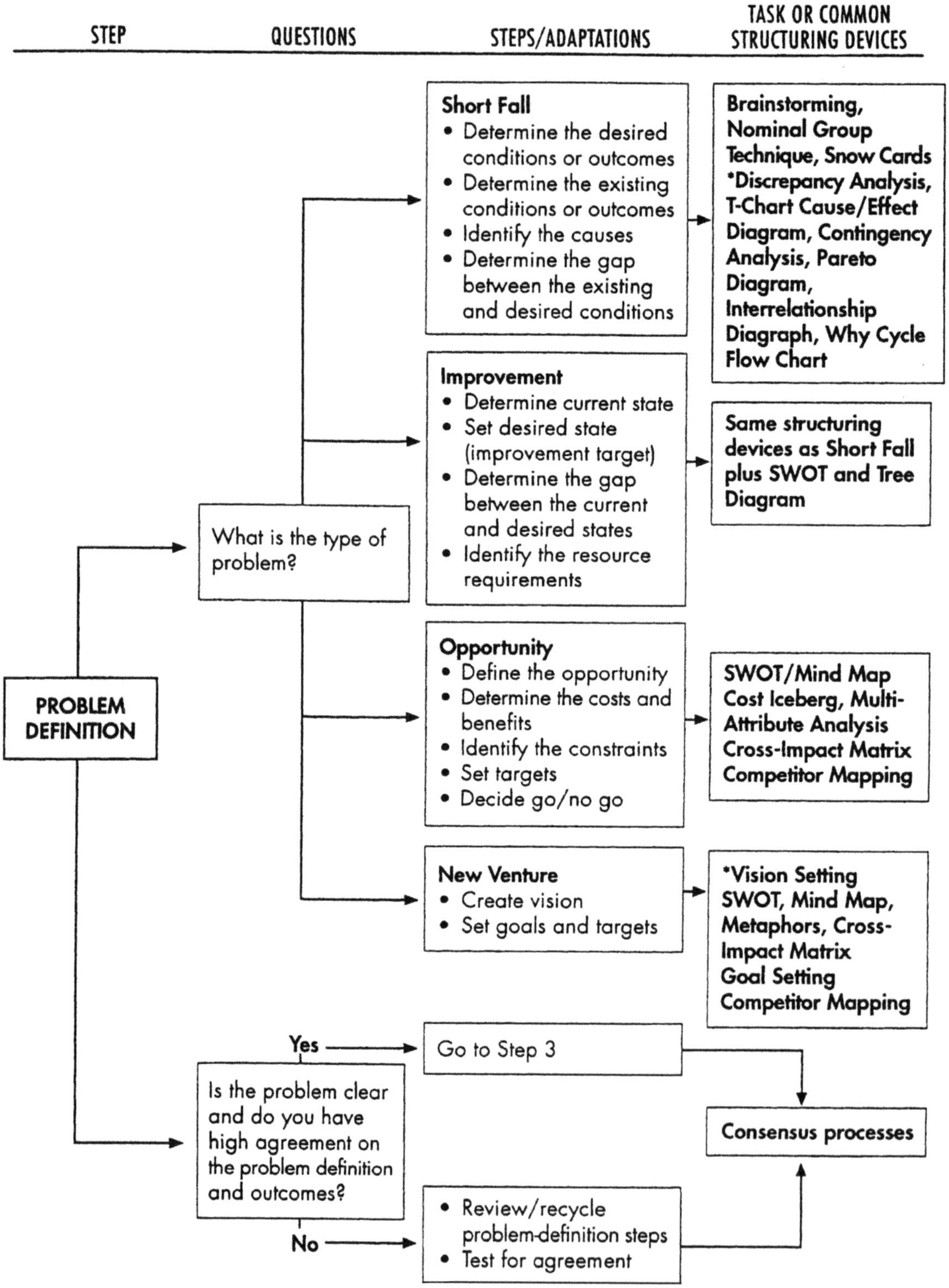

Figure 5.2. Problem Definition. *Author created (1st edition)*

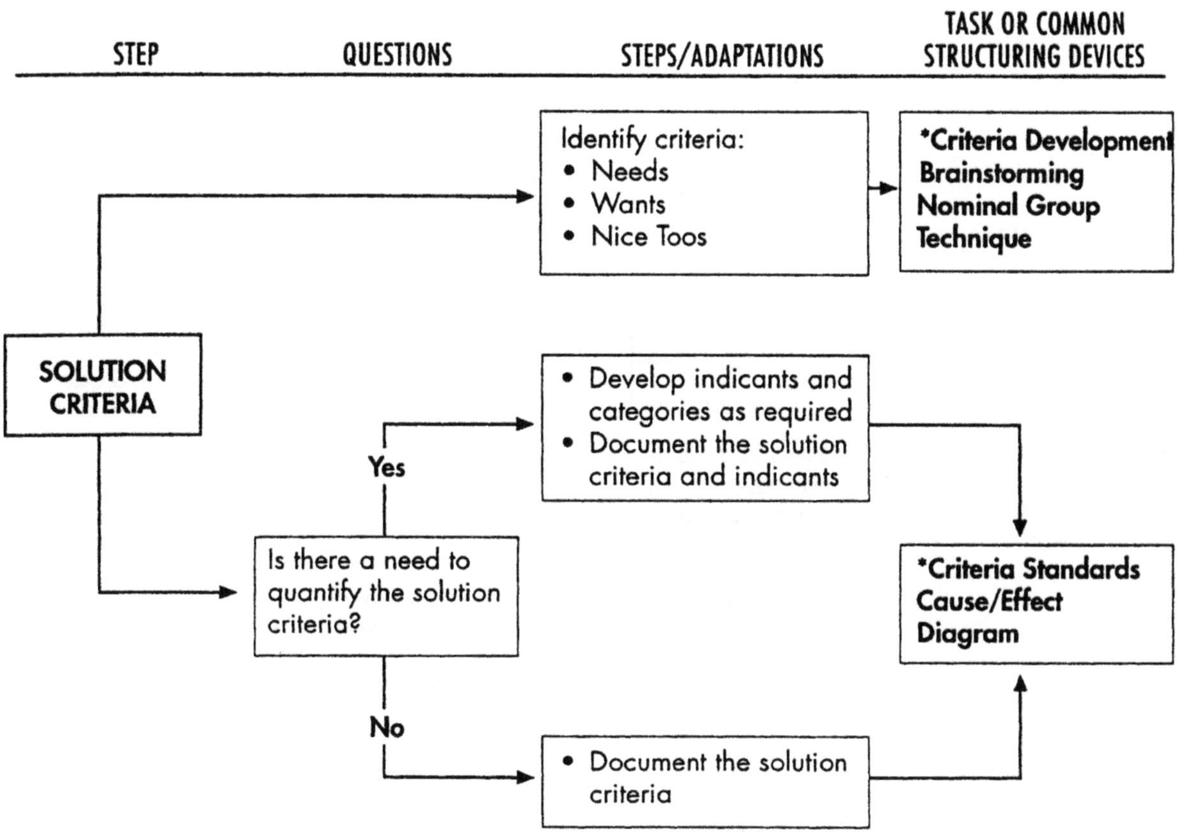

Figure 5.3. Solution Criteria. *Author created (1st edition)*

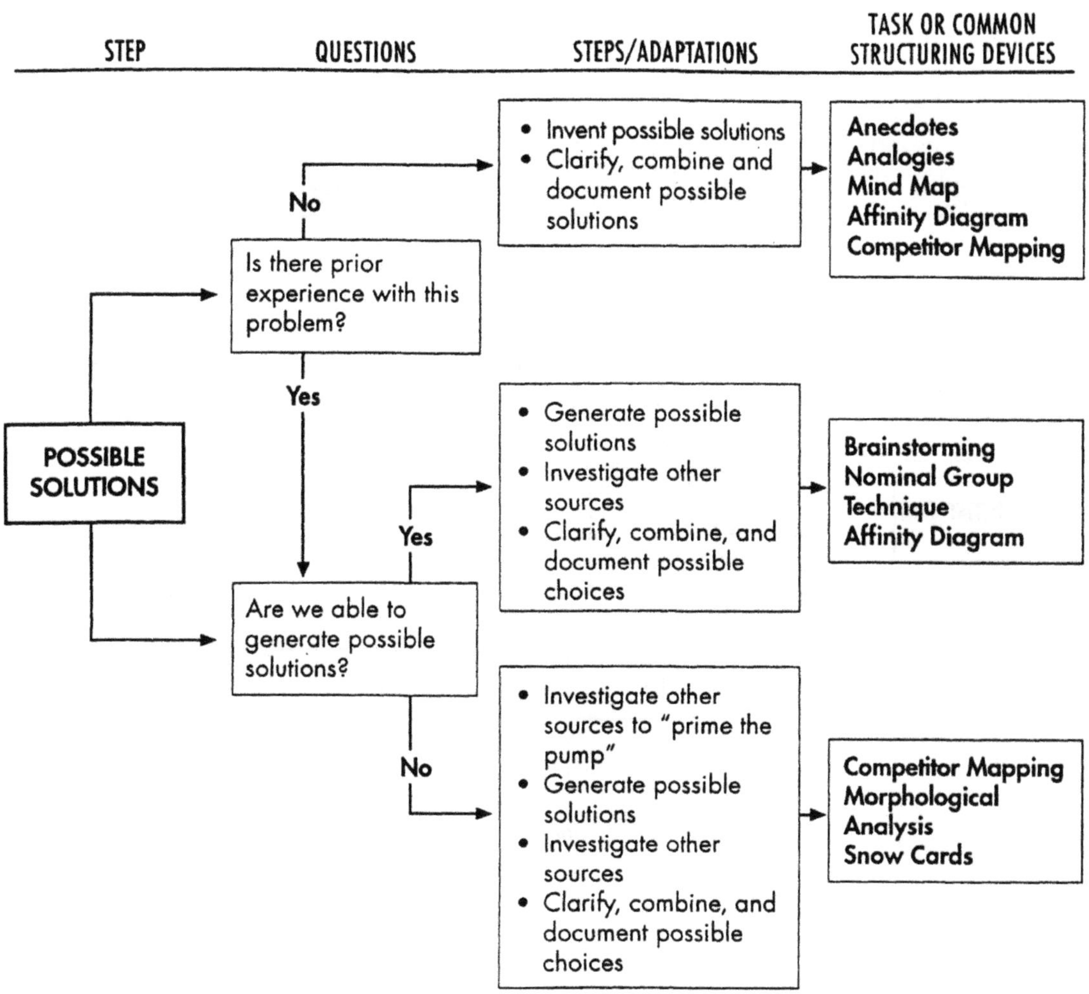

Figure 5.4. Possible Solutions. *Author created (1st edition)*

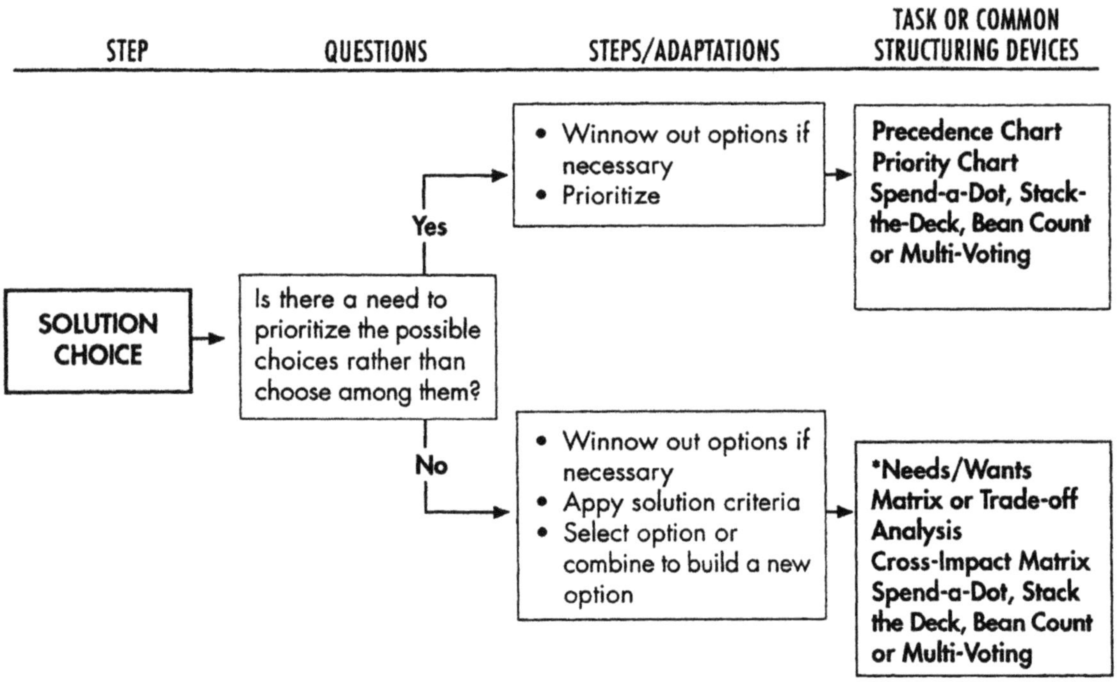

Figure 5.5. **Solution Choice.** ***Author created (1st edition)***

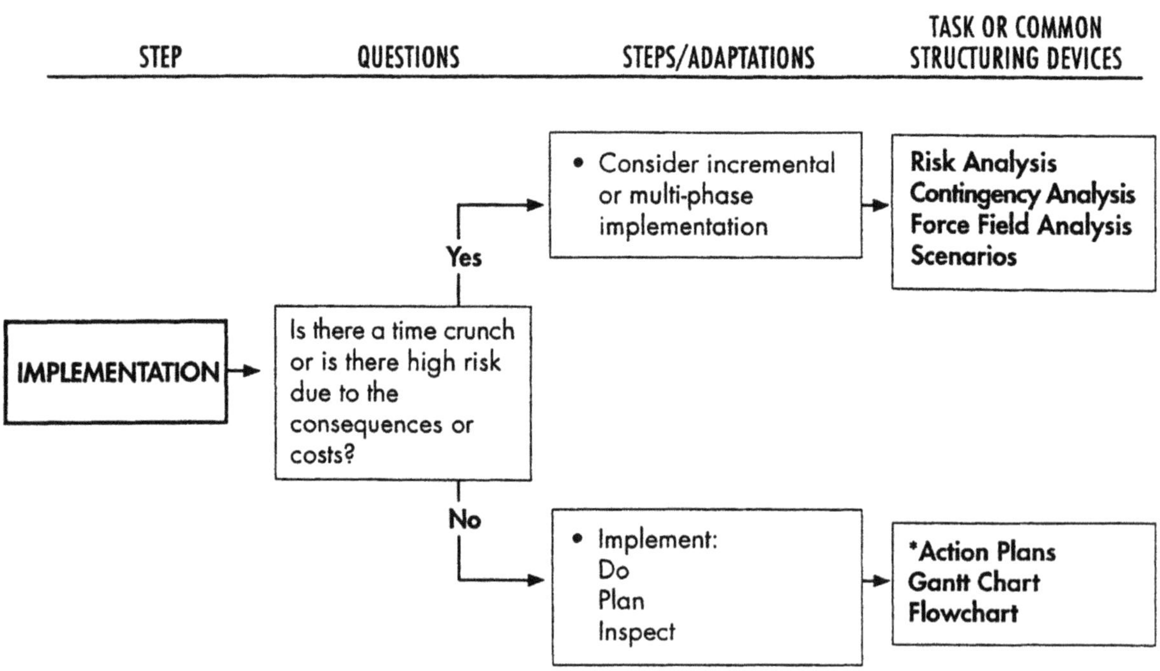

Figure 5.6. **Implementation.** ***Author created (1st edition)***

Chapter Six

Structuring Devices

This chapter is unlike any of the other chapters in this book. Its long-term worth to you will be mostly as a reference piece, a catalog of structuring devices. We recommend that you read through the devices to understand how each works. In the future, you will simply reread those devices that fit your decision conditions. In using this reference chapter, you should be aware of the following:

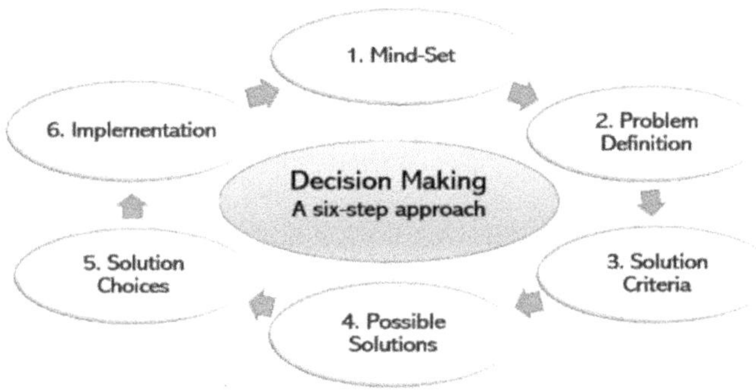

Figure 6.1. Decision Making: A Six-Step Approach. ***Author created (updated from 1st edition)***

1. The structuring devices are presented in alphabetical order for ease of access; we did not group them by decision steps because some devices are appropriate to multiple decision needs.
2. We have included the organizing tables from the previous chapters in this chapter also; this will facilitate your association of each device with decision steps and needs.
3. Each device is presented in a similar template; the template contains the following:
    a. Description
    b. Application or illustration of use
    c. Time, materials, and other considerations
    d. Procedural steps
    e. Variations
    f. Cautions
    g. Examples
    h. References
4. In this edition, we also include nondigital and digital methods to present each structuring device. The recommendations for incorporating digital methods, or groupware devices, is offered to increase participant engagement. While ongoing updates to groupware and devices may enhance future opportunities, some options may become obsolete. Not all structuring devices include or require the use of digital methods. In these cases, the method is omitted.
5. Feel free to use any of the worksheets or templates for your use in decision making (DM); the copyright associated with this book only limits your appropriation of the templates of these structuring devices for personal profit for publication.

Enjoy these structuring devices and use them in good health (tables 6.1–6.5).

Table 6.1. Structuring Device and Application to Decision Step (1 of 5). ***Author created (1st edition)***

STRUCTURING DEVICE	*DESCRIPTION*	*STEP 1 MIND-SET*	*STEP 2 PROBLEM DEFINITION*	*STEP 3 SOLUTION CRITERIA*	*STEP 4 POSSIBLE SOLUTIONS*	*STEP 5 SOLUTION CHOICE*	*STEP 6 IMPLEMENT*
ACTION PLAN	This device is a chart displaying who does what by when and how. A must in implementation.						X
ADVOCACY TEAMS	This device calls on individuals to argue for and against a solution. It opens people to viewpoints of others.					X	
AFFINITY DIAGRAM	A device that organizes ideas into categories or groupings.		X		X		
ANALOGY	A playful approach to looking at a problem by making an analogy; "this problem is like . . ."				X		
ANECDOTE	Participants apply past experiences to current SiTNAs.	X		X	X	X	
BEAN COUNT	Participants use beans to identify their preferences among a variety of possibilities.					X	
BOUNDARY-SETTING MISSION STATEMENT	This device is used to ensure that the decisions being made are congruent with the mission of the organization.	X					
BRAINSTORMING	Brainstorming is used to generate possibilities and ideas in a free flow process; also has variations.		X	X	X		
CAROUSEL BRAINSTORMING	This form of brainstorming asks participants to move from chart to chart to generate ideas. Best used when issue has multiple parts or subissues.		X	X	X		
CAUSE/EFFECT DIAGRAM	This fishbowl diagram helps participants identify and categorize causes of problems.		X	X			

Table 6.2. Structuring Device and Application to Decision Step (2 of 5). ***Author created (1st edition)***

STRUCTURING DEVICE	*DESCRIPTION*	*STEP 1 MIND-SET*	*STEP 2 PROBLEM DEFINITION*	*STEP 3 SOLUTION CRITERIA*	*STEP 4 POSSIBLE SOLUTIONS*	*STEP 5 SOLUTION CHOICE*	*STEP 6 IMPLEMENT*
COMPETITOR MAPPING	This device calls on participants to identify and visit "best of class" competitors to better understand own deficiencies and possible solutions.		X		X		
CONTINGENCY ANALYSIS	This TQM tool identifies causes of problems and potential ways to prevent these causes.		X				X
COST ICEBERG	Participants identify obvious and hidden costs for a project or process.		X				X
CRITERIA DEVELOPMENT	This technique helps individuals identify "must" and "want" criteria during solution criteria stage.			X			
CRITERIA STANDARDS	Individuals establish quantitative levels (indicants) for each solution criterion. Used where qualification is necessary.			X			
CROSS-IMPACT MATRIX	This device is used to examine the interaction of potential future events.		X			X	
DECISION TREE ANALYSIS	This graphic device displays the consequences of possible solutions or action steps to aid in solution choice. Each possibility has "branches" of consequences.					X	X
DISCREPANCY ANALYSIS	This device examines the differences between desired states and actual states.		X				
FLOWCHART	The Flowchart is a graphic means of laying out or mapping the stages of a process.		X				X
FORCE FIELD ANALYSIS	This approach identifies two sets of forces: those that drive change and those that resist it. Useful in developing action strategies.						X
GANTT CHART	This device reports the tasks, responsibilities, and time schedule for accomplishment of a project.						X
GOAL SETTING	This device is used to help groups to construct goals in SITNAs where new goals are needed.		X				

Table 6.3. Structuring Device and Application to Decision Step (3 of 5). ***Author created (1st edition)***

STRUCTURING DEVICE	*DESCRIPTION*	*STEP 1 MIND-SET*	*STEP 2 PROBLEM DEFINITION*	*STEP 3 SOLUTION CRITERIA*	*STEP 4 POSSIBLE SOLUTIONS*	*STEP 5 SOLUTION CHOICE*	*STEP 6 IMPLEMENT*
HUMAN SOCIOGRAMS	This structured experience calls on decision makers to move around a room, as a representation of their opinions about issues.					X	
INTERRELATIONSHIP DIGRAPH	This charting process represents the interconnectedness of various problem causes.		X				
MAGNITUDE ESTIMATION ANALYSIS	This scaling device is used for setting priorities. It is mostly used in surveys.					X	
METAPHOR	Individuals create visual representations of a problem and discuss what they say about the problem.		X				
MIND MAP	This free-form display is used to represent the element of a problem.		X		X		X
MORPHOLOGICAL ANALYSIS	This device is used to generate a large array of possibilities in an analytical, nonemotional way.				X		
MULTI-ATTRIBUTE ANALYSIS	This device compares costs to benefits of proposed solutions.					X	
MULTI-VOTING	Multi-voting is used to narrow down lists of possibilities.					X	
NEEDS/WANTS CRITERIA MATRIX	This device calls on participants to compare solution possibilities against needs/wants criteria.					X	
NOMINAL GROUP TECHNIQUE	This is an alternative idea-generating device to brainstorming; it relies on individual, silent generation of ideas in the beginning.		X	X	X		
PAPER PLATE EXCHANGE	This structured questioning activity encourages discussion through question-and-answer exchanges.		X				

Table 6.4. Structuring Device and Application to Decision Step (4 of 5). ***Author created (1st edition)***

STRUCTURING DEVICE	*DESCRIPTION*	*STEP 1 MIND-SET*	*STEP 2 PROBLEM DEFINITION*	*STEP 3 SOLUTION CRITERIA*	*STEP 4 POSSIBLE SOLUTIONS*	*STEP 5 SOLUTION CHOICE*	*STEP 6 IMPLEMENT*
PARETO CHART	The Pareto Chart is used to identify problems and causes that require the most energy and focus.		X			X	
PARTICIPATIVE MANAGEMENT TREE	This device identifies which of four decision approaches is most useful in a given setting: consultation, command, consensus, or convenience.	X					
PAYOFF MATRIX	This device examines the probable outcomes of various different contingencies; it is highly quantitative.					X	
PERSONAL POWER GRID	This tool explores with participants things they can and cannot control throughout the decision process.	X					
POSITIVE CONTEXT	This device creates a common set of beliefs, behaviors, and conditions needed for an effective decision process.	X					
PRECEDENCE CHART	This is a priority-setting device. It is based on binary comparison of variables.					X	
PRIORITY MATRIX	This priority-setting approach involves rating each solution possibility according to its importance and feasibility and placing the possibilities in a matrix format.					X	
RISK ANALYSIS	Risk analysis is used to look at the potential risks in selecting a choice.					X	X
SCENARIO BUILDING	This device uses narrative description of some situation or setting to understand that situation. Scenarios involve storytelling.		X			X	X
SNOW CARD	This technique is useful for: 1) generating ideas and 2) categorizing those ideas. This is done through a visual display of index cards/post-it notes.		X	X	X		

Table 6.5. Structuring Device and Application to Decision Step (5 of 5). ***Author created (1st edition)***

STRUCTURING DEVICE	*DESCRIPTION*	*STEP 1 MIND-SET*	*STEP 2 PROBLEM DEFINITION*	*STEP 3 SOLUTION CRITERIA*	*STEP 4 POSSIBLE SOLUTIONS*	*STEP 5 SOLUTION CHOICE*	*STEP 6 IMPLEMENT*
SPEND-A-DOT	Participants use colored adhesive dots to identify priority items.					X	
STACK THE DECK	This device narrows down solution possibilities through the use of index cards.					X	
STAKEHOLDER ANALYSIS	As the name suggests, this device identifies who holds some investment in the decisions being made.	X					
STRAW POLLING	This is a "show-of-thumbs" exercise for eliciting group feelings about a solution possibility.					X	
SWOT	SWOT examines the strengths, weaknesses, opportunities, and threats involved in a SiTNA.	X	X				
T CHART	This device helps participants look at factors working for or against a possible solution.		X			X	
TRADE-OFF ANALYSIS	This highly useful tool compares solution possibilities against solution criteria.					X	
TREE DIAGRAM	This is a visual display of causes of problems representing a tree diagram.		X				
VISION SETTING	This device is aimed at helping participants create an organizational vision.		X				
WHY CYCLE	Sometimes called "Five Times Why," it involves recurrent questioning through the word *why*. It is a questioning device.		X				

COLLABORATIVE SOFTWARE ("GROUPWARE") AND DEVICES

The following list contains potential resources to consider using when working collectively to make a decision. The application software and devices listed below are intended to incorporate engaging, tech-based opportunities for collaboration. As evidenced by the J curve, these applications and devices may undergo improvements or even become obsolete in the near future. We invite you to check out our Tech Tip section contained within each structuring device and use when applicable.

Collaborative Document

A collaborative document application allows users to write, edit, or contribute to a document with the goal of creating a single final version through collaboration. This can (but not always) replace chart paper. Examples include the following:

- Microsoft Word Online
- Google Docs
- Quip
- Paper by Dropbox

Collaborative Spreadsheet

Similar to the collaborative document, collaborative spreadsheets allow users to create, edit, or contribute to a group spreadsheet. These are especially helpful when the use of formulas are required for running both simple and more complex calculations. Examples include the following:

- MS Excel Online
- Google Sheets
- Zoho Sheets
- Air Table

Collaborative Presentation

Collaborative presentation applications allow for groups to create a collaborative presentation. These applications typically utilize a slide format that can incorporate multimedia, graphs, tables, and simple text. Examples include the following:

- MS PowerPoint
- Google Slides
- Prezi
- Visme
- Keynote

Whiteboard Collaborative Tools

Whiteboard collaborative tools allow users real-time collaboration in a cloud-based environment. Users can sketch, rearrange, group, and edit ideas. These tools work in small or large groups. This can (but not always) replace chart paper, note cards, or post-it notes. Examples include the following:

- Jamboard
- Padlet
- Limnu
- Deskle
- Note.ly
- Cardsmith

Video Communication/Conferencing Tools

Video communication/conferencing tools allow users in different locations the ability to meet face to face in small or large groups. There are several embedded applications within many of these tools such as shared screens, whiteboard, and group surveys. Examples include the following:

- Zoom
- GoToMeeting
- Google Meet
- Cisco WebEx
- Microsoft Teams

Other Applications

Examples of other interactive applications that can help engage, gather data, or organize a team include the following:

- Kahoot
- Quizlet
- Nearpod
- Electronic calendars

Devices

Devices can also contribute to providing a high-quality and engaging visual experience in the decision-making process. These technologies can range in cost, size, and availability. Examples include the following:

- Responders
- Tablet computer
- Smartboard
- Samsung Flip
- Large format display (LFD)

ACTION PLAN

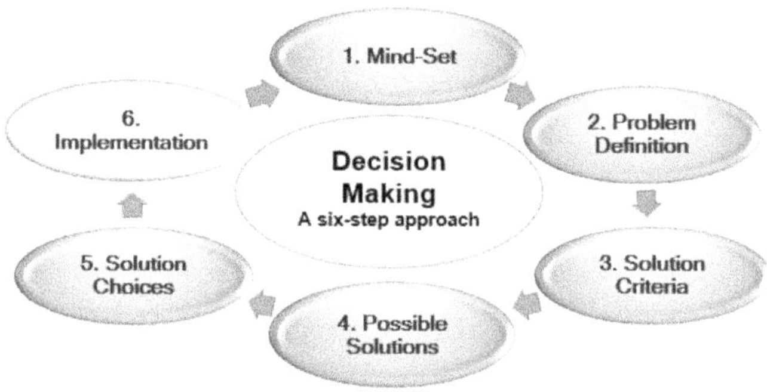

Figure 6.2. Decision Making: A Six-Step Approach: Action Plan. *Author created (updated from 1st edition)*

Description

A decision does not become a reality until it is put into action. The Action Plan is a device that structures action steps to facilitate decision implementation. The Action Plan identifies and defines tasks, responsibilities, and other considerations (who does what, by when, and how). The Action Plan is a record of information describing how the plan will be implemented.

Application or Illustration of Use

- Use an action plan for implementation after a decision is made. Table 6.6 shows what an action plan looks like.

Table 6.6. Action Plan: Application or Illustration Use (Image). *Author created (1st edition)*

GOAL:

WHAT IS TO BE DONE?	*WHO IS INVOLVED?*	*WHO IS RESPONSIBLE?*	*RESOURCES NEEDED?*	*HOW EVALUATED?*	*WHEN COMPLETED?*

Time, Materials, and Other Considerations

Time: Approximately 30–90 minutes to develop an action plan, depending on the complexity of the implementation process.
Materials: See table 6.7.

Table 6.7. Tech Table: Action Plan. ***Author created (updated from 1st edition)***

Nondigital	*Digital*
• Flip chart	• Collaborative Document (e.g., Google Docs, Microsoft Word Online)
• Pens, markers	• Whiteboard Collaborative Tools (e.g., Jamboard)
• Tape	• Devices (e.g., Interactive LFD)
• Worksheet (provided)	• Digital calendars

Procedural Steps

1. Make copies of the six-column Action Plan worksheet included in this book (see table 6.8).
2. Across the top row of the chart, write the title of the decision or goal.
3. In the column on the far-left side of the chart ("What Is to Be Done?"), list the tasks that must be accomplished to implement the decision. Try to list them in a natural sequence of activities. If the task is complex, you might use another process to generate the activities. You then need to sequence them.
4. Go to the second column and identify all of the people or groups involved in that particular task.
5. Next, go to the third column and assign responsibilities for each of the tasks.
6. At the fourth column, identify the resources needed (money, materials, time, facilities, etc.)
7. When the group is ready to move on to the evaluation step, they will need to discuss and identify what the accountability steps will be.
8. Set a deadline for completion for each task in the "When Completed?" column.
9. When completed, double check that the Action Plan will accomplish the intended purpose. See table 6.9 for an example of a completed action plan.

Cautions

Although it takes time and seems like an extra step after the decision has been made, always take the time to develop an action plan in order to better ensure implementation of a decision. Remind the group that actions may change over time and as circumstances change. The user should feel free to expand the action plan in any way useful. This could include adding columns or splitting columns.

Action Plan: Worksheet

See table 6.8 for a worksheet template.

Table 6.8. Action Plan: Worksheet. ***Author created (1st edition)***

GOAL:

WHAT IS TO BE DONE?	*WHO IS INVOLVED?*	*WHO IS RESPONSIBLE?*	*RESOURCES NEEDED?*	*HOW EVALUATED?*	*WHEN COMPLETED?*

Action Plan Worksheet: Example

See table 6.9 for an example worksheet.

Table 6.9. Action Plan Worksheet: Example. ***Author created (1st edition)***

GOAL: To create an ethnic studies center at Crescent Community College

WHAT IS TO BE DONE?	*WHO IS INVOLVED?*	*WHO IS RESPONSIBLE?*	*RESOURCES NEEDED?*	*HOW EVALUATED?*	*WHEN COMPLETED?*
• Form diversity task force	Pres Cabinet	Pres	Time	Budget	Oct. 22, 2021
• Include seed $ in budget	VP for business; president	Pres	$20,000		Oct. 30–Feb. 1
• Task force meets	9 members (3 fac, 3 admin, 3 students)	Facilitator (TBA)	Time		Nov. 7, 2021
• Task force visits other schools	Task force		Time: $500		Nov. 2021
• Tenets, vision program of work created	Task force		Time	Pres will monitor	Jan. 3, 2022
• Approved by senate	Task force, senate meeting		Majority vote	Senate minutes	Feb. 2022
• Approved by board of trustees	Pres; board, task force	Pres	Consensus	Trustee minutes	Mar. 19, 2022
• Hire director of center	Pres, task force	Pres	$10,000 (part of step 2)	Pres monitors	Mar.–Apr. 2022
• Announcement of center and its intended activities	Director of center	Director	$500 (part of step 2)	Local newspapers; press monitors	May 2022

ADVOCACY TEAMS

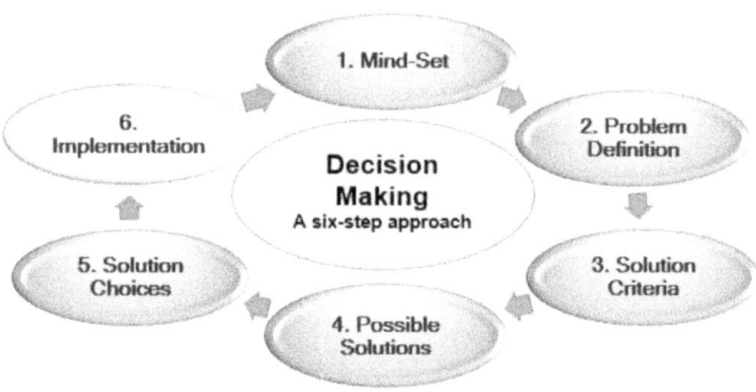

Figure 6.3. Decision Making: A Six-Step Approach: Advocacy Teams. ***Author created (updated from 1st edition)***

Description

Advocacy Teams is a structured experience that allows individuals or groups to advocate for or against a solution or decision. The use of this device encourages individuals (or groups) to "dig out" or surface facts and to establish a common level of communication. Furthermore, advocacy forces members to define terms, clarify positions, articulate, and justify a solution choice. It opens members to the viewpoints of others.

Applications or Illustrations of Use

- Use Advocacy Teams when there are strong feelings for or against a possible solution that is highly emotional.
- Use Advocacy Teams if a point of view is underrepresented.
- Use when the group is making a major "cultural" change (e.g., whether or not to implement shared governance as a decision-making format).
- Use when deciding to eliminate specific services or programs.

Time, Materials, and Other Considerations

Time: Approximately 15–30 minutes.
Materials: See table 6.10.

Table 6.10. Tech Table: Advocacy Teams. ***Author created (updated from 1st edition)***

Nondigital	*Digital*
• Flip chart	• Collaborative Document (e.g., Google Docs, Microsoft Word Online)
• Pens, markers	• Whiteboard Collaborative Tools (e.g., Cardsmith)
• Tape	• Devices (e.g., Interactive LFD)
• Participant data	

Procedural Steps

- Divide the participants into teams or pairs.
- Present the possible solution(s) to be discussed.
- Assign individuals or teams to research one side of a solution to look for evidence in favor of that side. One side argues for the solution; the other side argues against the solution. We usually assign people to sides that do not represent their true positions.
- Have each team present its data and argument. This can be done with or without discussion. Do this for each solution.
- Have a recorder note the salient points on a flip chart.
- Discuss salient points.

Caution

- Remind the Advocacy Teams that they are to argue for their assigned solution position and not attack other team members.

References

Koberg and Bagnall (1981, 84).
Van Gundy (1988, 233).

AFFINITY DIAGRAM

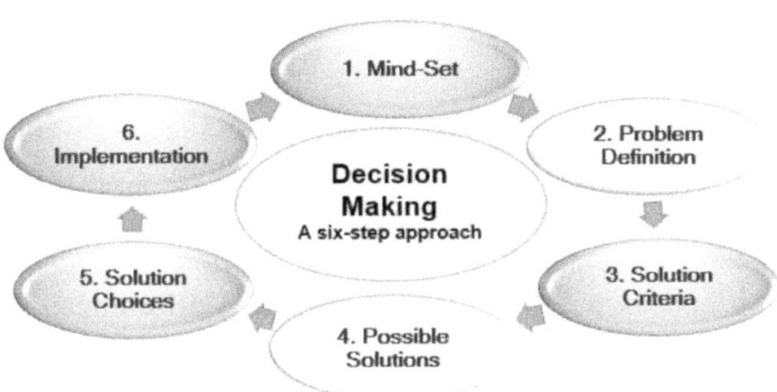

Figure 6.4. Decision Making: A Six-Step Approach: Affinity Diagram. ***Author created (updated from 1st edition)***

Description

The Affinity Diagram, just as its name implies, is a technique that organizes ideas into natural categories. This device is generally used following the generation of a long list of ideas (e.g., after brainstorming). The Affinity Diagram looks at relationships among identified problems, objects, and possible solutions and categorizes them into manageable groups according to a likeness or affinity. Because the Affinity Diagram has an individual component that requires silence, it allows participants an opportunity to give input without concern for judgment. The discussion that follows the grouping helps define ideas so that there is common understanding among the participants. The Affinity Diagram is useful when the team is large, more than 10 to 12, but it can be used with smaller groups.

Applications or Illustrations of Use

- Use the Affinity Diagram following brainstorming when you need to organize a wide array of possibilities.
- Use the Affinity Diagram when consensus is important. Because each individual has to "get involved," each person shares in the responsibility for grouping.
- Use when the group is analytical and creativity is desired.
- Use if the group is argumentative; affinity grouping requires silence-time to think.

Time, Materials, and Other Considerations

Time: Approximately 15–30 minutes.
Materials: See table 6.11.

Table 6.11. Tech Table: Affinity Diagram. ***Author created (new for 2nd edition)***

Nondigital	*Digital*
• Post-it notes	• Whiteboard Collaborative Tools (e.g., Jamboard)
• Pens, markers	• Devices (e.g., Interactive LFD)

Procedural Steps

Use Affinity Diagram following an activity in which a list of ideas is generated (as in brainstorming):

1. Record each idea onto a post-it note or card. This may be done by individuals or the group leader.

2. Post the ideas on to a wall or chart (randomly).
3. Remind the members that they are to move without discussion. The silence provides time for participants to think and give input without concern for judgment.
4. Each person goes to the wall or chart and silently moves (sorts) the cards into groupings or categories. One person may move another's ideas to a different category.
5. When it appears that the team is satisfied with the placement of the cards, give the grouping or category a header card (name) that encapsulates the general idea. Variation: If a person wants to move a card after the groupings are made, the facilitator asks the team if an idea can be moved to another category.
6. Open discussion by asking for clarification of ideas that seem unclear. The discussion that follows the grouping defines ideas and creates common understanding.
7. Discuss the following question: "Which grouping seems most appropriate?"
8. Once the team has a common understanding, decide on the next steps (e.g., prioritizing, solution criteria, solution possibilities).

Variation

- See Snow Cards as another version of Affinity Diagram.

Cautions

- Do not use Affinity Grouping if the problem definition is unclear.
- Keep an eye on the process so that participants are not rushing through the process. People want to prematurely end the process before the team has agreed on the categories.
- Do not allow the number of ideas in the categories to drive the decision.
- Be sure to allow participants time to reflect on their ideas.
- Allow time for clarification.

Example

Table 6.12 is an example of the Affinity Diagram for an international service organization that is seeking to determine new programs for funding.

Table 6.12. Possible New Programs. ***Author created (updated from 1st edition)***

Possible New Programs			
Eye Programs	*Disaster Relief*	*Family Services*	*Citizenship*
• Eye Bank • Program for the Blind • Glaucoma Testing	• Earthquake Relief • Flood Relief • Tornado/ Hurricane Relief • Famine Relief • Medical Services for Players • AIDS Support	• Family Awareness • Youth Service • Battered Women's Shelter • Elder Houses	• Citizenship

References

Brassard and Ritter (1994, 12).
Chang and Niedzwiecki (1994, 15).
Klubnik and Greenwood (1994, 146).
Viability Corporate HR, Performance Development Division (1994).

ANALOGY

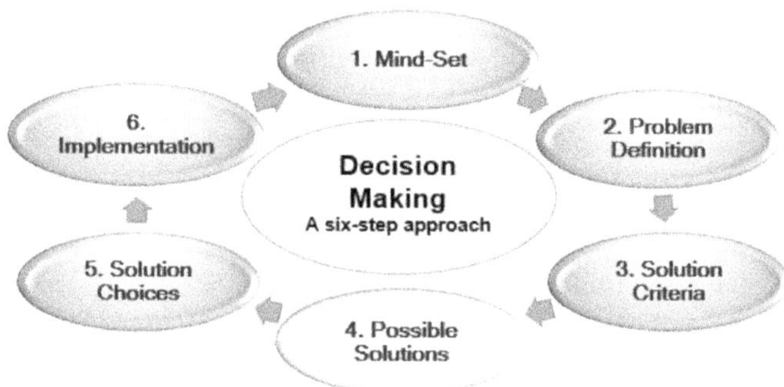

Figure 6.5. Decision Making: A Six-Step Approach: Analogy. ***Author created (updated from 1st edition)***

Description

Analogies are structured experiences that allow the decision makers to tap into their creativity to develop possible solutions. The decision makers move from an abstract concept to a concrete solution by comparing and associating relationships and differences of unlike items.

Application or Illustration of Use

- Use the Analogy when the decision-making group seems to be "stuck" in generating alternatives or when you want to stimulate their creativity.

Time, Materials, and Other Considerations

Time: Approximately 30–60 minutes.
Materials: See table 6.13.

Table 6.13. Tech Table: Analogy. ***Author created (new for 2nd edition)***

Nondigital	*Digital*
• Chart paper	• Collaborative Document (e.g., Google Docs, Microsoft Word Online)
• Pens, markers	• Whiteboard Collaborative Tools (e.g., Cardsmith)
• Post-it notes	• Devices (e.g., Interactive LFD)
• 8.5-inch x 11-inch writing paper	

Procedural Steps

1. Identify the problem or situation that requires a solution.
2. Ask the group to create an analogy that is similar to the problem. For example: "Coming up with a solution is like finding a toothpick in a haystack" or "Arriving at a solution is like rolling around on a bed of marshmallows."
3. Ask the group to describe all of the characteristics or aspects of this situation by describing such things as the following:

   a. How does it look?
   b. What does it feel like?
   c. How does it taste?
   d. What are its parts?
   e. What are its functions?

4. Identify what approaches you could use to solve the analogy/problem (find the toothpick or solidify the marshmallows).
5. Ask the group to transfer application of the analogy to the real problem or situation. Record the ideas.
6. Discuss and review the possible solutions.

Example

A leadership team wants to explore and expand on its image as a customer-oriented business. The leader makes the analogy: "Working with our company is like a giant dessert tray." The group then explores the following questions:

1. What kind of dessert are we?
2. Can there be too much of a good thing?
3. Are we seen as a necessary part of our customer's meal?
4. How do we taste? Look? Smell?
5. How could we make a better dessert?

By way of a playful analogy, the company can examine what it does and how important it is to the customer.

ANECDOTE

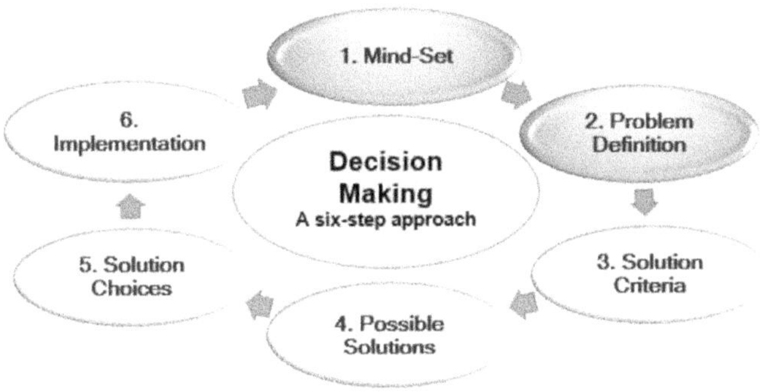

Figure 6.6. Decision Making: A Six-Step Approach: Anecdote. ***Author created (updated from 1st edition)***

Description

The Anecdote allows the decision maker to use his or her creativity. The participants apply past experiences (their own or others) to the current situation. This device allows the decision maker to approach the situation from another point of view, examine past experiences, and explore future settings.

Application or Illustration of Use

- Use the Anecdote when the group is more mature and experienced and the situation lends itself to past comparisons.

Time, Materials, and Other Considerations

Time: Approximately 30–60 minutes.
Materials: See table 6.14.

Table 6.14. Tech Table: Anecdote. ***Author created (new for 2nd edition)***

Nondigital	*Digital*
• Timer	• Digital Timer • Devices (e.g., Interactive LFD)

Procedural Steps

1. Define the current situation.
2. Have team members reflect on a similar problem/decision in the past.
3. Pose the question: "What happened?" Allow discussion.
4. Pose the next question: "What did you do?" Go through the situation step by step.
5. Ask the group to look at the current problem and respond to the first question: "What has happened so far?"
6. Ask these questions:
   - What did the previous situation teach us?
   - What can be transferred to this situation?
   - How is this situation different?

Caution

- Do not use Anecdote with participants who have no related experience.

BEAN COUNT

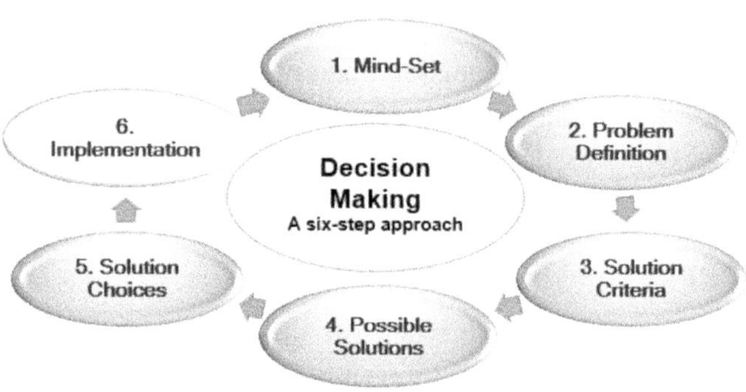

Figure 6.7. Decision Making: A Six-Step Approach: Bean Count. ***Author created (updated from 1st edition)***

Description

The Bean Count is a useful device that allows a decision-making group to prioritize a number of ideas or solution possibilities. The Bean Count is a quick and easy way to involve all the participants in the prioritizing or winnowing process without fear of judgment. Participants use beans to identify their preferences; the number of beans "counted" under a specific idea or option helps identify the most important thoughts selected by the group.

Applications or Illustrations of Use

- Use when the group has many ideas, for example, following brainstorming.
- Use the Bean Count as one way to involve each person in the group with the prioritizing process.
- Use a different colored bean to surface feelings of opposition quickly.

Time, Materials, and Other Considerations

Time: Approximately 5–10 minutes.
Materials: See table 6.15.

Table 6.15. Tech Table: Bean Count. ***Author created (new for 2nd edition)***

Nondigital	*Digital*
• Chart paper	• Collaborative Document (e.g., Google Docs, Microsoft Word Online)
• Pens, markers	• Devices (e.g., Interactive LFD)
• Beans (light and dark)	
• Containers to catch the beans	

Procedural Steps

Once a list is generated, complete the following steps:

1. Write each idea listed on the chart onto a separate piece of paper (chart or card).
2. Post or place the cards on or above tables around the room. Place a container (cup/plate) under the idea.
3. Give a number of beans to each person, depending on the number of ideas generated (usually five or six beans per person.) Typically, we use a ratio of

one bean for every five ideas generated. You could also use one bean of a different color. This single bean represents an idea that they cannot tolerate.

4. Have the group members wander around and place one or more of their beans in the containers for the ideas they value until all of their beans are gone. If you use different-colored beans (i.e., light-colored beans represent ideas that cannot be tolerated; dark-colored beans affirm the idea), remind them that they can place the light-colored bean under the idea they are not willing to accept. They do not have to use all of their beans.
5. When all members have distributed their beans, count the number of beans under each idea.
6. Identify the ideas with the most beans (usually the top five).
7. Identify and discuss the ideas that have light beans.
8. Discuss and affirm the ideas with the most beans as priority issues and/or solutions.

Variations

- Use covered cups with a hole in the cover to pass the bean through. This prevents participants from being influenced by seeing the number of beans in the containers.
- Use the different color bean as a mega-vote, your most highly prized choice.
- Use poker chips (white as the standard vote, blue as the "absolutely not" vote, and red as the mega-vote).
- Use play money.

Caution

- This is not a vote or a final decision or solution, simply a prioritization or winnowing tool.

BOUNDARY-SETTING MISSION STATEMENT

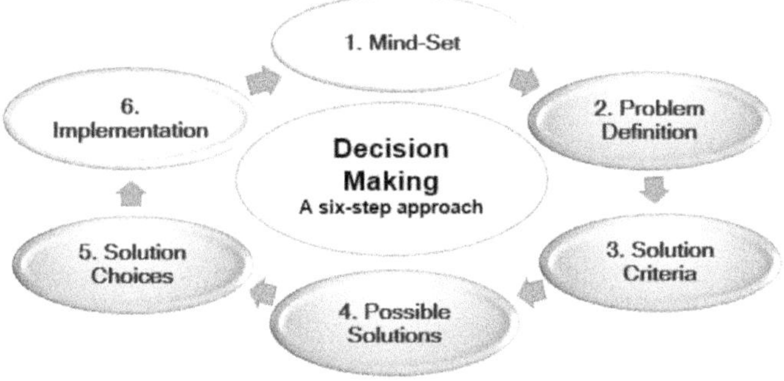

Figure 6.8. Decision Making: A Six-Step Approach: Boundary. ***Author created (updated from 1st edition)***

Description

The Boundary-Setting Mission Statement is a statement that identifies the starting point of the decision-making process. By describing the mission and identifying the specific purpose of the organization, the team commits to focus on the issue at hand in the context of the purpose of the organization. The Boundary-Setting Mission Statement serves as a template that identifies the product and customer. This statement keeps the team aligned with their original purpose as the team works through every step of the decision-making process.

Application or Illustration of Use

- Use the Boundary-Setting Mission Statement at the beginning of the decision process to ensure that the decisions being made are congruent with the mission of the organization.

Time, Materials, and Other Considerations

Time: Approximately 15–30 minutes.
Materials: See table 6.16.

Table 6.16. Tech Table: Boundary-Setting Mission Statement. ***Author created (new for 2nd edition)***

Nondigital	*Digital*
• Chart paper	• Collaborative Document (e.g., Google Docs, Microsoft Word Online)
• Pens, markers	• Whiteboard Collaborative Tools (e.g., Jamboard)
• Tape	• Devices (e.g., Interactive LFD)

Procedural Steps

Through discussion with the group, complete the following steps:

1. Identify the primary product or process of the organization or subunit.
2. Identify clients of the organization or subunit.
3. Ask "What is the purpose of the organization's or subunit's existence?"
4. Discuss until there is common agreement on steps 1, 2, and 3 above.

Write the mission as: The mission of the _______ is to _______ so that the _______ customer/client can _______.

Keep the Boundary-Setting Mission Statement present throughout the decision-making process.

Example

The mission of the Ajax Software Company is to produce quality software for financial planning so that the customer can plan individual long-term financial stability for his family without needing to consult a financial advisor.

Caution

- If you use this device, be sure to keep the mission statement posted during the decision-making process to redirect the team as necessary.

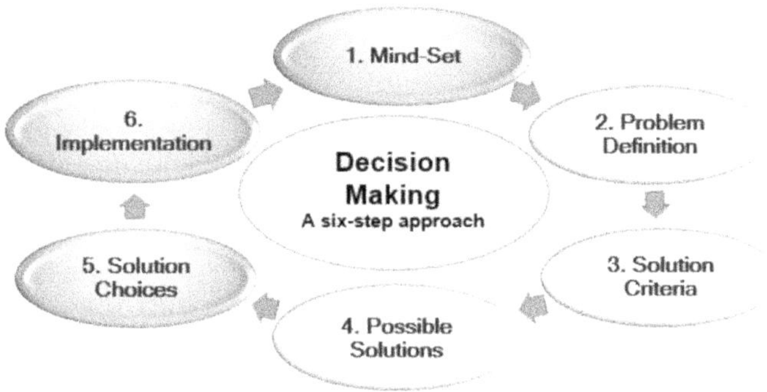

Figure 6.9. Decision Making: A Six-Step Approach: Brainstorming. *Author created (updated from 1st edition)*

BRAINSTORMING

Description

Brainstorming is a popular device among decision makers because of its ease of use and quick results. Brainstorming frees thinking by engaging the creative mind of the participants. Participants are encouraged to "think beyond the box" and to generate as many ideas related to a specific topic or issue as they can. The rules of Brainstorming specify that every idea is a good idea; hence, participants are encouraged to be creative without fear of censure. In Brainstorming, there is no "stupid idea" so that the "brainstormers" are able to bring out a number of ideas and create a list of ideas, solutions, and such.

Applications or Illustrations of Use

- Use Brainstorming when the need exists to generate many possibilities and ideas.
- Use Brainstorming at the beginning of the decision-making process as a way to define the problem or decision to be made.
- Use Brainstorming when you want people to be open minded, when their ideas are "stuck," and when you want people to look at problems in different ways.

Time, Materials, and Other Considerations

Time: Approximately 5–20 minutes.
Materials: See table 6.17.

Table 6.17. Tech Table: Brainstorming. ***Author created (new for 2nd edition)***

Nondigital	*Digital*
• Flip chart	• Collaborative Document (e.g., Google Docs, Microsoft Word Online)
• Pens, markers	• Whiteboard Collaborative Tools (e.g., Jamboard)
• Post-it notes	• Devices (e.g., Smartboard)
• Timer	• Digital timer
• Rules of Brainstorming	

Procedural Steps

1. Discuss the purpose of brainstorming and review the rules of brainstorming (provided).
2. Post a large chart pad to capture ideas.
3. Ask participants to propose ideas. It will usually start slowly and then move quickly (like a popcorn popper). Allow time for the right brain to kick in so that participants may build and add to the ideas, "no holds barred." Crazy is okay.
4. On the chart, write down every idea the way that participants say it.
5. After a list is generated, clarify, examine, discuss, and discard ideas. Focus on having a product when finished that may be used in relationship with other techniques.
6. Leave the visuals up for others to see and to reference.
7. After the list is generated, the ideas may be grouped (e.g., Affinity Diagram).

Variations

The following list describes focused variations of brainstorming:

- *Bouncing Ball Brainstorming* is a variation of brainstorming that manages the flow of ideas through the use of a ball. Have the group stand in a circle. Follow steps 1 and 2 above. Remind the group that participants may not throw out an idea until they have the ball in hand. Toss the ball from person to person, or participants may call for the ball. Participants may speak if they are in possession of the bouncing ball: "No ball—No Talk." At this point, follow Brainstorming steps 6 and 7.
- *Polarized Brainstorming* encourages the participants to propose ideas that are focused on a particular perspective of an issue (e.g., the pros or cons, pluses or minuses, what worked or what didn't work, etc.). Have the participants respond to one side (pole) at a time.
- *Possibility Thinking Brainstorming* gets people to think in terms of visions, to generate ideas and solution criteria. At step 3, have the participants think of a vision and create a list of possibilities from those thoughts.
- *Round Robin Brainstorming* controls the flow of ideas so that responses are solicited in a "round-robin" style with each person contributing an idea until all ideas are exhausted. Participants are allowed the right to "pass" on presenting an idea.
- *Sentence Completion Brainstorming* has participants share their ideas orally or on a slip of paper. As they respond, they must complete the sentence by adding an ending (e.g., "I see this problem as _______").
- *Wild Card Brainstorming* encourages participants to think of far-out examples or ideas. At step 3, ask the participants to use their imaginations to think of wild ideas. Participants propose the wildest ideas they can generate.

Other Variations

- Have participants silently brainstorm on post-it notes for "equity of voice."
- Reporting out to large group depends on a non-threatening and nonjudgmental environment. Break the large group into smaller groups for brainstorming. Then, during the reporting out period, have the large group add on to small group list.

Cautions

- Be sure to allow participants adequate time to generate ideas. If people stop too soon, while the group is still throwing out ideas, rich ideas won't come out.
- The size of the group can be a creativity and time "limiter." In large groups, people may try to hide so that there is not full involvement. To circumvent this from happening, use smaller groups to minimize risks.
- Make sure that everyone understands the "rules of Brainstorming"—no one evaluates or discusses the ideas as they are generated because it will kill creativity (see table 6.18).
- Because of brainstorming's speed, there may not be the richness or depth, resulting in superficial ideas. Be sure to allow time to elaborate on the ideas.
- Because of the popularity of this device, it may be overused and abused. Be sure to understand its purpose before using Brainstorming.
- You might want to use two or three recorders to keep the flow of ideas quick and smooth. You don't want to lose ideas because the recorder is too slow.
- Be cautious of using Brainstorming in volatile or conflictual situations.

Table 6.18. Brainstorming Ground Rules. ***Author created (updated from 1st edition)***

- Be creative; everyone "freewheels"; no holding back; the more ideas the better.
- Let the ideas flow without discussion. You will have a chance to revisit and clarify later.
- Withhold judgment of ideas. (Watch your body language.) Have fun, be positive, and encourage everyone's ideas to flow.
- Hitchhike and build on others' ideas. "Piggybacking" is OK.
- Make sure that your idea is posted correctly. Check for accuracy.

References

Brassard and Ritter (1994, 19).
Chang and Kelly (1993, 96).
Doyle and Straus (1986, 232).
Fisher, Ury, and Patton (1991, 62).
Klubnik and Greenwood (1994, 140).
Higgens (1994, 118).
Koberg and Bagnall (1981, 68).
Quinlivan-Hall and Renner (1990, 85).
Scholtes et al. (1994, 2–41).
Van Gundy (1988, 24).

CAROUSEL BRAINSTORMING

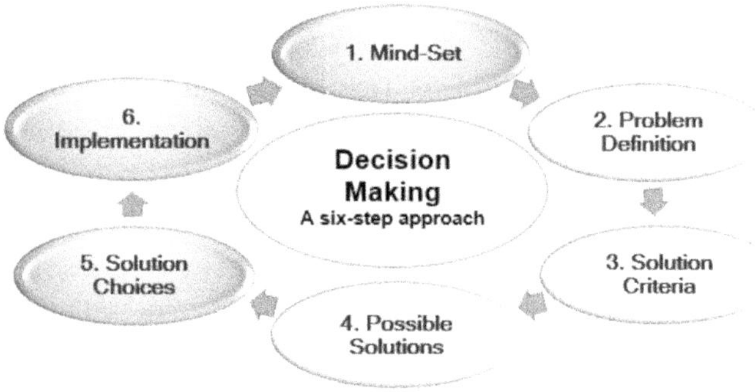

Figure 6.10. Decision Making: A Six-Step Approach: Carousel Brainstorming. ***Author created (updated from 1st edition)***

Description

Carousel Brainstorming is a variation of Brainstorming that provides for smaller group involvement and extends and triggers thinking in small groups. Carousel Brainstorming is a novel and fun way to generate ideas. The same principles of Brainstorming are used, but people are actively involved and moving. Instead of calling out individual responses in a large group setting, smaller groups "carousel" and move to different questions posted on charts in different parts of the room. Within the small groups, individuals address questions that focus discussion. The primary use for carouseling is when the issue has multiple parts or subissues.

Applications or Illustrations of Use

- Use Carousel Brainstorming in a SWOT Analysis. It is an ideal device to look at strengths, weaknesses, opportunities, and threats to a program.
- Use Carousel Brainstorming to generate ideas to address a problem or to identify possible solutions.
- Use Carousel Brainstorming to generate internal causes for concern (e.g., personnel issues, budget issues, facilities).
- Use Carousel Brainstorming as a time-saving device, especially when working with a large group.
- Use Carousel Brainstorming as a team builder and when a need exists to create small-group interaction.

Time, Materials, and Other Considerations

Time: Approximately 20–60 minutes (depends on the number of charts).

Materials: See table 6.19.

Table 6.19. Tech Table: Carousel Brainstorming.
Author created (new for 2nd edition)

Nondigital	*Digital*
• Multiple flip charts	• Whiteboard Collaborative Tools (e.g., Jamboard)
• Pens, markers	• Devices (e.g., multiple LFDs)
• Post-it notes	

Procedural Steps

1. Make a chart for each idea, question, or topic and set the charts around the room. Be sure that charts are spread around the room to prevent "traffic jams."
2. Post the rules of Brainstorming (see table 6.18). Remind the group that you want them to generate honest responses. There is no ownership so that participants aren't intimidated by superiors.
3. Instruct groups (not individuals) to move around from chart to chart, sharing ideas at the facilitator's signal.
4. Give 10 to 15 minutes to record the ideas as they are generated. Allow participants "stop and think" time so that they may build on and add to the ideas.
5. On the second signal, groups rotate to the next chart (clockwise).
6. The group reviews what is written and adds to the list (5–10 minutes).
7. Repeat this until each group addresses each chart.
8. Allow time for each group to rotate through the entire set of charts one more time to read and review all charts. Carousel Brainstorming can be adjusted to allow more time for discussion, particularly if the issues are complex.

Cautions

- Timing is important. Be careful—don't leave the people at one chart too long or they will lose their focus.
- Be sure that the topic word or question (on the chart) is a real concern or possibility. Charts must have distinct differences.

Variation

- *Same Idea Carousel:* Have the group generate a brief list of four or five ideas. Participants "piggyback" ideas as they follow steps 4 through 8.

Examples

- In strategic planning, you could set four charts in four corners of a room. The heading of the first chart would be "Strengths." The other charts would be labeled "Weaknesses," "Opportunities," and "Threats." Four groups would be rotated around the room, one at each chart.
- In a change analysis, you could place three charts around a room labeled with the headings: "Proponents," "Opponents," and "Neutrals." The group can then maintain who will be the key actors in the change process.

CAUSE/EFFECT DIAGRAM (AKA FISHBONE AND ISHIKAWA'S FISH)

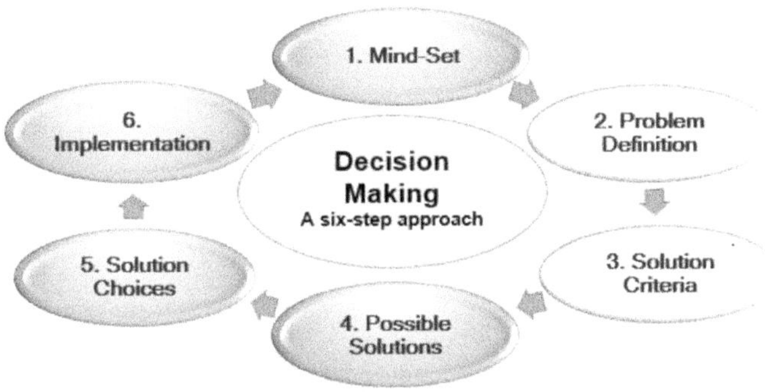

Figure 6.11. Decision Making: A Six-Step Approach: Cause/Effect. ***Author created (updated from 1st edition)***

Description

The Cause/Effect Diagram, sometimes called a Fishbone Diagram, is a visual representation of identified problem causes. This device allows decision makers to analytically lay out potential sources of the causes of the problem. Through this device, the decision makers are able to identify the relationship between symptoms and causes as well as the elements and factors that contribute to a problem or goal. The Cause/Effect Diagram charts and categorizes likely causes of problems and emerging themes. The Cause/Effect Diagram is useful to define the problem, clarify issues, sort, and "put faces" on thought processes. The Cause/Effect Diagram is a useful tool when consensus is important and helps people articulate the problem.

Applications and Illustrations of Use

Use the Cause/Effect Diagram

- To start off a project and to get the team to define the problem, rather than symptoms.
- When the group needs direction to gather more information.
- When the issue revolves around a quality concern.
- When the group is unable to draw linkages and/or connections and you want to get them there.
- If it is a problem and a need exists to bring out many aspects or potential causes and their impact on the problem.

Time, Materials, and Other Considerations

Time: Approximately 1–2 hours, depending on the complexity of the problem.
Materials: See table 6.20.

Table 6.20. Tech Table: Cause/Effect. ***Author created (new for 2nd edition)***

Nondigital	*Digital*
• Multiple flip charts	• Whiteboard Collaborative Tools (e.g., Jamboard)
• Pens, markers	• Devices (e.g., Smartboard)

Procedural Steps

1. Start with a clear definition of the problem (effect). Write the problem (effect) in a box to the right, then draw a horizontal line with an arrow leading to the problem (effect). See figure 6.12.

Figure 6.12. Cause/Effect: Procedural Step 1. ***Author created (updated from 1st edition)***

2. Identify and discuss logical categories for the major "bones" or elements (usually three to six). When the problem area has a recognized process or set of repetitive activities, you can use the major steps in the process as the major bones in the diagram. When there is no recognized process, simply analyze the subelements of the problem.

3. Draw as many bones as you have major categories and label each bone with a category label. See figure 6.13.

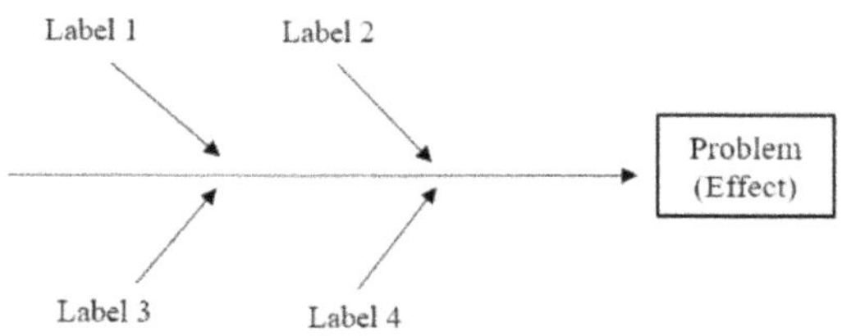

Figure 6.13. Cause/Effect: Procedural Step 2. ***Author created (updated from 1st edition)***

4. Identify the primary (first-level) causes for each bone. Add these to the diagram as an arrow pointing to a major bone.
5. Once you have identified the primary causes, look at each one and determine if there are subcauses (second level). If there are, add these as arrows pointing to the primary cause.
6. If the problem is complex you may need to look for the third-, fourth-, or even fifth-level causes and add them to your diagram See figure 6.14.

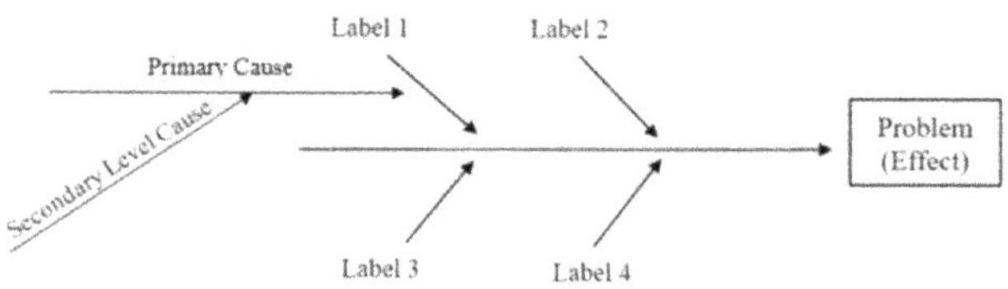

Figure 6.14. Cause/Effect: Procedural Step 3. ***Author created (updated from 1st edition)***

7. Once the diagram is complete discuss it to find out if you can determine if there are one or more of the causes that are the root cause(s). If so, circle the root cause(s).

Caution

- Be sure that the focus is on what you want (as an outcome) and not what you do *not* want.

Example

In this example, the grade-level coordinators were exploring causes for students' excessive tardiness to school. They were able to determine primary and secondary causes (see figure 6.15).

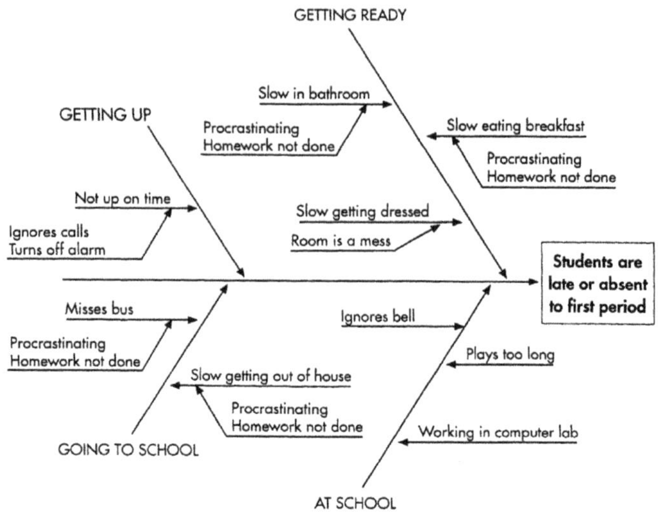

Figure 6.15. Cause/Effect: Example. ***Author created (1st edition)***

References

Brassard and Ritter (1994, 23).
Chang and Kelly (1993, 97).
Klubnik and Greenwood (1994, 151).
Scholtes et al. (1994, 2–30).

COMPETITOR MAPPING

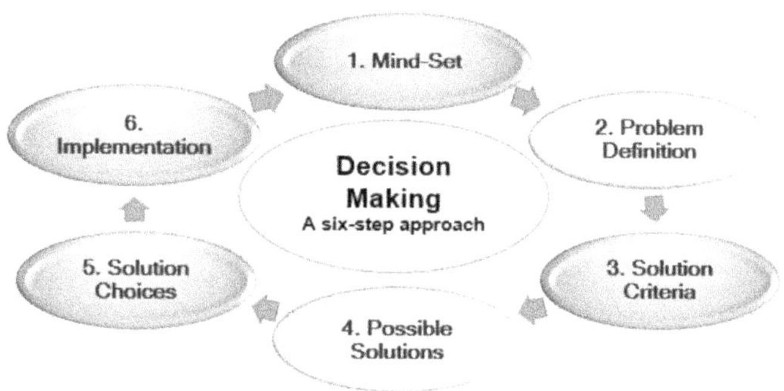

Figure 6.16. Decision Making: A Six-Step Approach: Competitor Mapping. ***Author created (updated from 1st edition)***

Description

Competitor Mapping is a structured research technique that allows decision makers to identify and compare quality and expectations against competitor standards. Competitor Mapping applies the concept "don't reinvent the wheel" by examining what others are doing in a similar field. This device presents a picture of what others in the field are doing well and hence acts as a comparison base. It allows the decision makers to set a standard or benchmark for high quality.

Application or Illustration of Use

- Use this technique to compare and emulate successful organizations or products.

Time, Materials, and Other Considerations

Time: Be sure that resources (time, money, personnel) are available that will allow freedom to visit other organizations. Visitations can take from two to eight hours and may involve multiple visits, travel time, and expenses.

Procedural Steps

1. Collect data through an external scan to identify similar organizations that are recognized as "Best of Class."
2. Make arrangements to visit the organizations to collect information about their process and product development. Identify what it is you want to know (i.e., success factors).
3. During the visit, observe and ask questions using the Sherlock method (who, what, where, why, when, how).
4. When you return to your own site, compare the "Best of Class" with your own organization.
5. Identify gaps.

Caution

- Adapt, don't adopt.

CONTINGENCY ANALYSIS

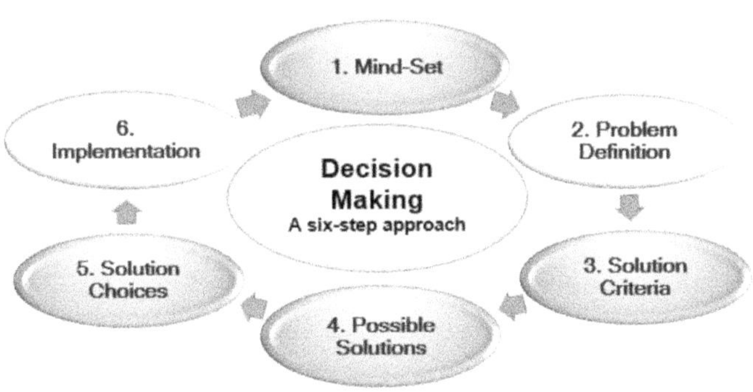

Figure 6.17. Decision Making: A Six-Step Approach: Contingency Analysis. ***Author created (updated from 1st edition)***

Description

The Contingency Analysis is a Total Quality Measurement (TQM) quality tool that presents a diagram of all of the things contributing to the error or problem. The Contingency Analysis allows the decision makers to analyze the causes of the problem. Furthermore, the Contingency Analysis can assist the decision makers to create a prevention checklist. The Contingency Analysis helps a group monitor the implementation of a decision. The Contingency Analysis looks at the lack of payoffs, determines how contingencies can be covered, shows implications, and asks the questions: "What if?" and "How can we prevent further failures or problems?" It is a highly portable learning tool that doesn't require expertise.

Applications or Illustrations of Use

- Use the Contingency Analysis during the planning and implementation step of a decision.
- Use with personnel decisions.

Time, Materials, and Other Considerations

Time: Approximately 45–60 minutes, according to complexity.
Materials: See table 6.21.

Table 6.21. Tech Table: Contingency Analysis. ***Author created (new for 2nd edition)***

Nondigital	*Digital*
• Chart paper	• Whiteboard Collaborative Tools (e.g., Nearpod)
• Pens, markers	• Devices (e.g., Interactive LFD)

Procedural Steps

1. Identify the problem and record it on the top of the chart paper.
2. Draw a diagram of a half (crescent) moon on the right side of the paper. Label the crescent with the problem.
3. Draw rays "radiating" from the moon. Brainstorm and identify the contributing causes of the failure. Label each ray with the name of the cause. The rays indicate contributing causes of the failure.

4. With each contributing cause, evaluate importance as a cause. How strong are they? What is the impact of each cause on the problem? Usually the group will use an impact scale from 1 to 10.
5. Develop a checklist of preventions for each cause extending from the "ray."

Example

Problem: Poor internal communication between department heads (see figure 6.18).

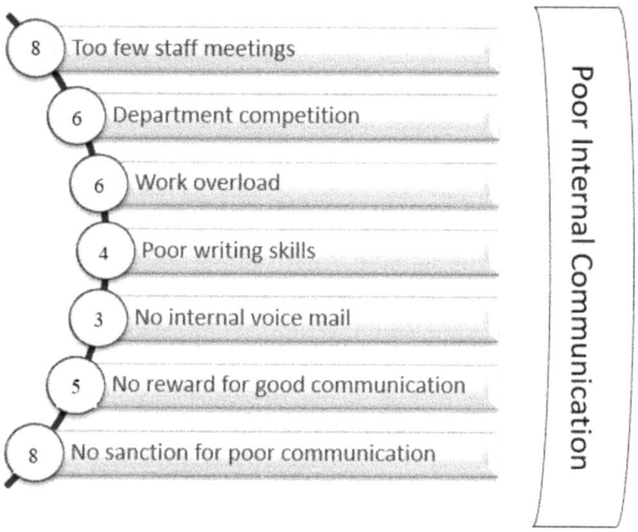

Figure 6.18. Contingency Analysis: Example. Author created *(updated from 1st edition)*

How can causes of the problem be prevented?

COST ICEBERG

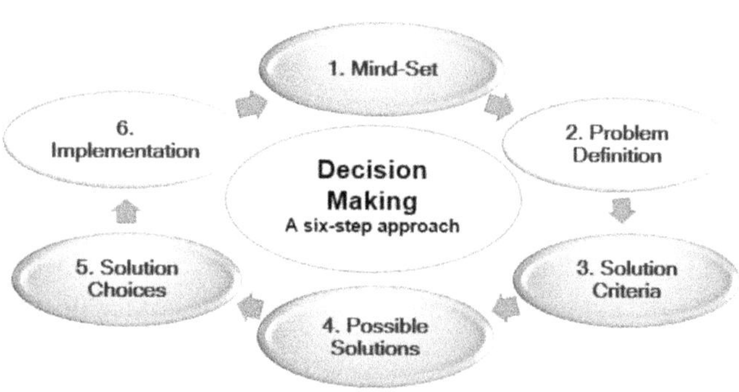

Figure 6.19. Decision Making: A Six-Step Approach: Cost Iceberg. *Author created (updated from 1st edition)*

Description

The Cost Iceberg is a device that helps the decision makers focus on the impact of a work process on costs. Decision makers develop an awareness of costs, both explicit and implicit.

Application or Illustration of Use

See figure 6.20 for an illustration.

- Use the Cost Iceberg to identify and isolate necessary costs and to develop an improvement plan to keep those costs at a minimum.

Figure 6.20. Iceberg image. *Author created (1st edition)*

Time, Materials, and Other Considerations

Time: Approximately 30–60 minutes.
Materials: See table 6.22.

Table 6.22. Tech Table: Cost Iceberg. *Author created (new for 2nd edition)*

Nondigital	*Digital*
• Flip chart	• Collaborative Document (e.g., Google Docs, Microsoft Online)
• Pens, markers	• Whiteboard Collaborative Tools (e.g., Cardsmith)
	• Devices (e.g., Smartboard)

Procedural Steps

1. Identify the problem area.
2. Label a chart with the headings "Obvious Costs" and "Hidden or Less Obvious Costs."
3. Have the group generate a list under each of the headings.

4. On another sheet of chart paper, draw an iceberg (like the example in figure 6.20) with a "water" line.
5. Label the tip of the iceberg "Obvious" and the portion below the water "Hidden or Less Obvious."
6. Diagram the costs onto the iceberg (by transferring the costs from the generated lists). Be sure that the more obvious of the costs are on a higher level than the less obvious.
7. Next, label a chart with the heading "Necessary" and "Unnecessary" and group the costs from step 6 under these headings.
8. Finally, develop a plan to minimize or eliminate costs that are unnecessary and to control necessary ones.

Variation

- Under step 7, in situations that involve product quality, you may want to use three categories of costs: "Prevention," "Inspection," and "Failures." To save time, you may want to have participants record obvious costs and hidden costs directly into the iceberg diagram. The same thing could be done for step 7.

CRITERIA DEVELOPMENT

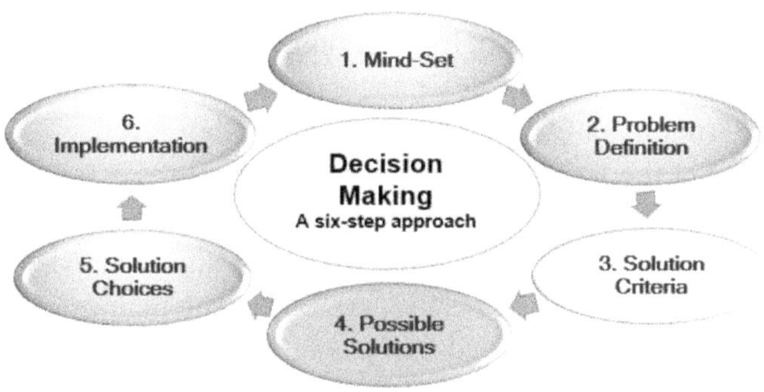

Figure 6.21. Decision Making: A Six-Step Approach: Criteria Development. ***Author created (updated from 1st edition)***

Description

Criteria Development is a technique that allows the decision makers to develop criteria that are most important to the organization. The criteria are the means by which the decision makers judge their solutions.

Application or Illustration of Use

- Use this device to help with the development of solution criteria.

Time, Materials, and Other Considerations

Time: Approximately 30–60 minutes.
Materials: See table 6.23.

Table 6.23. Tech Table: Criteria Development.
Author created (new for 2nd edition)

Nondigital	*Digital*
• Chart paper	• Collaborative Document (e.g., Microsoft Word Online)
• Pens, markers	• Devices (e.g., Interactive LFD)

Procedural Steps

1. Describe needs that the problem or decision will address.
2. Through discussion, define the goals of the solution.
3. Identify the characteristics that are essentials, the "musts." The "musts" are the characteristics that must be present for the solution to be acceptable. Record the "musts" on a separate chart.
4. Identify the characteristics that are preferences but are not required such as the "musts." These characteristics are the "wants."
5. Through discussion, come to agreement on the criteria.
6. Discuss results and decide on next steps.

Variation

- May have two levels of wants:
  - Wants
  - Nice-toos

Cautions

- Take time to clearly develop and specify criteria.
- Focus on solution needs, not positions.

Example

See table 6.24 for an example.

Table 6.24. Criteria Development: Example. ***Author created (updated from 1st edition)***

CRITERIA DEVELOPMENT	
PROBLEM: Improve production line process for Ajax Shoe Manufacturing.	
MUSTS	WANTS
1. Costs less than $50,000 2. Acceptable to union 3. Can be implemented by Dec. 10 4. Does not require additional personnel 5. Reduces long-term costs by 5%	1. Usable in other countries 2. Saves processing time 3. Reduces long-term costs by 10%

References

Scholtes et al. (1994, 5–43).
Fisher, Ury, and Patton (1991, 85).

CRITERIA STANDARDS

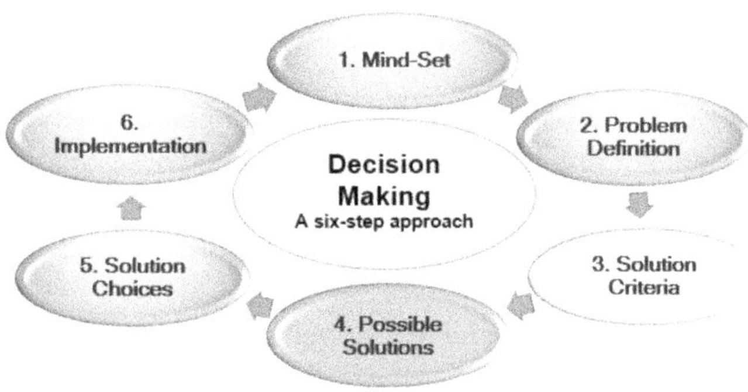

Figure 6.22. Decision Making: A Six-Step Approach: Criteria Standards. ***Author created (updated from 1st edition)***

Description

For some applications, it is appropriate to create indicants or quantifiable measures for solution criteria. This is particularly important with decisions related to money, quality, and equipment. This device is useful for setting standards for criteria when they are not obvious or when they are already set by other measures in the organization.

Application or Illustration of Use

- Use Criteria Standards to develop indicants for solution criteria involving money, quality, or any other criterion that requires quantification.

Time, Materials, and Other Considerations

Time: Approximately 30 minutes, depending on the number of criteria.
Materials: See table 6.25.

Table 6.25. Tech Table: Criteria Standards. ***Author created (new for 2nd edition)***

Nondigital	*Digital*
• Flip chart	• Whiteboard Collaborative Tools (e.g., Cardsmith)
• Index cards or post-it notes	• Devices (e.g., Interactive LFD)
• Pens, markers	

Procedural Steps

1. Develop a list of criteria.
2. Determine the appropriate number and type of measure. Types are descriptive (words) or quantitative (numbers of units, percentages, dollars, etc.).
3. Set the level for each measure (indicant).
4. Review the standards as a group to make sure that you have not set up an impossible situation. Make sure that the measures are sufficient to meet the requirements (needs) of a solution.

Variation

- Use subgroups if there are many criteria or if criteria fall into expertise of subgroups within the problem-solving team.

Example

See table 6.26 for an example.

Table 6.26. Criteria Standards: Example. ***Author created (updated from 1st edition)***

Criteria Standards		
Criterion	*Measure*	*Indicant*
Cost	Dollars	$50,000 or less
Customer satisfaction	Satisfaction survey results	10% increase in satisfaction from former survey
Time efficiency	Time divided by outputs	Reduce processing time per output by 15%

CROSS-IMPACT MATRIX

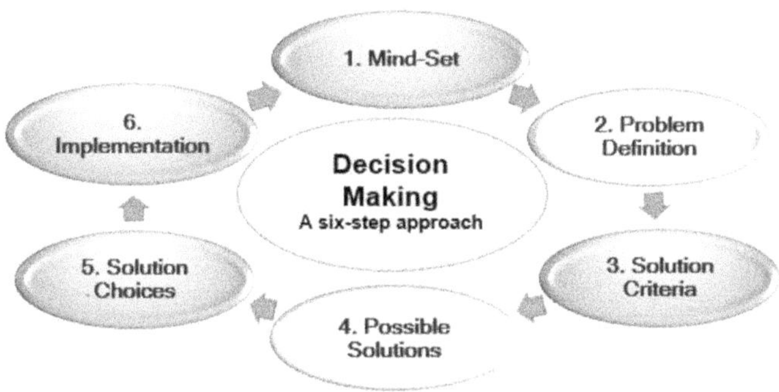

Figure 6.23. Decision Making: A Six-Step Approach: Cross-Impact Matrix. ***Author created (updated from 1st edition)***

Description

This is a device used in planning to understand the interaction of potential future events. It is built on the assumption that the change in the probability, or impact, of any one event will affect the probability or impact of all other events.

Applications or Illustrations of Use

- Use the Cross-Impact Matrix at the problem-definition or solution-choice step.
- Use the Cross-Impact Matrix for future planning.

Time, Materials, and Other Considerations

Time: Approximately 60 minutes.
Materials: See table 6.27.

Table 6.27. Tech Table: Cross-Impact Matrix. ***Author created (new for 2nd edition)***

Nondigital	*Digital*
• Blank Matrix	• Collaborative Spreadsheet (e.g., Google Sheets)
• Flip chart	• Devices (e.g., Interactive LFD)
• Pens, markers	

Procedural Steps

1. Choose a series of present or potential future events.
2. Put them in a matrix format with the events represented on both dimensions of the matrix (see table 6.28).

Table 6.28. Cross-Impact Matrix: Procedure. ***Author created (1st edition)***

	El	E2	E3	E4	E5
E1	X				
E2		X			
E3			X		
E4				X	
E5					X

3. On a scale from 1 to 10, estimate what will be the impact of El on E2 if El should occur. Do the same for E3, E4, E5, and so on. If the impact is to be positive, use a plus (+) sign, if negative, use a minus (–) sign.
4. Continuing the process in step 3, on a scale of 1 to 10, estimate the impact on E2 on E1 if E2 were to occur. Continue across the matrix to calculate the impact of E2 on E3. Repeat for each factor.
5. When all cells are filled, add across rows. Use absolute value. Then add down columns. Use absolute values.
6. The row totals will describe how strong each event is an "actor," something that affects other events. The column total will describe each event as a "reactor," something that is affected by other events. Actors are those factors that affect most strongly the other events in the display. That is to say, when you cause a change in an "actor" variable everything else is usually affected. A reactor variable is one that is affected by everything else.

Causing a change in a reactor variable does little to affect the other factors in display. If you want to effect change, work with actor variables. Take your strong actor variables and decide what they say about the problem at hand.

Example

See table 6.29 for an example.

Table 6.29. Cross-Impact Matrix: Example. ***Author created (1st edition)***

	E1	E2	E3	E4	E5	E6	Total of Reactors
E1	X	.3	.3	.4	–7	.7	24
E2	–6	X	3	+6	+7	+4	26
E3	–8	0	X	+1	+4	+4	17
E4	.4	+6	+8	X	+8	+10	36
E5	–8	+7	+8	0	X	+10	33
E6	0	0	+1	+3	+3	X	7
Total of Reactors	26	16	23	14	29	35	7

E5 and E4 are strong actors.
E6 is a strong reactor.

DECISION TREE ANALYSIS

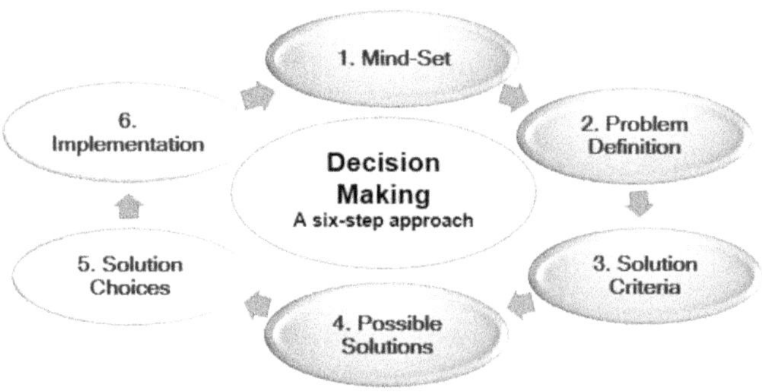

Figure 6.24. Decision Making: A Six-Step Approach: Decision Tree Analyses. ***Author created (updated from 1st edition)***

Description

The Decision Tree Analysis is a device that graphically displays the action steps of a decision. The various tasks are placed on "branches" so that the final product resembles a tree. The Decision Tree Analysis is also used to identify the consequences of a solution choice. By reviewing the possible results of following through with the decision, the decision makers will be able to anticipate possible opportunities or roadblocks.

Applications or Illustrations of Use

- Use the Decision Tree Analysis to help the decision makers understand the consequences of a possible solution.
- Use the Decision Tree Analysis to initiate implementation by identifying the action steps.

Time, Materials, and Other Considerations

Time: Approximately 30–90 minutes, depending on the complexity of the decision.
Materials: See table 6.30.

Table 6.30. Tech Table: Decision Tree Analysis. ***Author created (new for 2nd edition)***

Nondigital	*Digital*
• Flip chart	• Other application (e.g., Padlet)
• Pens, markers	• Devices (e.g., Interactive LFD)
• Post-it notes	

Procedural Steps

1. Determine the context of the decision tree. Does it represent a project, solution possibilities, or something else? Write one or more words that represent the task in the left center of the paper. Draw a line under these words with an arrow to the right, then draw a small circle or box at the end of the arrow. This becomes the root node of the tree.
2. Determine the taxonomy of decisions that you will use for the remaining nodes of the tree. Order these nodes in the way that they most logically interact with each other. For example, if the decision tree was to look at various options for training on computers you might decide that the taxonomy would be type of training, mode of delivery, and who delivers the training, in that order.
3. Determine the tasks, options, or subcategories for the first item in your taxonomy. Add them to the root node of the tree by drawing a line with an arrow on the end for each one and writing the task, option, or subcategory on the line. Add a small box or circle to the end of the line to make the next

node. For example, you might determine that the types of training that are possible in your situation are a one-week in-house training, a three-day off-site conference, and six one-day in-house training sessions over four months. See figure 6.25.

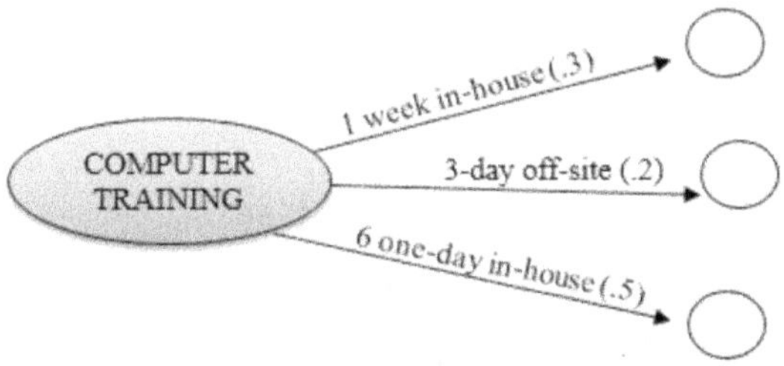

Figure 6.25. Decision Tree Analysis: Procedure 1. ***Author created (1st edition)***

4. Determine the probability or desirability factor for each one of these occurring and assign each a number from 0 to 1. The total of all of the probability/desirability factors for all of the items that branch off from one node must add up to 1. Write the factor for each option on the line next to the type.
5. Determine the tasks, options, or subcategories for the next level of your taxonomy based on the previous level. Do this one node at a time. These may be the same for all of the nodes off from the prior level, or they may be different. Add the tasks, options, or subcategories to each of the nodes by drawing a line with an arrow on the end and write the name of the task, option, or subcategory on the line. If this is not the last item in your taxonomy, add a small box or circle to the end of each line for the node. In our example, the next level is mode of delivery. For the one-week in-house training, we determined that the modes of delivery available to us are a computer-based training (CBT) course and a workshop using a trainer. Adding these, the tree would appear as shown in figure 6.26. Continue with the three-day and six one-day options.

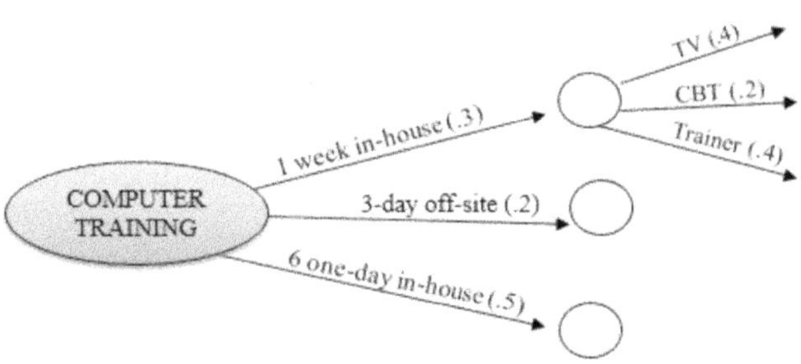

Figure 6.26. Decision Tree Analysis: Procedure 2. ***Author created (1st edition)***

6. Determine the probability or desirability factor for each one of these happening and assign each a number from 0 to 1. Again, the total of all of the probability/desirability factors for all of the items that branch off from one node must add up to 1. Write the factor for each option on the line next to the type.
7. Repeat steps 5 and 6 for the remaining items in your taxonomy.
8. Once you have completed the entire tree compute the overall probability/desirability factor for each branch of the tree. This is done by multiplying the factors for each line on the branch. (See the two examples in figures 6.27 and 6.28 for these overall factors.)
9. Look at the overall factors for the branches. The ones with the highest number(s) are the most probable or desirable branches (options).
10. Discuss the results.

Example 1

The following example deals with implementation of a project (see figure 6.27).

What is the best pathway?

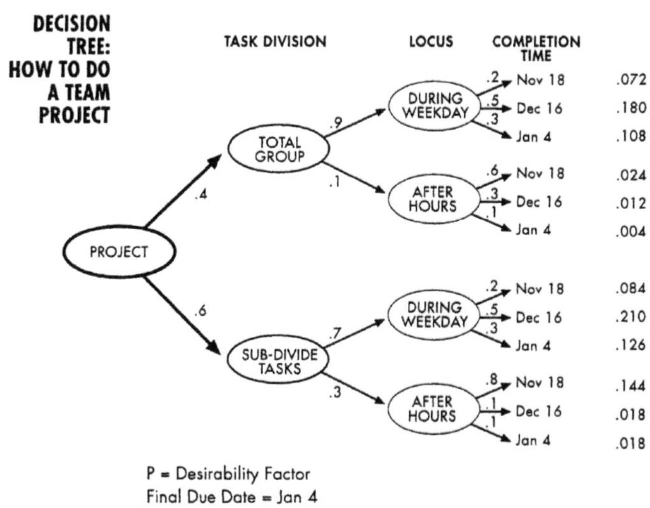

Figure 6.27. Decision Tree Analysis: Example 1. ***Author created (1st edition)***

Example 2

The following example deals with how to meet the learning needs of employees (see figure 6.28):

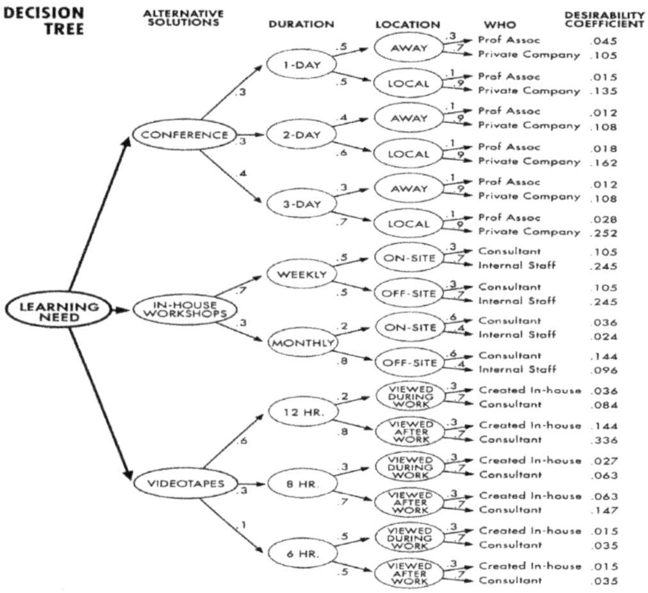

Figure 6.28. Decision Tree Analysis: Example 2. ***Author created (1st edition)***

The best single path is to use twelve hours of video viewed after work and have a consultant do them (.336 probability). The second-best path is to use internal workshops weekly with workshops given by consultants on- or off-site (.245 probability).

DISCREPANCY ANALYSIS

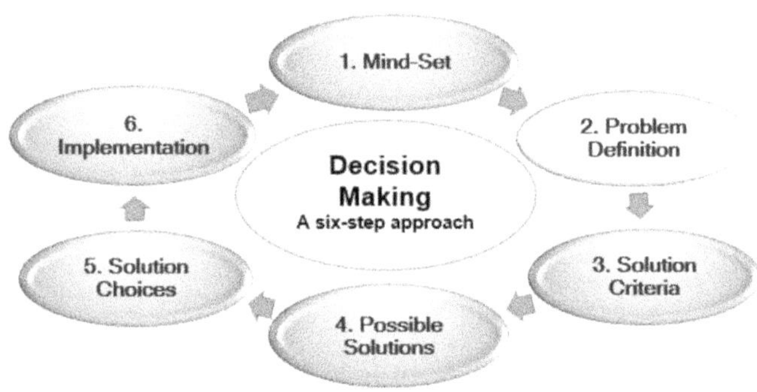

Figure 6.29. Decision Making: A Six-Step Approach: Discrepancy Analysis. ***Author created (updated from 1st edition)***

Description

The Discrepancy Analysis is a device that examines the differences between desired states and actual states. By identifying where a discrepancy, or gap, exists between the desired and actual states, the decision makers are better able to identify and understand problems or situations that need attention (SiTNAs).

Application or Illustration of Use

- Use the Discrepancy Analysis to define the problem, particularly if the problem involves a gap between actual states and expectations.

Time, Materials, and Other Considerations

Time: Approximately 30–60 minutes.
Materials: See table 6.31.

Table 6.31. Tech Table: Discrepancy Analysis. ***Author created (new for 2nd edition)***

Nondigital	*Digital*
• Flip chart	• Whiteboard Collaborative Tools (e.g., Jamboard)
• Pens, markers	• Devices (e.g., Interactive LFD)

Procedural Steps

1. Define the decision situation.
2. Ask participants to define the ideal state. This can be done as a general description, a scenario, or as a series of variables that can be numerically evaluated for desirability.
3. Ask participants to define the current or actual state (at this point in time).
4. Examine the gaps between ideal and actual.
5. Ask participants, "What do these gaps tell us about what problems we have?"

Variation

- This could be done as a must/wants discrepancy or a desirable/feasible discrepancy.

Examples

In the following examples, we used a survey format to determine if there was a difference in perceptions toward service orientation (see figure 6.30). We quantified the perceptions by adding a scale of 1 to 7. The most desired rating is a 7 while a 1 is the least desired. In the first chart, a discrepancy, or gap, exists between the way the organization sees itself currently and the most desired state. Hence, a problem exists. In the second chart, the desired and actual state received the same rating; hence, there is no gap or problem.

EXAMPLE 1.
TO WHAT DEGREE ARE WE CLIENT-CENTERED?

Desired State	1	2	3	4	5	6	(7)
Actual State	1	2	3	(4)	5	6	7

EXAMPLE 2.
TO WHAT DEGREE DO WE INVOLVE STAFF IN DECISION MAKING?

Desired State	1	2	3	4	5	(6)	7
Actual State	1	2	3	4	5	(6)	7

Figure 6.30. Discrepancy Analysis: Example 1 and 2. ***Author created (1st edition)***

FLOWCHART

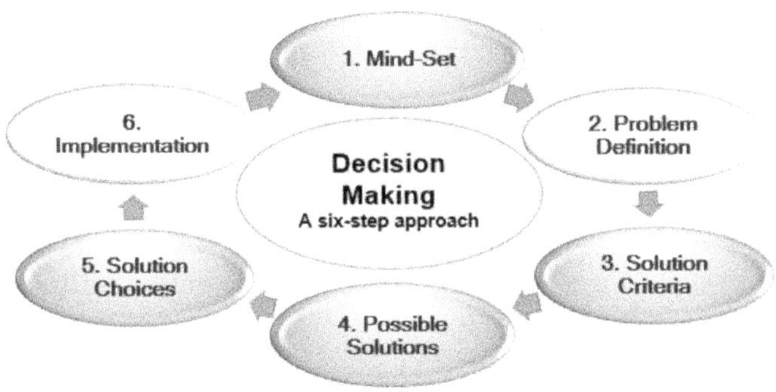

Figure 6.31. Decision Making: A Six-Step Approach: Flowchart. ***Author created (updated from 1st edition)***

Description

The Flowchart is a graphic means of laying out or mapping the steps of a process. It indicates where the process starts and ends and differentiates between process activity and a decision point. The flowchart provides details about the current condition of a process. It is useful for defining the problem and identifying events leading up to the problem. While there are many symbols used in flowcharting, you can represent

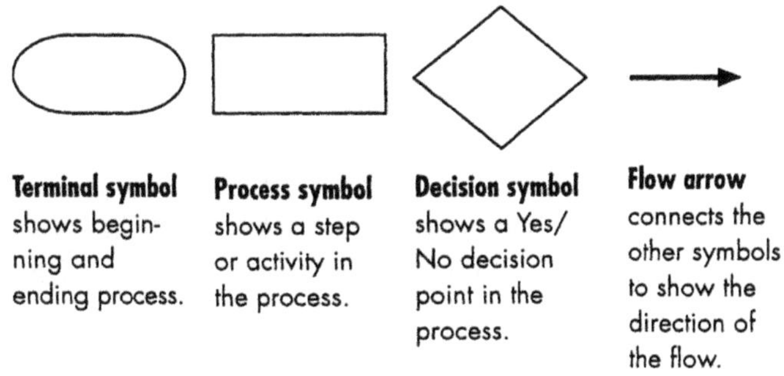

Figure 6.32. Flowchart: Description Image. ***Author created (1st edition)***

most activities with three symbols, connected with flow lines (see figure 6.32).

Applications or Illustrations of Use

- Use the Flowchart to elaborate on the steps needed to implement a decision.
- Use the Flowchart to document work processes and to identify roadblocks.
- Use the Flowchart when the decision-making group is an analytical group of linear thinkers who "think in bullets."

Time, Materials, and Other Considerations

Time: Time depends on the complexity of the process.
Materials: See table 6.32.

Table 6.32. Tech Table: Flowchart Analysis.
Author created (new for 2nd edition)

Nondigital	*Digital*
• Chart paper	• Collaborative Document (e.g., Google Docs, Microsoft Word Online)
• Pens, markers	• Whiteboard Collaborative Tools (e.g., Limnu)
• Post-it notes	• Devices (e.g., Samsung Flip)

Procedural Steps

1. Identify the steps or activities in the process. Be sure to include any decisions that determine the sequence of the steps.
2. Put the steps in order.
3. Draw a flowchart of the steps and decisions using the flowchart symbols.

Variation

- You can add "responsibility" to a flowchart by listing across the top of the chart the major "players" (people, departments, etc.) in the process. As the flow moves from process to process, it can also move between columns, therefore showing who does the process.

Caution

- Flowcharts can be difficult if the purpose or mission is unclear.

Examples

See figure 6.33 for flowchart examples.

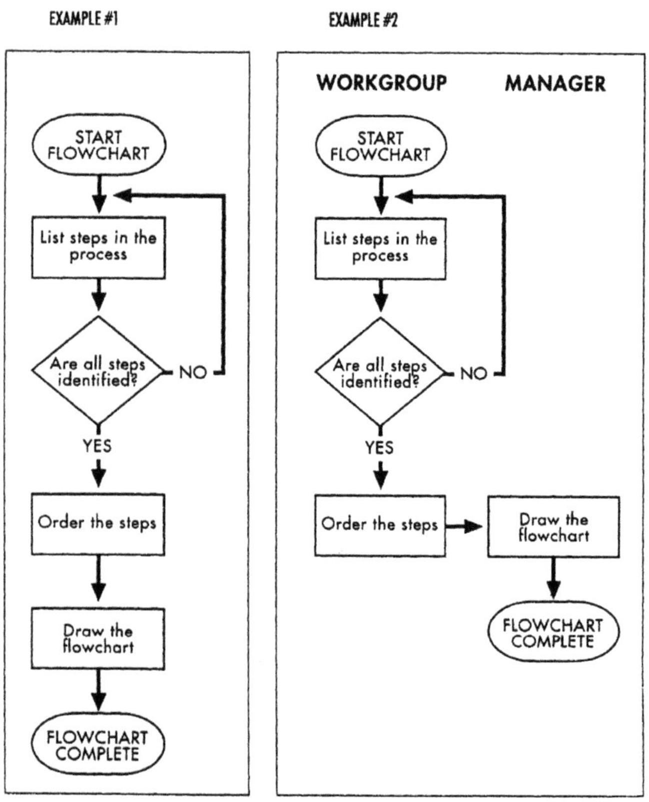

Figure 6.33. Flowchart: Examples 1 and 2. ***Author created (1st edition)***

References

Brassard and Ritter (1994, 56).
Scholtes et al. (1994, 2–22; 7–16).
Xerox (n.d., 104).

FORCE FIELD ANALYSIS

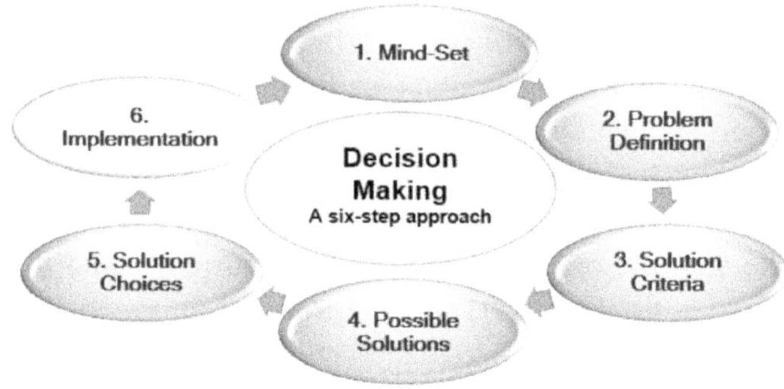

Figure 6.34. Decision Making: A Six-Step Approach: Force Field Analysis. ***Author created (updated from 1st edition)***

Description

Kurt Lewin's Force Field Analysis distinguishes between two types of forces that can affect implementation of a decision: forces that restrain change or forces that drive change. The Force Field Analysis identifies factors that contribute to the program and actions needed to counteract resistance and obstructions. It is a device that can help the decision makers focus energy on reducing forces by determining if the solutions will get support.

Applications or Illustrations of Use

See figure 6.35 for an illustration.

- Use this device for "soft" issues that have little data available (i.e., when morale is low).
- Use the Force Field Analysis when a solution needs a reality test in the action-planning and implementation phase. This can be completed individually or with a group.

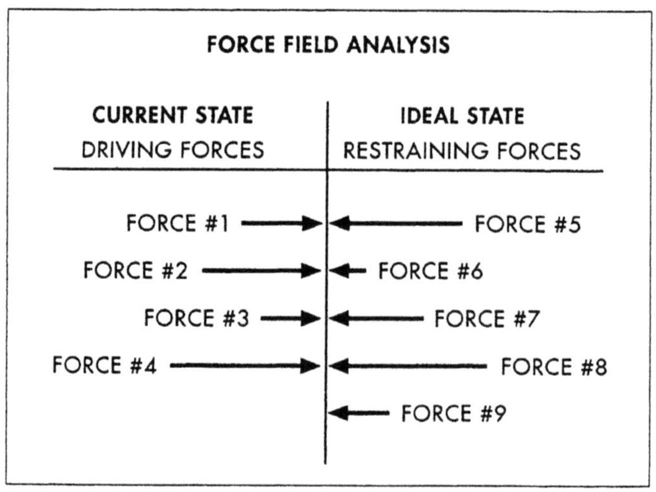

Figure 6.35. Force Field Analysis: Application Image. ***Author created (1st edition)***

Time, Materials, and Other Considerations

Time: Approximately 30 minutes to 1 hour.
Materials: See table 6.33.

Table 6.33. Tech Table: Force Field Analysis. ***Author created (new for 2nd edition***

Nondigital	*Digital*
• Force Field Analysis worksheet	• Collaborative Document (e.g., Microsoft Word Online, Google Docs)
• Pens, markers	• Devices (e.g., Smartboard LFD)

Procedural Steps

1. Identify a particular objective.
2. Draw a T down a page.
3. Identify the current state on the left side of the diagram.
4. Identify where you want to be (ideal or desired state) on the right side of the diagram.
5. Identify the restraining forces or factors that are restraining (hindering) the move to the ideal state.
6. Identify the driving forces or factors that are driving (influencing) the move to the ideal state.
7. Plot the restraining and driving forces on the chart for visual clarity.
8. Determine and discuss the strengths of each force (usually on a scale from 1 to 5 or 1 to 10).
9. Draw arrows toward the center. The length of the arrow denotes the strength of pressure. Record the numerical value on the arrow.
10. Develop a strategy to deal with the two sets of forces. Ask: "What would we have to do to increase the driving forces? To decrease the restraining forces?" Limiting the restraining forces is more desirable than increasing driving forces.
11. Evaluate your strategies to determine their effects as you move toward the desired state.

Variation

- Use with Pluses and Minuses with a 1-3-5 Likert scale indicating the strength of the item.

Caution

- The Force Field Analysis is subjective and not scientific because it does not tell how much resistance or support actually exists.

Example

See figure 6.36 for an example.

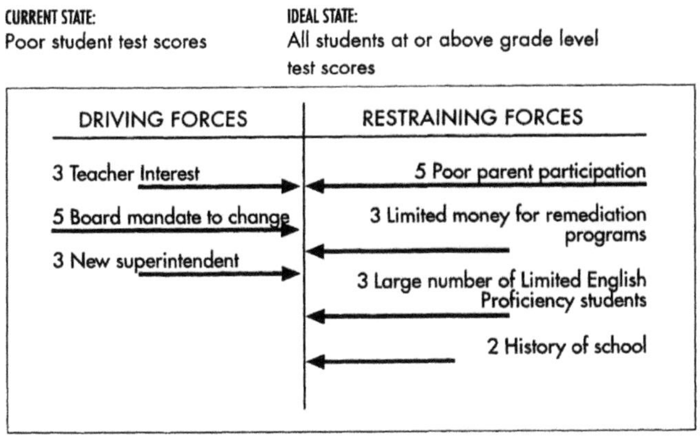

Figure 6.36. Force Field Analysis: Example. ***Author created (1st edition)***

Force Field Analysis: Worksheet

See table 6.34 for the worksheet template.

Table 6.34. Force Field Analysis: Worksheet. ***Author created (updated from 1st edition)***

Current State:

Ideal State:

Driving Forces	Restraining Forces

References

Brassard and Ritter (1994, 63).
Chang and Niedzwiecki (1994, 37).
Higgens (1994, 194).
Lewin (1951).
Moody (1983, 78–80).
Quinlivan-Hall and Renner (1990, 68).
Viability Corporate HR, Performance Development Division (1994).

GANTT CHART

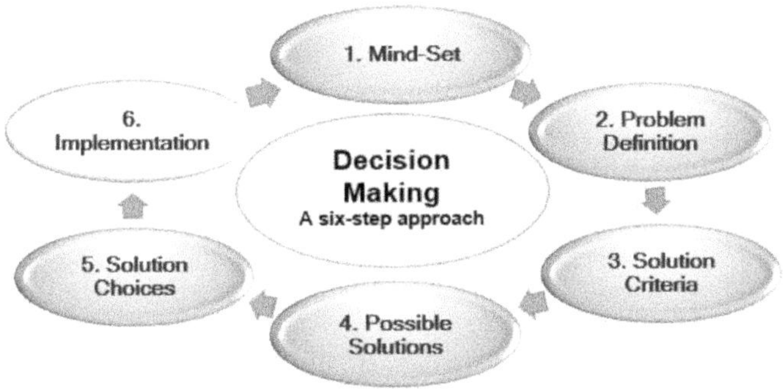

Figure 6.37. Decision Making: A Six-Step Approach: Gantt Chart. ***Author created (updated from 1st edition)***

Description

The Gantt Chart is a device that displays the tasks, responsibilities, and time schedule for the accomplishment of a project. The Gantt Chart documents the action plan by outlining roles, responsibilities, time, milestones, and dates. The matrix uses bars that indicate when the action begins and ends.

Application or Illustration of Use

- Use the Gantt Chart for planning action for long-range plans such as a three-year change effort.

Time, Materials, and Other Considerations

Time: Approximately 45–60 minutes.
Materials: See table 6.35.

Table 6.35. Tech Table: Gantt Chart.
Author created (new for 2nd edition)

Nondigital	*Digital*
• Chart paper	• Collaborative Spreadsheet (e.g., Google Sheets)
• Pens, markers	• Collaborative Document (e.g., Google Docs)
	• Devices (e.g., Interactive LFD)

Procedural Steps

1. Introduce the purpose of the Gantt Chart.
2. Identify all the tasks or events necessary to achieve the project's completion. Record those on a chart.
3. Clarify and review all of the tasks to be sure that no step is excluded.
4. Order the tasks.
5. Using the Gantt Chart worksheet (see table 6.36), list tasks or events in ordered sequence in the left column of the chart.
6. Across the top of the chart, list the time line in an incremental (monthly and weekly) format.
7. Determine how much time will be allotted to each task.
8. Mark the time period on the chart that each task will take. Draw a bar from start point to end point.
9. The group must agree on the final product. Post and communicate the chart.

Variations

- You can add responsibilities to the Gantt by writing the names of the people involved.
- To include milestones, place a triangle symbol (Δ) at a location that is a milestone.

Example

The GANTT Chart shown in figure 6.38 is an example of a ten-month change effort in a small business involving implementing technology. The decision makers identified all the necessary steps, ordered them, and then indicated a time line for beginning and ending the task.

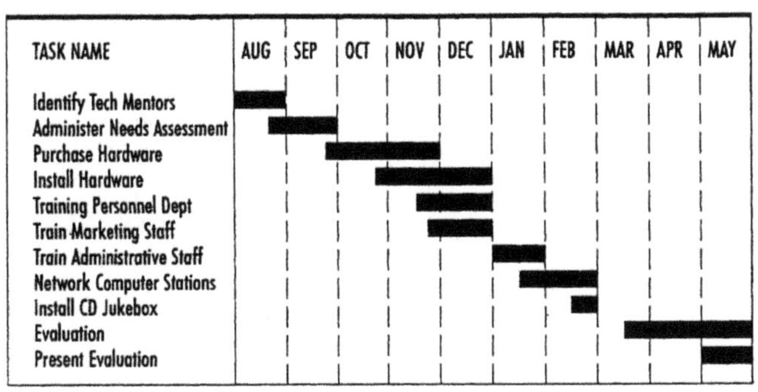

Figure 6.38. Gantt Chart: Example. ***Author created (1st edition)***

Gantt Chart: Worksheet

See table 6.36 for a template of the Gantt Chart worksheet.

Table 6.36. Gantt Chart: Worksheet. ***Author created (1st edition)***

Tasks													

References

Brassard and Ritter (1994, 9).
Xerox (n.d., 43).

GOAL SETTING

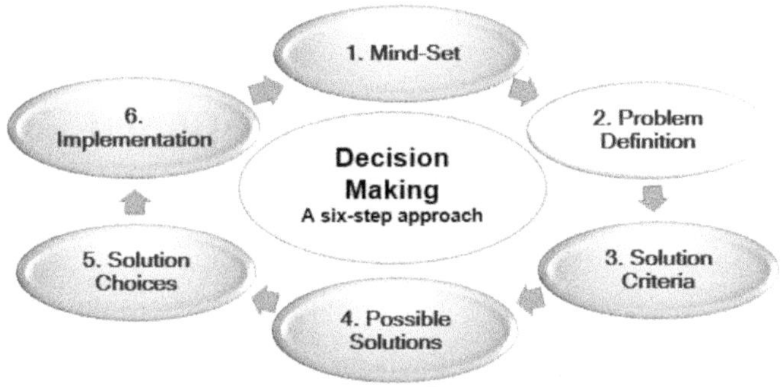

Figure 6.39. Decision Making: A Six-Step Approach: Goal Setting. ***Author created (updated from 1st edition)***

Description

In DM that involves planning, it is often necessary to set goals for future action. Goals may be set in terms of situations to be achieved or programs and/or services to be created. The former are outcome goals and the latter process goals.

Applications or Illustrations of Use

- Use Goal Setting during planning.
- Use if goals are not already present.
- Use if you are dealing with a new venture or opportunity.

Time, Materials, and Other Considerations

Time: Approximately 1–3 hours.
Materials: See table 6.37.

Table 6.37. Tech Table: Goal Setting.
Author created (new for 2nd edition)

Nondigital	*Digital*
• Chart paper	• Collaborative Document (e.g., Google Docs, Microsoft Word Online)
• Pens, markers	• Devices (e.g., Interactive LFD)

Procedural Steps

1. Determine the focus of the goals.
2. Determine if the goal relates to outputs or processes to achieve an output.
3. If it is an output:
   a. Ask the group to describe what the outputs (outcomes) are of the organization. Record them on a flip chart.
   b. Ask the group to define what changes, if any, they would like to see in these outcomes (i.e., additional outputs or improved quality of current outputs).

   If it is a process:

   a. Ask the group to describe key programs and/or processes that create these outputs.
   b. Ask the group to define what changes they would like to see in these programs/processes (i.e., either additional programs/processes or improved quality of current programs/processes).
4. Write goal statements for items identified.
5. Check goal statement to see if it is clear, specific, and future oriented.

Examples

It is our goal to

- Create TQM staff development programs by January 1.
- Expand our market to Japan and China.
- Shorten delivery time of our computers to one week.
- Improve student math test scores by fifty points by June 2024.

HUMAN SOCIOGRAMS

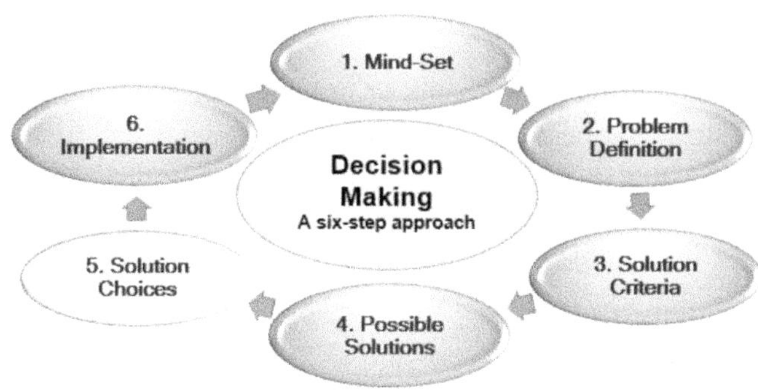

Figure 6.40. Decision Making: A Six-Step Approach: Human Sociograms. ***Author created (updated from 1st edition)***

Description

Human Sociogram is a structured experience that involves physical movement of the decision makers so that a group can discuss issues. People move around the room to demonstrate their attitudes or feelings about a decision. The Human Sociogram is a tool that results in a visual depiction of people's feelings.

Applications or Illustrations of Use

- Use Human Sociograms as a way to indicate support or disagreement with possible solutions.
- Use Human Sociograms if individuals do not feel free to express feelings verbally.

Time, Materials, and Other Considerations

Time: Approximately 30–45 minutes.
Materials: Charts stating "For" and "Against" (optional). See table 6.38.

Table 6.38. Tech Table: Human Sociograms. ***Author created (new for 2nd edition)***

Nondigital	*Digital*
• Chart paper	• Whiteboard Collaborative Tools (e.g., Jamboard)
• Pens, markers	• Devices (e.g., Interactive LFD)

Procedural Steps

1. Tell participants that they will be moving without discussion.
2. State the problem or pose the question or option.
3. Create a continuous line across the room with "totally for" and "totally against" as the two end points.
4. Direct the participants to move to the point on the line that best fits their feelings.
5. Follow up with discussion, posing the question "What would it take to move you closer to either end?"

Variations

- Indicate points in the room (various corners) that represent multiple discrete positions. Instruct participants to line themselves around the room wherever he/she stands on an issue.
- When the issue involves a dichotomous choice (yes/no), have people stand up when their alternative is described.

INTERRELATIONSHIP DIAGRAPH

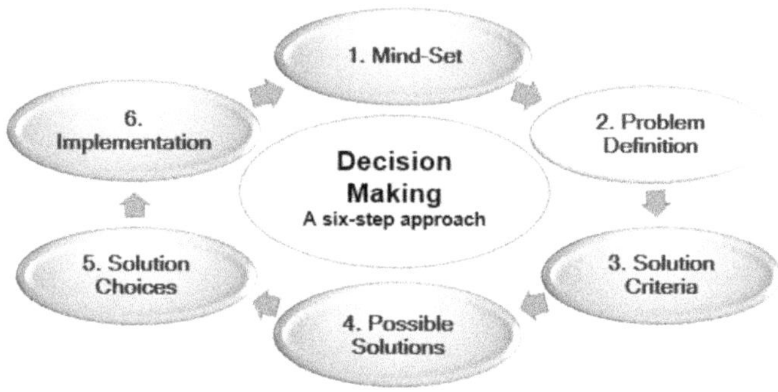

Figure 6.41. Decision Making: A Six-Step Approach: Interrelationship Diagraph. ***Author created (updated from 1st edition)***

Description

The Interrelationship Diagraph is a chart that represents the interconnectedness of various problem causes. It is a structuring device that answers these questions: "Do these things interrelate with each other? Do they cause or affect others?" The Interrelationship Diagraph identifies where the big problems or bottlenecks are and, in doing so, allows the group to understand the input and output of each activity. It looks at ideas in terms of relationship between each pair.

Applications or Illustrations of Use

- Use the Interrelationship Diagraph to identify primary causes of defects/problems.
- Use the Interrelationship Diagraph after grouping or categorizing ideas (i.e., affinity).

Time, Materials, and Other Considerations

Time: Approximately 1–3 hours.
Materials: See table 6.39.

Table 6.39. Tech Table: Interrelationship Diagraph. ***Author created (new for 2nd edition)***

Nondigital	*Digital*
• Chart paper	• Whiteboard Collaborative Tools (e.g., Jamboard)
• Pens, markers	• Devices (e.g., Interactive LFD)

Procedural Steps

See figure 6.42 for an illustration of the procedure.

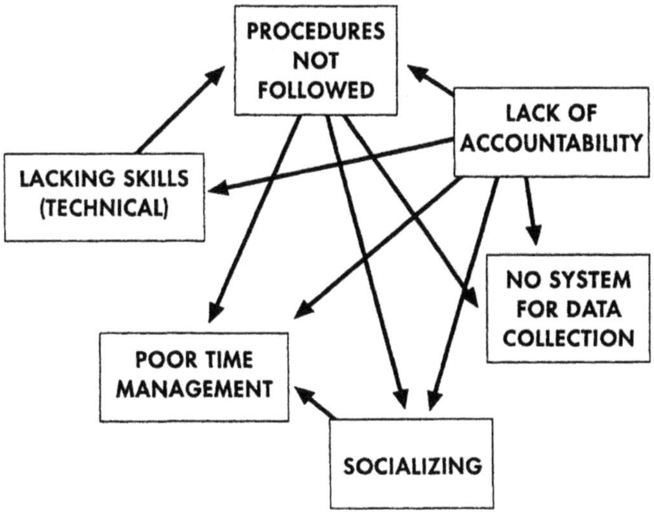

Figure 6.42. Interrelationship Diagraph: Procedure. ***Author created (1st edition)***

1. Have the group generate and categorize causes of the problem.
2. Place the categories in a circle formation on a sheet of chart paper.
3. Ask these questions of each category:
    - Is there a cause or influence relationship (from one category to the other)?
    - If yes, draw an arrow in the direction (to or from) of cause or influence. Make sure the arrows from each category go in one direction only. You will end up with a map of arrows.
4. Assess strength of arrows on a 1 to 10 scale. Write this value on the arrow line.
5. Assess causes. The categories with the highest or strongest arrows away from are causes or key drivers. You can either choose the arrow with the highest value or choose the cause with the highest total value of all arrows. The key driver is the variable that has the strongest impact on the various other factors in the display.
6. Discuss key drivers.

Example

See figure 6.43 for an example.

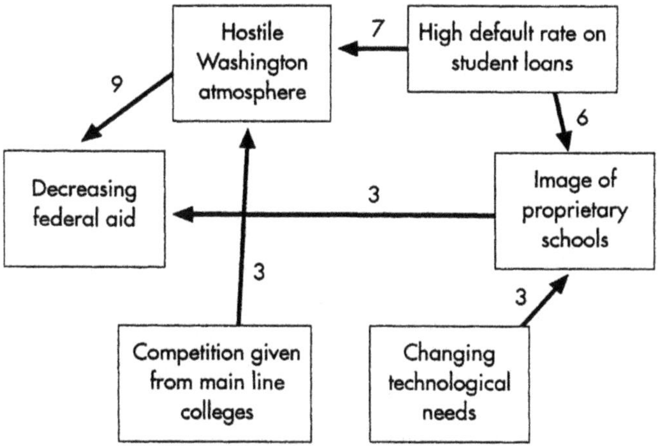

Figure 6.43. Interrelationship Diagraph: Example. ***Author created (1st edition)***

References

Brassard and Ritter (1994, 76).

MAGNITUDE ESTIMATION ANALYSIS

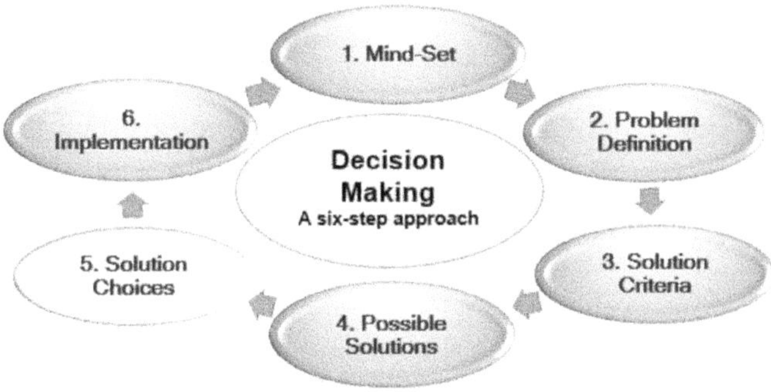

Figure 6.44. Decision Making: A Six-Step Approach: Magnitude Estimation Analysis. ***Author created (updated from 1st edition)***

Description

This is a useful scaling device to set priorities. It involves the use of ratio data to establish a range of ordered values. It is often used in surveys.

Application or Illustration of Use

- Use the Magnitude Estimation Analysis to force a set of ordered priorities.

Time, Materials, and Other Considerations

Time: 10–25 minutes; survey time can vary.
Materials: See table 6.40.

Table 6.40. Tech Table: Magnitude Estimation. ***Author created (new for 2nd edition)***

Nondigital	*Digital*
• Chart paper	• Collaborative Spreadsheet (e.g., Microsoft Excel Online)
• Pens, markers	• Devices (e.g., Interactive LFD)
• Calculator	

Procedural Steps

1. Post the generated list of possible solution choices that need to be prioritized.
2. Take the first possible solution choice and give it a value of 100.
3. Ask respondents to rate each possible solution relative to the baseline alternative that has been given a score of 100. They can use any positive value.
4. Compute a geometric mean for each possible solution. Computing geometric means requires that the scores be converted to logarithms. As a result, a calculator can be useful.
5. Divide each derived mean by 100 to determine a power ratio.
6. Display possible solutions in order of power ratios. The possible solutions are now not only in order but also in ratio with each other. Possible solutions with a power ratio of 2.5 are 2.5 times as strong a priority as the lower ratio of 1.0.

Example

See table 6.41 for an example.

Table 6.41. Magnitude Estimation: Example. ***Author created (1st edition)***

Support Program	*One Example of Personal Responses*	*Group Geometric Mean*	*Power Ratio*
Staff Development	100	100	1.00
Marketing	150	173	1.73
Customer Satisfaction	500	322	3.22
TQM	60	94	.94
Organization Development	75	36	.36

The customer satisfaction program is the most important program and is almost twice as important as the next alternative, marketing. The least important program is organizational development, which is nearly one-tenth as important as customer satisfaction.

References

S. S. Stevens (1956).

METAPHOR

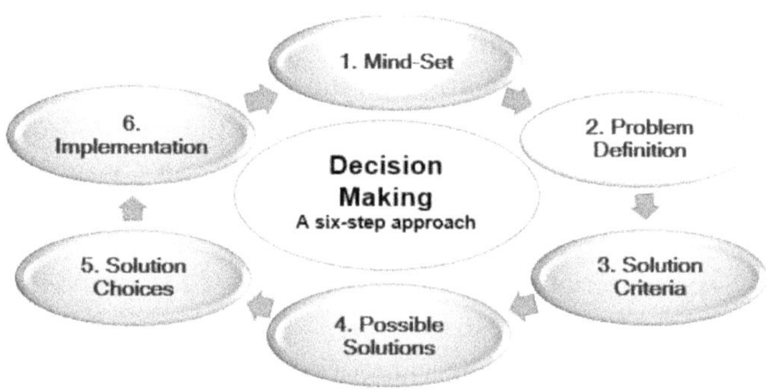

Figure 6.45. Decision Making: A Six-Step Approach: Metaphor. ***Author created (updated from 1st edition)***

Description

The Metaphor is a structuring device that stimulates thinking and encourages the creation of an analogy. Because it involves the use of creativity, participants have an opportunity to have fun and look at the decision from an intuitive perspective. The Metaphor can help the decision makers to clarify and identify the problem.

Applications or Illustrations of Use

- Use the Metaphor if the problems are sensitive and difficult for the people to talk about directly.
- Use the Metaphor with analytical thinkers to open up insight about a problem/topic.
- Use the Metaphor to develop a vision.
- Use the Metaphor in problem definition as a device to define gaps.

Time, Materials, and Other Considerations

Time: Approximately 45–60 minutes.
Materials: See table 6.42.

Table 6.42. Tech Table: Metaphor. ***Author created (new for 2nd edition)***

Nondigital	*Digital*
• Chart paper	• Devices (e.g., Samsung Flip)
• Pens, markers	
• Makerspace supplies (see variation)	

Procedural Steps

1. Post the problem or decision to be made and ask the individuals to look at the problem. In doing this, ask them to explore the more creative, right side of the brain as they look at the problem.
2. Distribute materials. Individually or within small teams, have them draw or design a logo, emblem, picture, or a coat of arms that resembles the problem.
3. Have a representative from each group share their visual representation and their perceptions of the problem.
4. Have the group discuss what this says about the needs of the problem.

Caution

- To avoid confusion later, be sure to spend time up front explaining the purpose of the exercise. (Some people will be more involved with the game than the intent.)

Variation

- Give the individuals a bag of items (e.g., toothpicks, pipe cleaners, Legos, rubber bands, straws, etc.) and have them build a model that represents the problem.

References

Higgens (1994, 61).
Van Gundy (1988, 106).

MIND MAP

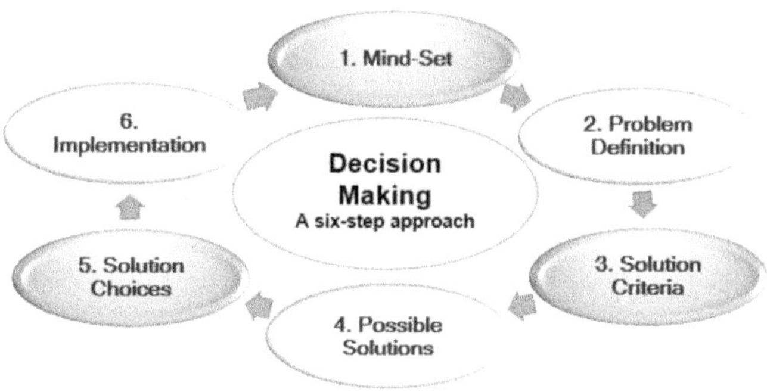

Figure 6.46. Decision Making: A Six-Step Approach: Mind Map. ***Author created (updated from 1st edition)***

Description

A Mind Map is a free-form display that represents various elements of a topic or thought. They are also called Learning Maps because they are invaluable tools for learning. These maps help you simplify complex ideas and can trigger all three of the primary learning modalities: visual, verbal, and kinesthetic. Mind Maps can help the members of a problem-solving team release their creativity and to view situations in new and creative ways.

Applications or Illustrations of Use

- Use during problem definition to help map the components of the problem.
- Use any time you are attempting to identify categories, tasks, or ideas.
- Use to help discover the tasks and concerns of implementation.
- Use to help focus complex ideas on a single graphic. This way you can take it in all at once.

Time, Materials, and Other Considerations

Time: The time will vary with the use and complexity of the application; however, it usually takes less than 20 minutes to do a typical Mind Map.

Materials: See table 6.43.

Table 6.43. Tech Table: Mind Map. ***Author created (new for 2nd edition)***

Nondigital	*Digital*
• Chart paper	• Collaborative Document (e.g., Microsoft Word Online, Google Docs)
• Colored pens, markers	• Devices (e.g., Smartboard)
• Tape	

Procedural Steps

1. Start in the center with the central topic or key idea for the map. This might be the problem statement itself if you are going to map the components of the problem.
2. Branch off from the center with other main ideas, steps, activities, and such. Add subtopics to the main ones as required.
3. Add, for example, symbols, graphics, color, or different styles of writing to highlight and add impact to the map. Remember, the intent of a completed map is to quickly highlight key ideas for those who are referring to it.
4. Make the map large so that you can "post" it for future reference.

Variation

- You can add meaningful graphics to the map, such as a small organization chart, to add other key information to the map.

Example

The example shown in figure 6.47 is a learning map of the problem-solving approach presented in this book. It demonstrates the use of a graphic representation of the steps in the model to quickly "jog" your memory.

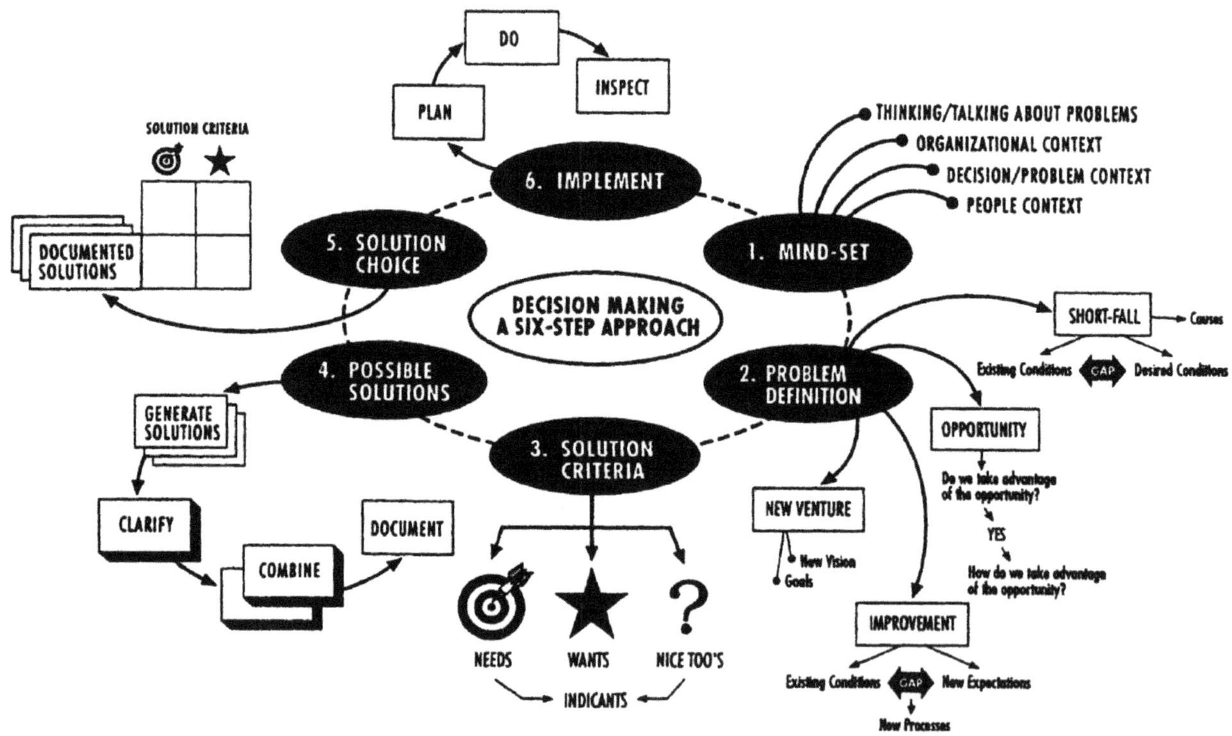

Figure 6.47. Mind Map: Example. ***Author created (1st edition)***

MORPHOLOGICAL ANALYSIS

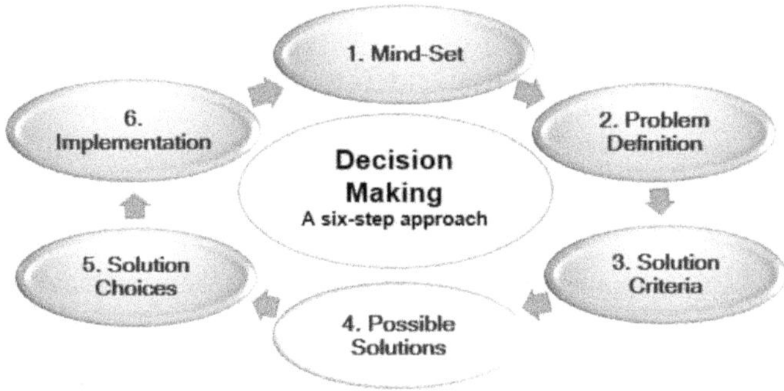

Figure 6.48. Decision Making: A Six-Step Approach: Morphological Analysis. ***Author created (updated from 1st edition)***

Description

The Morphological Analysis is a creative, exploratory technique that clarifies all possible relationships among the objects being considered. It is an unbiased approach that does not place value on the desirability or feasibility of an alternative. The Morphological Analysis generates a large array of alternatives. This device can "spark thinking" so that all solutions are considered as possibilities until they are proven impossible. This device is useful in generating possibilities in an analytical, nonemotional way.

Applications or Illustrations of Use

- Use the Morphological Analysis to generate an array of possible solutions as well as understanding the true extent of possibilities.
- Use to develop new products and processes.

Time, Materials, and Other Considerations

Time: Approximately 3–6 hours.
Materials: See table 6.44.

Table 6.44. Tech Table: Mind Map. ***Author created (new for 2nd edition)***

Nondigital	*Digital*
• Chart paper	• Devices (e.g., Samsung Flip, responders)
• Pens, markers	
• Tape	

Procedural Steps

1. Concisely state the problem or decision to be made.
2. Identify all of the parameters of the problem. A parameter is a defining characteristic of the product or process, for example, the structure, time, environment, politics, and resources.
3. List all the possible elements for each of the parameters.
4. An element is a facet of each parameter.
5. Calculate the number of possible alternatives excluding contradictory elements across the parameters through a math permutation. (For example, three parameters with two elements each would be $2 \times 2 \times 2 = 8$.)
6. Randomly select an element from each parameter to create an alternative. Repeat this as often as is useful (probably eight to fifteen scenarios).
7. Discuss to clarify, group, or eliminate. Do not be quick to reject any alternative as a possibility.

Example

A morphological display relies on the delineation of parameters of major decisions or plans and then the determination of the possible elements that could occur within each parameter. This morphology does not attempt to display all elements, just likely ones. The data shown in tables 6.45 and 6.46 were derived from the members of a college's Financial Planning Committee.

Table 6.45. Morphological Analysis: Chart 1. ***Author created (1st edition)***

	E01	*E02*	*E03*	*E04*
P1:	E11	E12	E13	E14
P2:	E21	E22	E23	
P3:	E31	E32		
P4:	E41	E42		
PS:	E51	E52		
P6:	E61	E62		
P7:	E71	E72	E73	
P8:	E81	E82	E83	
P9:	E91	E92	E93	
P10:	E101	E102	E103	
P11:	E111	E112		

With these 11 parameters (shown in table 6.45), the number of possible solutions is 31,104 (4 × 3 × 2 × 2 × 2 × 2 × 3 × 3 × 3 × 3 × 2). The point of a morphology is to randomly choose several possibilities and see what they look like.

Table 6.46 shows three examples of scenarios (randomly selected):

Table 6.46. Morphological Analysis: Chart 2. ***Author created (1st edition)***

A.	E12	E22	E31	E41	E51	E62	E73	E83
	E91	E102	E112					
B.	E12	E23	E32	E42	E52	E62	E72	E82
	E91	E103	E111					
C.	E13	E21	E31	E42	E51	E62	E11	E81
	E92	E101	E111					

In scenario A, the college will have a 5 percent undergrad enrollment increase with a 300 percent graduate increase, 0 percent doctoral and certificate increase, and 10 percent law school increase. This will occur with no new marketing personnel, meeting 600 percent of students' need, little capital outlay, meeting targeted grant receipts, and giving more financial aid to adults. What does this scenario tell you?

What do scenarios B and C say?

MULTI-ATTRIBUTE ANALYSIS (MAA)

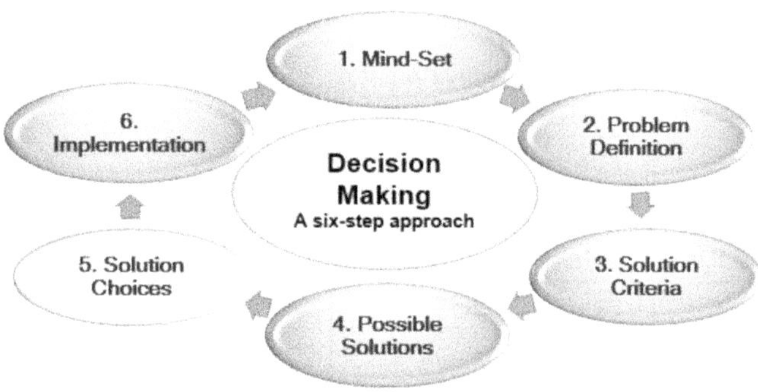

Figure 6.49. Decision Making: A Six-Step Approach: Multi-Attribute Analysis. ***Author created (updated from 1st edition)***

Description

The Multi-Attribute Analysis (MAA) is a device that compares costs in relation to the benefits of proposed solution possibilities. The structured nature of this device allows the decision makers to leave their emotions behind as they prioritize their proposed alternatives. The MAA is a form of cost-benefit analysis with the expansion of cost factors beyond money.

Applications or Illustrations of Use

- Use the MAA when considering large expenditures or budget cuts and various stakeholder groups that will be affected by the cuts.
- Use to examine the consequences of alternatives.

Time, Materials, and Other Considerations

Time: Approximately 1–3 hours.
Materials: See table 6.47.

Table 6.47. Tech Table: Multi-Attribute Analysis. ***Author created (new for 2nd edition)***

Nondigital	*Digital*
• Flip chart	• Collaborative Spreadsheet (e.g., Microsoft Excel Online, Google Sheets)
• Pens, markers	• Devices (e.g., Interactive LFD)
• Tape	

Procedural Steps

1. Construct two matrices of two dimensions each (one will be a cost matrix and the other a benefit matrix) or use the worksheets provided (see tables 6.50 and 6.51).
2. On each of the matrices, list each of the proposed alternatives down the side.
3. Assign a weight to each cost factor (which we will call X) (as noted under step 5) according to its perceived level of importance. We suggest that you assign weights from .5 (low) to 5 (high).
4. Assign a weight to each benefit factor (which we will call Y) (as noted in step 6 below) according to its perceived level of importance. Use the same ranges of weights as in step 3.
5. Determine the Cost Factors, using a 1–5 scale value (see table 6.48).

   C1 Money: direct and indirect costs (excluding personnel)
   C2 Personnel time: hours × cost per hour
   C3 Opportunities lost: forgone income or irretrievable opportunities

Table 6.48. Multi-Attribute Analysis: Cost Matrix. ***Author created (1st edition)***

Comparative Cost Matrix					
Variable Weights	*1*	*2*	*.5*	*1*	*0*
	Money	*Time*	*Opportunity Lost*	*Negative Secondary Effects*	*Other*
Retreat	$635	5 people × 16 hrs $1,600			
	1	3	0	2	0
Retreat	$2,500	5 people × 24 hrs $2,400			
	4	4	0	1	0

C4 Negative secondary effects: on satisfaction and subsequent job completion
C5 Other (Each organization should decide if it has some unique cost it wishes to include.)

6. Determine Benefit Factors using a 1–5 scale value (see table 6.49).

B1 Quality of outcome: achievement of objective
B2 Positive secondary effects on climate
B3 New opportunities gained
B4 Other (Each organization should decide if it has some unique benefits it wishes to include.)

7. Insert determined values into the following formula:

COST = C1(X1) + C2(X2) + C3(X3) + C4(X4) + C5(X5)
BENEFIT = B1(Y1) + B2(Y3) + B4(Y4)

8. Determine the Benefit-to-Cost Ratio for each alternative by computing the formula.

Table 6.49. Multi-Attribute Analysis: Benefit Matrix. ***Author created (1st edition)***

Comparative Benefit Matrix				
Variable Weights	*2*	*1*	*.5*	*0*
	Objectives Achieved	*Positive Climate*	*New Opportunity*	*Other*
On-Site A1	4	3	2	0
Off-Site A2	5	4	3	0

It should be noted that the higher the calculated value, the better the possible solution.

Variation

- See also Trade-Off Analysis.

Example

The problem in the following example is whether or not to have an off-site retreat or an on-site retreat.

The data in the two matrices are then converted into a formula:

C1(X1) + C2(X2) + C3(X3) + C4(X4) + C5(X5)

Wherein each C1 or C2 or C3 stands for the cost in a cell and X1 stands for the weight of that cell. In this case, the money cost for an on-site retreat is very limited so it is rated as 1. The weight of this variable is also a 1 (very limited). The result is 1 × 1 or written as 1(1) in the formula. For time, the rating is 3 with a weighting of 2 for a result of 3(2) or 6. This is carried through mathematically for each cell of each possibility. The resulting formula appears as follows:

A1: On-Site Retreat
Cost = 1(1) + 3(2) + 0(.5) + 2(1) + 0 = 9
Benefit = 4(2) + 3(1) + 2(.5) + 0 = 12
Benefit/Cost Ratio = 12/9 = 1.33

A2: Off-Site Retreat
Cost = 4(1) + 4(2) + 0(.5) + 1(1) + 0 = 13
Benefit = 5(2) + 4(1) + 3(.5) + 0 = 15.50
Benefit/Cost Ratio = 15.50/13.00 = 1.19

As you can see, the benefits are higher for an off-site retreat (15.5) but so are the costs (13). The ratio of benefits to costs favors the on-site retreat.

Multi-Attribute Analysis Worksheet: Costs

See table 6.50 for a "costs" worksheet.

Table 6.50. Multi-Attribute Analysis Worksheet: Costs. ***Author created (1st edition)***

Alternatives	*Money*	*Personnel Time*	*Opportunities Lost*	*Negative Secondary Effects*	*Other*
A_1					
A_2					
A_3					
A_4					

Multi-Attribute Analysis Worksheet: Benefits

See table 6.51 for a "benefits" worksheet.

Table 6.51. Multi-Attribute Analysis Worksheet: Benefits. ***Author created (1st edition)***

Alternatives	*Quality of Outcomes*	*Positive Secondary Effects*	*New Opportunities Gained*	*Other*
A_1				
A_2				
A_3				
A_4				

MULTI-VOTING

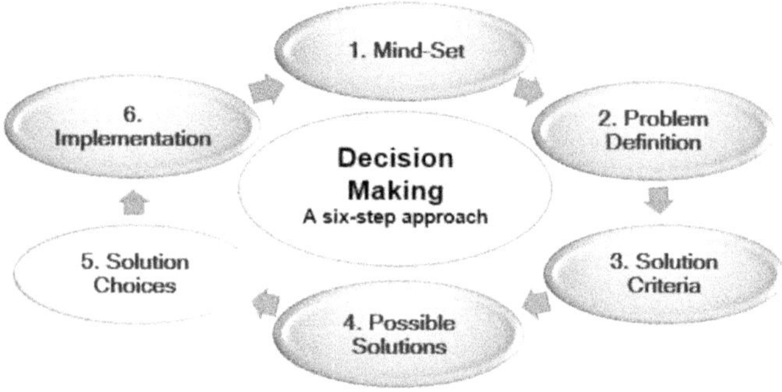

Figure 6.50. Decision Making: A Six-Step Approach: Multi-Voting. ***Author created (updated from 1st edition)***

Description

Multi-Voting is a descriptive term for several devices that prioritize or winnow items. Multi-Voting is also used to narrow down lists of possibilities. Three devices are noted here: N/3 Voting, Divide by 2, and 10-5-2-1.

Applications or Illustrations of Use

- Use Multi-Voting to eliminate items on a list.
- Use to prioritize.

Time, Materials, and Other Considerations

Time: Approximately 10–15 minutes.
Materials: See table 6.52.

Table 6.52. Tech Table: Multi-Voting. ***Author created (new for 2nd edition)***

Nondigital	*Digital*
• Chart paper	• Whiteboard Collaborative Tools (e.g., Jamboard)
• Pens, markers	• Other application (e.g., Poll)
• Tape	• Devices (e.g., Samsung Flip, responders)

Procedural Steps

N/3 Voting

1. Present the list of possibilities.
2. Have the participants vote by dividing the list by three (e.g., if you start with thirty possibilities, you must pick ten). Each person selects the designated number of possibilities from the list.
3. Have each person report out his/her choices and put a mark next to the choice.
4. Identify the possibilities that are most often selected.
5. Share that the most often selected will be priority considerations.

Divide by 2

This variation operates the same as N/3 Voting, but the process is repeated twice.

1. Present the list of possibilities.
2. Have the participants individually divide the list by two (e.g., if you have forty possible alternatives, the individuals must come up with twenty choices).
3. Each person reports his/her choices. Put a mark next to the choice.
4. Once all individuals have shared all their choices, identify the top choices (one-half of the original list).
5. Repeat steps 2–4. The remaining list will be priority considerations.

10-5-2-1

1. Present the list of possibilities.
2. Ask individuals to choose their top ten choices.
3. Next, ask them to pare that list (step 2) from their top ten to their top five choices.
4. Have them select their top two of the five choices (in step 3).
5. Finally, have them select their top choice.

NEEDS/WANTS CRITERIA MATRIX

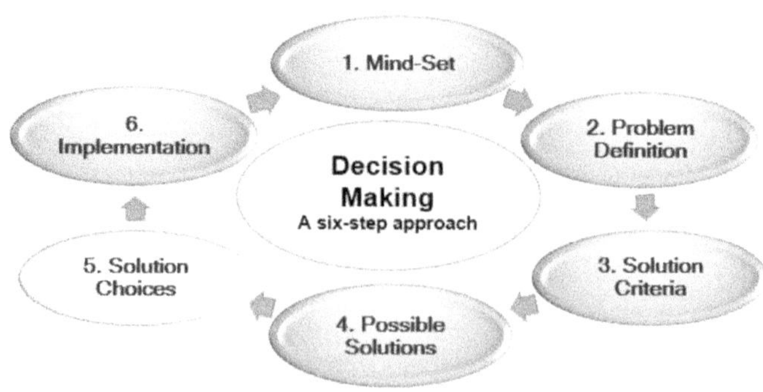

Figure 6.51. Decision Making: A Six-Step Approach: Needs/Wants Criteria Matrix. ***Author created (updated from 1st edition)***

Description

The Needs/Wants Criteria Matrix is a structuring device that allows the decision makers to establish the objectives wanted for the solutions. The objectives are divided into "needs" and "wants" and then compared against the criteria. The Needs/Wants Criteria Matrix causes the decision makers to come up with quality analytical solutions rather than solutions based on emotions.

Application or Illustration of Use

- Use the Needs/Wants Criteria Matrix to establish criteria when evaluating possible solutions.

Time, Materials, and Other Considerations

Time: Approximately 60 minutes.
Materials: See table 6.53.

Table 6.53. Tech Table: Needs/Wants Criteria Matrix. ***Author created (new for 2nd edition)***

Nondigital	*Digital*
• Chart paper	• Collaborative Spreadsheet (e.g., Zoho Sheets, Google Sheets)
• Pens, markers	• Devices (e.g., Interactive LFD)
• Tape	

Procedural Steps

1. Make a matrix (grid) with three sections.
2. Label each section: Needs, Wants, and Nice-toos. "Needs" are the mandatory criteria or requirements. For example, in teacher selection, candidate characteristics could be "must have math credential," "eight years teaching experience," or "bilingual." "Wants" are desirable qualities. "Nice-toos" are those qualities that are nice to have but neither mandatory nor desirable.
3. List the possible solutions (e.g., teacher applicants' names) in a column on the left side of the matrix.
4. List the various "needs" criteria across the top of the matrix (in the "Needs" section).
5. Write the "wants" criteria in the next section across the top of the matrix. Assign a weight to each "Wants" from 5 to 10 (5 = somewhat important; 10 = extremely important).
6. Write the "nice-toos" in the third section across the top of the matrix. Assign a weight to each "nice-too" from 1 to 4 (1 = slightly desirable; 4 = desirable). The "nice-toos" should have a lower weight than the "wants."
7. Compare the possible solutions against the "needs" criteria. If the solution doesn't match the criteria, cross it off of the list. This step takes the possible solution list down to fewer options.
8. Using the remaining solution list, compare solutions against the "wants" criteria. Record weights on the grid.
9. Next, compare the possible solutions to the "nice-toos" criteria. Record weights on the grid.
10. Add the weights for each solution. The highest score is the most favorable solution.
11. Discuss the remaining solution. Is there agreement among the team members? Does everyone feel the same?
12. Discuss and determine the next step.

Caution

- Although the criteria matrix is "dispassionate" DM, the final decision must "feel" right. Be sure to check feelings with other team members.

Example

Table 6.54 depicts a Needs/Wants Criteria Matrix used to select a new math teacher.

Table 6.54. Needs/Wants Criteria Matrix: Example. ***Author created (updated from 1st edition)***

	Needs				Wants		Nice-Toos		Total
Criteria *(Weights)*	*Bilingual*	**Exp.: 2 Years Min.**	*Math* **Major**	*Coach* **Sport**	**Sci** *(5)*	*Comp. Lit.* *(7)*	*Female* *(1)*	**Grant Writer** *(4)*	
B. Blade	X			X					0
S. Ludlow	X	X	X	X	5		I	4	10
A. Smith	X	X	X	X	5	7	I		13

In this example, Blade was not a consideration because he did not meet the "needs" criteria. Ludlow and Smith were the top choices because they met the "needs" criteria: bilingual, experienced, math major, and coached sports. Both of the candidates met the "wants" criteria by having a science background; however, Ludlow lacked computer literacy skills. Both of these candidates met some of the "nice-toos" criteria; however, Ludlow had an advantage over Smith with grant-writing experience. This "nice-too" was not as heavily weighted as a "want." Hence, as you look at the total weighting, Smith was the top candidate meeting all the needs/wants criteria.

References

Doyle and Straus (1986, 210 [Criteria Checkerboard]).
Klubnik and Greenwood (1994, 180 [Criteria Matching]).

NOMINAL GROUP TECHNIQUE

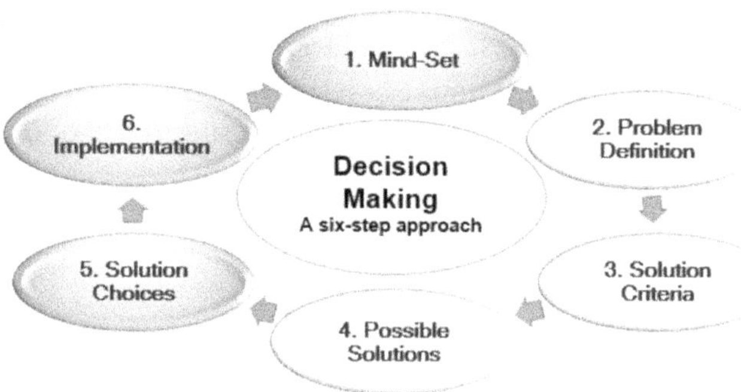

Figure 6.52. Decision Making: A Six-Step Approach: Nominal Group Technique. ***Author created (updated from 1st edition)***

Description

Nominal Group Technique is an idea-generating device similar to brainstorming but is a more formalized and structured approach than brainstorming. This device promotes and balances participation by structuring a way for participants to share and have a voice. The Nominal Group Technique can help filter out biases by using silent individual generation of ideas at the beginning of the process.

Applications or Illustrations of Use

- Use the Nominal Group Technique if dominating personalities are in the group or trust is low and needs to be built.
- Use Nominal Group Technique when the group has introverts, cliques, or subgroups.
- Use Nominal Group Technique if the group is diverse and members have different personal agendas that may be a source of conflict or controversy.
- Use this technique to generate criteria needs if criteria are unclear.

Time, Materials, and Other Considerations

Time: Approximately 30–60 minutes.
Materials: See table 6.55.

Table 6.55. Tech Table: Nominal Group Technique. ***Author created (new for 2nd edition)***

Nondigital	*Digital*
• Chart paper	• Collaborative Document (e.g., Google Docs, Microsoft Word Online)
• Pens, markers	• Other application (e.g., Padlet)
• Tape	• Devices (e.g., Smartboard)
• Index cards, post-it notes	

Procedural Steps

1. Present the problem or decision.
2. Tell the group that they will have a few minutes to think about the problem or decision.
3. Have the individuals silently generate and write their ideas (on a three-by-five card or post-it).
4. Gather ideas from each of the individuals in round-robin style and record them on a chart.
5. When all the ideas have been recorded, the group then discusses each idea in order to be sure that everyone has a common understanding of each idea. If the group is large, put the members into smaller groups to collaborate and collectively share information, merits, and demerits of each idea.
6. With the group's agreement, eliminate duplicate ideas and combine similar ones.

Variations

- You might want to protect anonymity of the participants if issues of power are evident or members seem reluctant to share out. Have participants record their ideas on a card. Collect the cards, shuffle, then distribute them so that participants are sharing others' ideas.
- Have the group come to the meeting with individually prepared lists so that they are warmed up and ready to share.
- Have the small groups share the merits and demerits of each idea.
- Get members involved by having them "pass the baton" (pass/play) to the next person. Members hold the baton to share or pass to the next person.
- Use the 1-3-6 method if the group is large. Follow procedural steps 1–3 individually. Then, form groups of three for steps 4–6. Once all the information is shared in the small group, form groups of six and repeat steps 4 through 6.

References

Brassard and Ritter (1994, 91).
Higgens (1994, 150).
Klubnik and Greenwood (1994, 147).
Nutt (1990, 362–365).
Quinlivan-Hall and Renner (1990, 102).
Scholtes et al. (1994, 2–45).
Viability Corporate HR, Performance Development Division (1994).

PAPER PLATE EXCHANGE

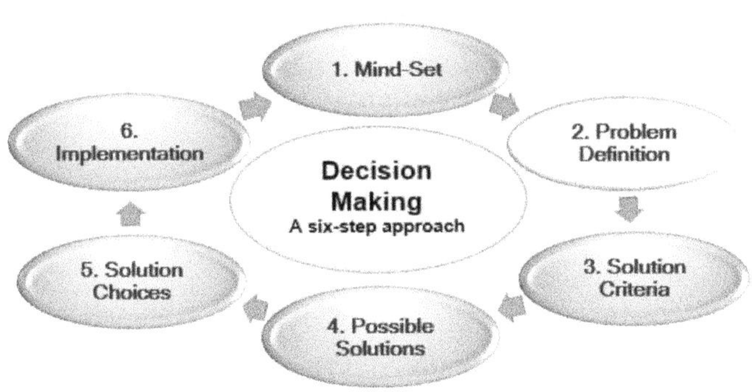

Figure 6.53. Decision Making: A Six-Step Approach: Paper Plate Exchange. ***Author created (updated from 1st edition)***

Description

The Paper Plate Exchange is a structured questioning activity to encourage discussion through question-and-answer exchanges. This device facilitates problem clarification.

Applications or Illustrations of Use

- Use the Paper Plate Exchange to create a "safe environment" to clarify problems.
- Use this device as an alternative to energize the group.

Time, Materials, and Other Considerations

Time: Approximately 10–15 minutes.
Materials: See table 6.56.

Table 6.56. Tech Table: Paper Plate Exchange. ***Author created (new for 2nd edition)***

Nondigital	*Digital*
• Small paper plates	• Whiteboard Collaborative Tools (e.g., Jamboard)
• Pens, markers	• Devices (e.g., Interactive LFD)

Procedural Steps

1. Distribute one paper plate to each individual.
2. Present a question, a problem to be solved, or a decision to be made.
3. Ask participants to write their questions of clarification on one side of the paper plate. Allow 3 minutes.
4. When the time allotted has been used, instruct the individuals to pass their plate to the person on their left.
5. Each person responds in writing to the questions on the other side of the plate and passes the plate on to the next person.
6. Repeat step 5 until every person in the group has an opportunity to respond.
7. Collect and share out. Post the plates for visual reference.
8. Discuss.

Variation

- If anonymity is desired, collect the plates, shuffle, and redistribute them for reporting out.

Example

A principal brought her teachers together to discuss parent involvement in the school. Several parents had expressed that they did not feel comfortable invading the teachers' space. The principal wanted to surface how the teachers were feeling and posed the question to the teachers on a paper plate. The teachers wrote their questions and feelings and exchanged them. Questions surfaced, such as, "How will this affect me?" and "Will we have confidentiality?" and "Will volunteers feel welcome?"

This experience opened the door to discussion of feelings and perceptions so that the staff could begin to address the problem and the feelings related to it.

PARETO CHART

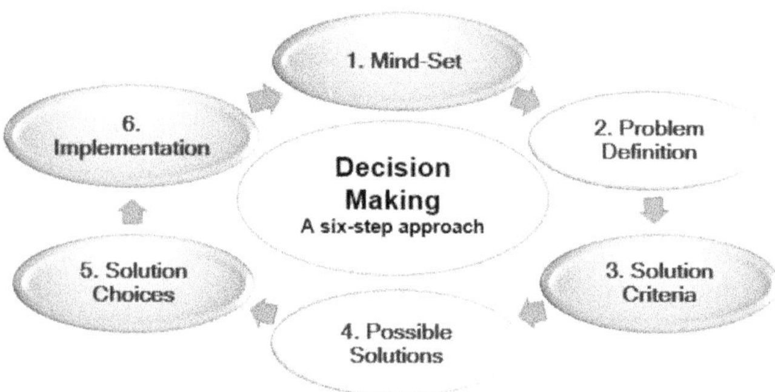

Figure 6.54. Decision Making: A Six-Step Approach: Pareto Chart. ***Author created (updated from 1st edition)***

Description

The Pareto Chart is a special form of a vertical bar chart that visually identifies the category or problem with the most occurrences. It can help you determine which cases of a problem to solve and in what order. The Pareto Chart is derived from a demographic study conducted in Italy. It involves the 80/20 rule, or Pareto principle, in which 80 percent of the costs are caused by 20 percent of the problems. The Pareto Chart is useful to identify problems that require the most energy and focus. It is a chart used to analyze a situation and identify the elements in that process that produce "headache." The Pareto Chart "separates the critical few from the trivial many issues." The Pareto Chart rank-orders facts in graphical display and displays all the data. The most important issue quickly becomes observable.

Applications or Illustrations of Use

- Use the Pareto Chart whenever a fault or cause analysis is needed.
- Use with a group of decision makers who are less sophisticated with problem analysis and who might have difficulty separating what is most important.
- Use to analyze a work process: "Which work process would give the most progress or improvement?"
- Use in sales to analyze customers, for example, "Which customers are creating the greatest heartburn?"

Time, Materials, and Other Considerations

Time: Time varies.
Materials: See table 6.57.

Table 6.57. Tech Table: Pareto Chart. ***Author created (new for 2nd edition)***

Nondigital	*Digital*
• Chart paper	• Collaborative Spreadsheet (e.g., Zoho Sheets, Google Sheets, Microsoft Excel Online)
• Pens, markers	• Devices (e.g., Smartboard)

Procedural Steps

1. Select a problem in which the causes or possible subproblems can be quantified and turned into percentages. These include such things as customer complaints, number of failures, referrals, defects, types of injuries, and such.
2. Identify each cause or subproblem.
3. Collect data on the occurrence of each cause or subproblem.
4. Draw a vertical line for the y axis and connected horizontal line for the x axis.
5. Put the frequency, quantity, or occurrences along the y axis and the labels for the categories along the x axis to the right. (See the example in figure 6.55.)

6. Draw a bar the height of which matches the frequency on the y axis to the left for each cause or subproblem.
7. Calculate a percentage of the total represented by each cause or subproblem. Draw a cumulative percentage line starting in the lower-left corner at 0 percent. Place a dot above each bar showing the cumulative percentage to that bar. Connect the dots to make the cumulative-percentage line.
8. Use the 80/20 principle to select the causes or subproblems that will give you the biggest payoff.

Caution

- Be sure that the data are measurable. The Pareto Chart is not efficient for intangible problems such as organizational development, personnel, or human issues.

Example

The example in figure 6.55 shows a Pareto Chart of customer complaints. There were 210 total complaints for the period, with 91 complaints of poor response time, 58 of late shipment, 28 of difficult installation, and 12 of poor documentation. There were 28 other complaints; however, these were a variety of complaints with no more than two of any type. The line graph of cumulative percentages shows that 43 percent of the complaints were in the first category (poor response time), 71 percent were in the first two categories, 84 percent in the first three categories, and so on. The Pareto principle (80/20 rule) would indicate that you should focus on resolving the first three causes, which will cut customer complaints by 84 percent.

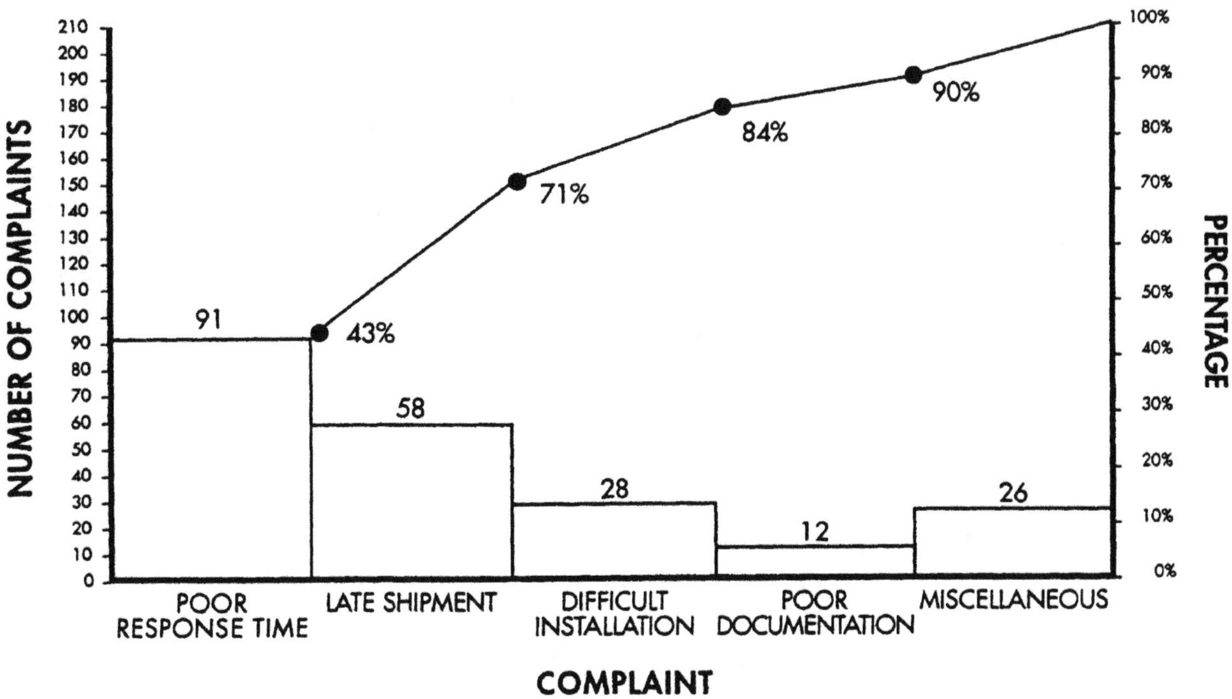

Figure 6.55. Pareto Chart: Example. ***Author created (1st edition)***

References

Brassard and Ritter (1994, 95).
Chang and Kelly (1993, 33–34).
Klubnik and Greenwood (1994, 170).
Scholtes et al. (1994, 2–29).
Xerox (n.d., 2).

PARTICIPATIVE MANAGEMENT TREE

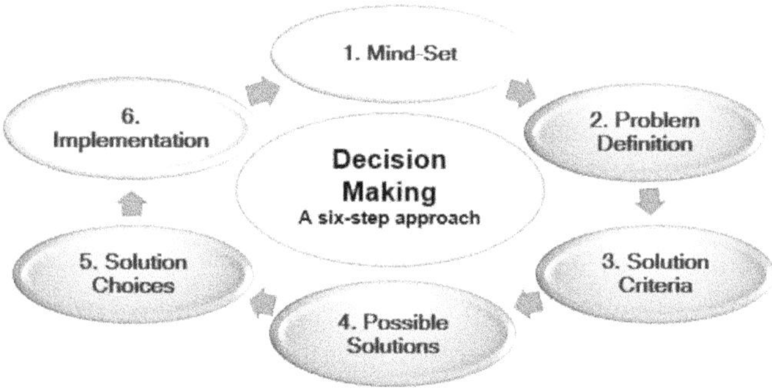

Figure 6.56. Decision Making: A Six-Step Approach: Participative Management Tree. ***Author created (updated from 1st edition)***

Description

The Participative Management Tree provides a way for a leader to determine the most appropriate approach for making a decision in a variety of situations. By answering a few simple questions in a decision tree, you arrive at one of four decision-making approaches: command, consultation, consensus, or convenience. These are called the Four Cs of DM.

According to Jones and Bearley (1986), each of the Four Cs has both assets and liabilities, and it is important to be aware of these when selecting them as strategies. In most cases, the liabilities can be overcome. A good rule is, "When in doubt, involve group members actively."

- *Consultation* means talking with individuals and/or the entire work group and then making the decision yourself. Benefits of this approach include being able to gather information to make a high-importance decision and to maintain efficiency in the decision-making process. Only people who have relevant information participate, and you make the decision yourself. It is vital in this method to make the rules clear. Others give information, not advice, and you make the decision. The problem with soliciting advice is that you may disagree with the advice, and your associates may become resentful and may not actively support your decision. When managing group consultation, be careful to point out that the meeting is only for the purpose of information input to you.
- *Command* means making the decision yourself, without prior discussions with the group. This method is quick, it capitalizes on the manager's knowledge and information, and the responsibility for the decision is clear. It may generate respect for you as a leader. On the other hand, command DM is easily abused by autocratic managers, and it often alienates those who have to live with the choice. It puts the leader in a power position, and this can inspire resistance. It is important not to put off decisions and then make them by command.
- *Consensus* means getting the group together and working toward substantial agreement. Unanimity often is not achievable, so the rule is to reach a level of substantial agreement without serious disagreement. Assets of this approach are that it generates high acceptance of the decision and it can produce synergistic teamwork. Some drawbacks are that bad group dynamics usually result in bad decisions, group decisions can reflect the pooling of ignorance, and consensus seeking is the slowest of the four methods.
- *Convenience* means making the decision in whatever manner seems to be the easiest. That may be through delegation, asking volunteers, or appointing someone to make the decision. In others, you ensure that no one makes a federal case over how the decision is made. Convenience methods are good for relatively unimportant decisions, such as where to place the water cooler. This approach avoids time-consuming participation and often is seen as a reward by individuals selected to make the decision. In low-trust situations, however, people often cause disruption over trivial decisions because they feel that were not involved. If you misjudge the significance of *importance* and *acceptance*, or you are largely unaware of the trust level in the group, you may find that you use the convenience method too frequently. You might encounter resistance, and you may be seen either as being indecisive or as playing favorites.

Application or Illustration of Use

- Use the Participative Management Tree to determine the appropriate approach for any decision you must make. If the indicated approach is consensus, or possible consultation, the leader should create a decision-making team to work on the decision situation.

Time, Materials, and Other Considerations

Time: The use of the Participative Management Tree takes only a few minutes unless the leader must collect some additional information in order to use the tree.

Materials: The only material required is a copy of the Participative Management Tree (see figure 6.57).

Procedural Steps

1. Clearly identify the decision or problem situation.
2. Move through the tree in figure 6.57, starting at the far left. Do this by answering the questions 1–5 as indicated by the tree. These questions relate to the considerations of time, trust, teamwork, importance, and acceptance.
3. When you get a "hit" on the appropriate decision-making approach, take action.

Example

See figure 6.57 for an example.

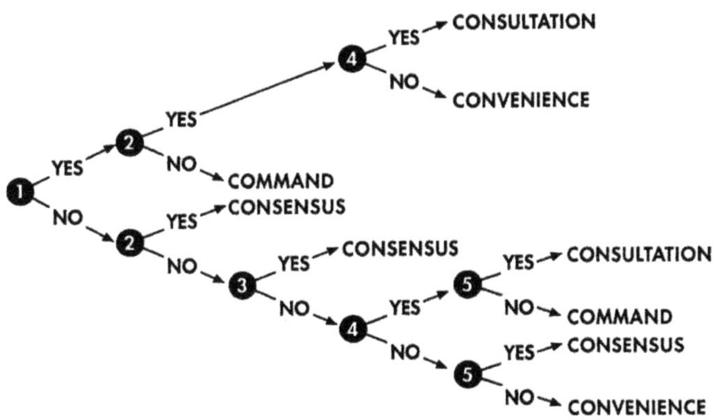

Figure 6.57. Participative Management Tree: Example. ***Author created (1st edition)***

Overriding Considerations

1. Time: Is there a time crunch—that is, must a decision be made right away?
2. Trust: Do the people affected by the decision trust each other in general?
3. Teamwork: Do you want to develop your work group toward a higher level of teamwork with this decision?
4. Importance: Is the decision crucial to the organization—that is, one that may result in clear benefits or harm?
5. Acceptance: Is it important to generate high acceptance of the decision—that is, are your people likely to have strong feelings about it and/or how it is made?

References

Jones and Bearley (1986).

PAYOFF MATRIX

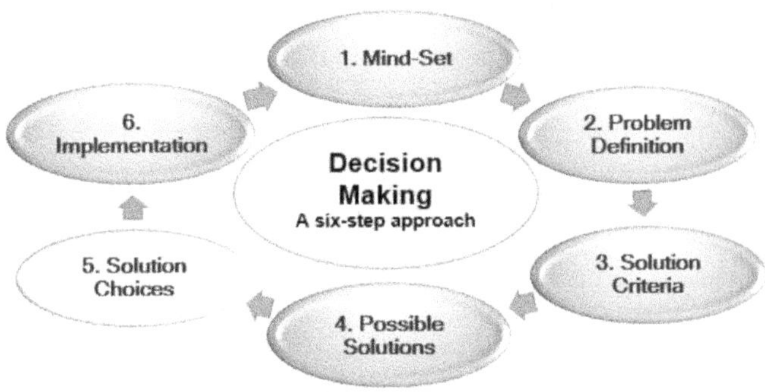

Figure 6.58. Decision Making: A Six-Step Approach: Payoff Matrix. ***Author created (updated from 1st edition)***

Description

This is a multifactor matrix that helps individuals understand the consequences of various "states of nature" relative to the payoffs for different possible solutions. "If this happens, then this will be my payoff (or outcome)." This quantitative device is useful where stakes are high and is a method for examining contingencies.

Application or Illustration of Use

- Use the Payoff Matrix to understand the consequences of decision choice.

Time, Materials, and Other Considerations

Time: Approximately 3–4 hours.

Materials: See table 6.58.

Table 6.58. Tech Table: Payoff Matrix. ***Author created (new for 2nd edition)***

Nondigital	*Digital*
• Matrix sheets	• Collaborative Spreadsheet (e.g., Google Sheets, Microsoft Excel Online)
• Pens, markers	• Whiteboard Collaborative Tools (e.g., Jamboard) • Devices (e.g., Interactive LFD)

Procedural Steps

1. List possible solutions down the side of the matrix (S1, S2 . . .). See figure 6.59.
2. Establish "states of nature or competitor strategies." These are factors beyond your control that affect the situation significantly. List these across the top of the matrix (N1, N2 . . .). Steps 1 and 2 create the basic payoff matrix.

CONCEPTUAL PAYOFF MATRIX COMPETITOR STRATEGIES (STATES OF NATURE)				
YOUR ALTERNATIVE STRATEGIES	N_1 (PROB)	N_2 (PROB)	N_3 (PROB)	N_N (PROB)
S_1	P_{11}	P_{12}	P_{13}	P_{1N}
S_2	P_{21}	P_{22}	P_{23}	P_{2N}
S_3	P_{31}	P_{32}	P_{33}	P_{3N}
S_N	P_{N1}	P_{N2}	P_{N3}	P_{NN}
P = Payoff ($ or Utility)				

Figure 6.59. Payoff Matrix: Procedure 1. ***Author created (1st edition)***

3. Next, determine the probability of each state of nature (prob). The total probability of all Ns should be 1.0 or 100 percent.
4. Three Approaches to Payoff Matrix:

   Under "certainty," just pick greatest payoff.
   Under "risk," compute expected value and add.
   Under "certainty," you need to go to personality types: optimist, pessimist, and pragmatist.

   a. Certainty
   If probability for one state of nature is 1.0 or 100 percent, then estimate the payoff or utility for each cell and pick the cell with the greatest payoff. Utility can be calculated through a trade-off analysis or by consensus. The issue of the cell value (utility) is one of the more difficult things to understand. It usually involves human judgment and human estimates. We often use numerical scales (1–5, 1–10, 1–100, or whatever) to approximate qualitative realities (e.g., on a 1–10 scale, how much do you love your spouse?).

   In the example shown in figure 6.60, a city is trying to decide whether to (1) maintain services, (2) privatize services, or (3) reduce services. The states of nature are stable revenues, reduced revenues, or increased revenues. These are things happening outside our control. If we assume that the likelihood of reduced revenue is 1.0 or 100 percent, then you would do a certainty condition payoff matrix. In this case, two variables, community reactions and organizational feasibility, have been used to determine utility and cell values. A group has determined that on a 0–50 scale for each variable what would be the best estimate for utility. Privatizing services would get a positive response from the public (40 points out of 50) but would get some strong negative employee response, but it would be easy to administer (10 out of 50). This makes the total cell 50. We did all cells in the same fashion.

PAYOFF MATRIX CERTAINTY CONDITION	
Maintain Service	10
Privatize	50
Reduce Services	20

Utility = Community Reaction + Organizational Feasibility (+ or – 100).
* Privatizing is best alternative.

Figure 6.60. Payoff Matrix: Example 1. ***Author created (1st edition)***

b. Risk

If the states of nature were reasonably predictable but spread in probability, then you would use a risk condition payoff matrix. Calculate cell values as before, then multiply cell value by probability of states of nature. Then add across cells. See figure 6.61.

PAYOFF MATRIX RISK CONDITION			
	CURRENT FISCAL STATE (.60)*	REDUCED REVENUE (.30)	INCREASED REVENUE (.10)
Maintain Service	50	10	90
Privatize	60	50	10
Reduce Service	-30	20	-90

UTILITY deals with Community Reaction + Organizational Feasibility (+ or – 100).

PAYOFF MATRIX EXPECTED VALUE RISK CONDITION				
	CURRENT	REDUCED	INCREASED	TOTAL
Maintain Service	30	3	9	42
Privatize	36	15	1	52
Reduce Service	-18	6	-9	-21

Privatizing is best alternative.

Figure 6.61. Payoff Matrix: Example 2. ***Author created (1st edition)***

c. Uncertainty

If states of nature cannot reasonably be estimated for their probability of occurrence, then use an uncertainty condition payoff matrix. Calculate cell values as in step 4b. If you are an optimist, you will pick alternatives with greatest cell value. If you are a pessimist, you pick alternatives where smallest payoff is the best. If you are a pragmatist, you use regret matrix (see figure 6.62), in which you subtract each payoff from maximum payoff for that state of nature. This is maximum regret and you choose the least of these.

REGRET MATRIX			
	CURRENT	REDUCED	INCREASED
Maintain Service	50	10	90
Privatize	60	50	10
Reduce Service	-30	20	-90
S1	10	40	0
S2	0	0	80
S3	80	30	180

S1 is minimum of maximum regrets.

Figure 6.62. Payoff Matrix: Example 3: Regret Matrix. ***Author created (1st edition)***

Optimist: uses largest cell or coefficient of optimism.

Pessimist: minimum payoff and chooses best.

Minimax: regret matrix. Subtract each payoff from maximum payoff for that state of nature. Compute maximum regret. Choose least of three.

Payoff Matrix: Worksheet

See table 6.59 for a worksheet template for the Payoff Matrix.

Table 6.59. Payoff Matrix: Worksheet. *Author created (1st edition)*

States of Nature (PROB) Possible Solutions	*N1 ( )*	*N2 ( )*	*N3 ( )*	*N4 ( )*
S1				
S2				
S3				
S4				
S5				

PERSONAL POWER GRID

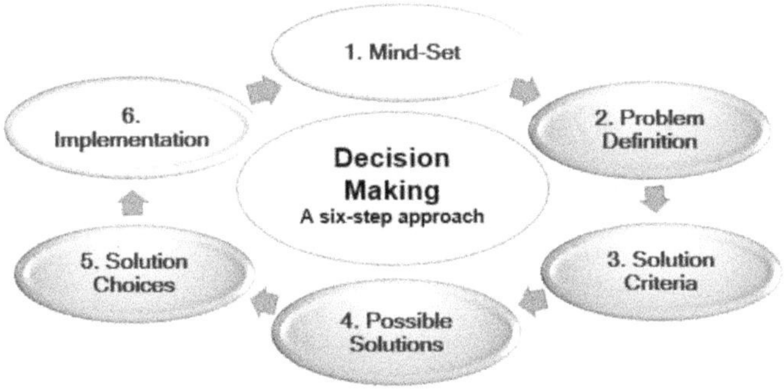

Figure 6.63. Decision Making: A Six-Step Approach: Personal Power Grid. ***Author created (updated from 1st edition)***

Description

The Personal Power Grid is a structured activity that identifies the group members' feelings of "power" over the things that they can and cannot control throughout the problem-solving or decision-making process.

Application or Illustration of Use

- Use the Personal Power Grid with cross-functional teams or when various levels of employees are involved in the decision-making process.
- Use in highly politicized decision settings.

Time, Materials, and Other Considerations

Time: Approximately 10–15 minutes.
Materials: See table 6.60.

Table 6.60. Tech Table: Personal Power Grid. ***Author created (new for 2nd edition)***

Nondigital	*Digital*
• Flip chart	• Collaborative Document (e.g., Google Docs, Microsoft Word Online)
• Pens, markers	• Other application (e.g., Padlet)
• Post-its	• Devices (e.g., Interactive LFD)

Procedural Steps

1. Identify the decision area.
2. On two sheets of the flip chart, write these headings: "Things That We Cannot Control or Change" and "Things We Can Control or Change."
3. Develop a list of items on the chart under the first heading (Things We Cannot Control).
4. Generate ideas under the second heading "Can Control" list.
5. Revisit the "Cannot Control" column and discuss what can be done to influence them.
6. Through discussion, come to agreement about "Things That Can Be Controlled."
7. Post this list during each meeting for reference.

References

Koberg and Bagnall (1981, 38).

POSITIVE CONTEXT

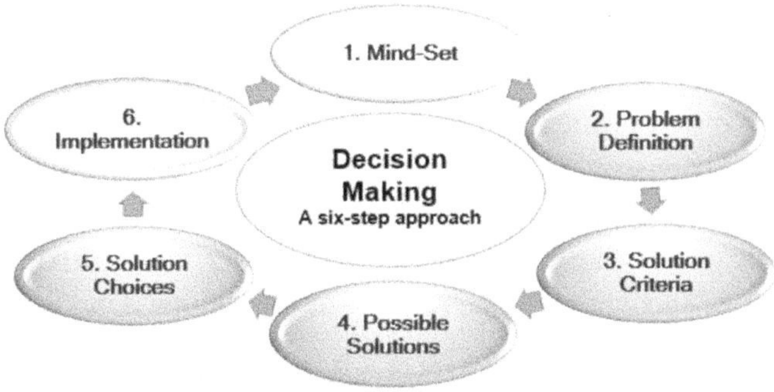

Figure 6.64. Decision Making: A Six-Step Approach: Positive Context. ***Author created (updated from 1st edition)***

Description

A key starting point for DM is establishing a positive context for participants to approach problems and issues. This device is useful in the mind-set stage by creating common focus and direction around beliefs, behaviors, and conditions that would be effective DM. This is a form of norm setting.

Application or Illustration of Use

- Use in opening meetings of new groups.

Time, Materials, and Other Considerations

Time: Approximately 15–30 minutes.
Materials: See table 6.61.

Table 6.61. **Tech Table: Positive Context.** *Author created (new for 2nd edition)*

Nondigital	*Digital*
• Chart paper	• Collaborative Document (e.g., Google Docs, Microsoft Word Online)
• Pens, markers	• Whiteboard Collaborative Tools (e.g., Limnu)
• Positive Context sheet	• Devices (e.g., Interactive LFD)

Procedural Steps

1. Ask participants to describe beliefs, behaviors, or conditions in the past that were helpful in effective DM. List these on a large piece of chart paper.
2. Ask participants to describe beliefs, behaviors, or conditions in the past that got in the way of effective DM. List these on a large piece of chart paper.
3. Discuss which positive beliefs, behaviors, and conditions were most important and productive.
4. Discuss which negative beliefs, behaviors, and conditions were most unproductive.
5. Write what would be the positive or mirror image of those beliefs, behaviors, or conditions described in step 4.
6. Record those positive beliefs, behaviors, and conditions described in steps 3 and 5 on the positive context sheet.
7. Review these with the group and then post them on a large poster board. These should be present and visible during all decision-making meetings.

Example

Positive Context Sheet

The following are beliefs, behaviors, and conditions we pledge ourselves to maintain during our decision-making process:

- Belief
    - We believe there is a mutually acceptable solution available.
    - We believe in the value of each participant.
    - We believe that conflict can be productive in DM.
- Behavior
    - What we say is what we mean; no game playing.
    - We will not bully our way to victory.
    - We will listen.
    - We will be on time to meetings.
- Conditions
    - There will be time to make a quality decision.
    - We will meet around a table.
    - We will keep committees between five and twelve people.

References

Harvey and Drolet (1994, chapter 3).

PRECEDENCE CHART

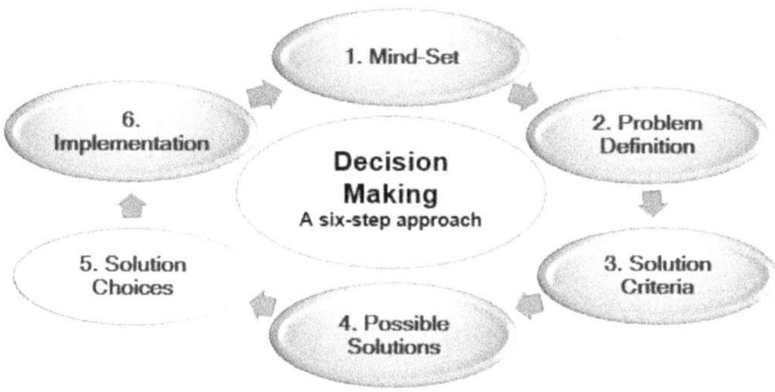

Figure 6.65. Decision Making: A Six-Step Approach: Precedence Chart. *Author created (updated from 1st edition)*

Description

The Precedence Chart is a device used for prioritization. The process allows decision makers to look at analytical data and make choices based on a binary comparison of variables. The Precedence Chart encourages participation and discussion throughout the narrowing-down process, which in turn builds consensus. This device operates on the theory that priorities can be set by comparing all possibilities, two at a time.

Application or Illustration of Use

- Use the Precedence Chart to set priorities.

Time, Materials, and Other Considerations

Time: Approximately 1–2 hours depending on the number of decision possibilities.
Materials: See table 6.62.

Table 6.62. Tech Table: Precedence Chart. ***Author created (new for 2nd edition)***

Nondigital	*Digital*
• Precedence Chart worksheets	• Collaborative Document (e.g., Microsoft Word Online)
• Pens, markers	• Collaborative Spreadsheet (e.g., Google Sheets)
• Post-it notes	• Devices (e.g., Interactive LFD)

Procedural Steps

1. Post your list of possible solutions (choices).
2. Use a copy of the matrix provided (see table 6.65).
3. List the choices in the row of "cells" across the top of the matrix. Label the choice A, B, C, D, and so on.
4. List the same choices in the column of "cells" on the left side of the matrix. Label each choice A, B, C, D, and so on, and in the same order as in step 3.
5. Start with the first row. Ask, "Do you prefer A over B?" If the group chooses A over B, put a 1 in that box. Then ask, "Do you prefer A over C?" If they do not, put a 0 in that box. Continue across the row until all of the pairs have been compared. (See the example in table 6.63.) Have each individual fill out the total Precedence Chart before the group discusses each cell.
6. For each alternative, total the number of "ls" across. Then, total the number of "0s" down. Add the two subtotals together for a total score.
7. The resulting sum totals will indicate a rank ordering of choices. The item with the highest total is the first priority. (See the example in table 6.63.)

Check quantitative results with group sense of priority.

Variation

- If you are doing this in a group setting, set a minimal level of consensus (e.g., two-thirds agreement means consensus for purpose of each cell). If there is a consensus, continue discussion; if no consensus can emerge, leave the cell blank.
- You could have the group do the procedure, without individuals doing it first (alteration to step 5).
- If money is involved, you may want to add a column that shows dollar implications of each possibility.

Cautions

- Be sure to allow time for discussion to assure consensus.
- If the group cannot come to consensus on a cell score, then leave it blank.

Example

In this example of seven potential foundation programs (table 6.64), programs for the blind received

Table 6.63. Precedence Chart: Procedure. ***Author created (1st edition)***

	A	*B*	*C*	*D*	*E*	*F*	*G*		*Total Is Across*	*Grand Total*
A	X	1	0	0	1	1	1		4	4
B		X	0	0	1	1	0		2	2
C			X	0	1	1	0		2	4
D				X	1	1	1		3	6
E					X	0	0		0	0
F						X	0		0	1
G							X		0	4
H										
I										
Total 0s Down	0	0	2	3	0	1	4			

Table 6.64. Precedence Chart: Example. ***Author created (1st edition)***

	1	*2*	*3*	*4*	*5*	*6*	*7*	*Total Is Across*	*Total*	*$*
1. Programs for Blind	X	I	I	I	I	I	I	6	6	500,000
2. Youth Outreach		X	0		I	I	I	3	3	50,000
3. Community Involvement			X	I	1	0	1	3	4	100,000
4. International Relations				X	0	0	I	I	I	75,000
5. Environmental Programs					X	0	0	0	1	40,000
6. Humanitarian Needs						X	I	I	4	130,000
7. Youth Campus							X	0	I	42,000
Total 0s Down	0	0	I	0	1	3	1			

the highest rating, followed by community involvement and humanitarian needs. The three lowest rated were programs of international relations, environment, and youth camps. If you had $600,000 to expend, you would have picked program 1 and 3. If you had $800,000, you would also have programs 6 and 2.

Precedence Chart: Worksheet

See table 6.65 for a Precedence Chart worksheet template.

Table 6.65. Precedence Chart: Worksheet. ***Author created (updated from 1st edition)***

	1	*2*	*3*	*4*	*5*	*6*	*7*	*8*	*9*	*10*	*Total 1s Across*	*Total*
A												
B												
C												
D												
E												
F												
G												
H												
I												
J												
Total 0s Down												

References

Moody (1983, 88–95).

PRIORITY MATRIX

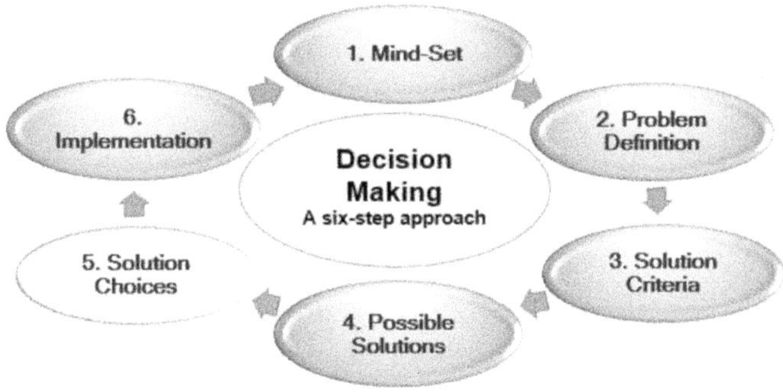

Figure 6.66. Decision Making: A Six-Step Approach: Priority Matrix. ***Author created (updated from 1st edition)***

Description

The Priority Matrix is a nonquantitative device that allows decision makers to prioritize their choices by comparing their relative importance and feasibility. The Priority Matrix presents a more rational way of analyzing data for prioritizing rather than depending on a "gut feeling."

Applications or Illustrations of Use

- Use the Priority Matrix to help the group decide where to begin, particularly if a team wants to tackle all the solutions.
- Use to evaluate the value of programs and activities.

Time, Materials, and Other Considerations

Time: Approximately 30–60 minutes.
Materials: See table 6.66.

Table 6.66. Tech Table: Priority Matrix. ***Author created (new for 2nd edition)***

Nondigital	*Digital*
• Priority Matrix worksheets	• Collaborative Spreadsheet (e.g., Google Sheets)
• Flip chart	• Whiteboard Collaborative Tools (e.g., Jamboard)
• Post-it notes	• Other application (e.g., Padlet)
• Pens, markers	• Devices (e.g., Interactive LFD)
• Tape	

Procedural Steps

1. Prepare a list of choices or projects and record them in the center of the chart paper or Priority Matrix worksheet (see table 6.67).
2. On the left side of the list, have the group determine (by consensus) the importance of each choice and then circle it (H, M, L).
3. On the right side of the list, have the group rate the feasibility of each solution choice or project and then circle it (H, M, or L).

IMPORTANCE				FEASIBILITY		
(H)	M	L	Choice A	H	M	(L)
H	(M)	L	Choice B	H	M	(L)
(H)	M	L	Choice C	(H)	M	L
(H)	M	L	Choice D	(H)	M	L
H	(M)	L	Choice E	(H)	M	L
H	M	(L)	Choice F	(H)	M	L
H	(M)	L	Choice G	H	(M)	L
H	M	(L)	Choice H	H	M	(L)

Figure 6.67. Priority Matrix: Procedural 1. ***Author created (1st edition)***

For example, in figure 6.67 choice A is marked of *high* importance but *low* feasibility.

4. Use the matrix provided and transfer the information to the corresponding matrix cells (i.e., high importance, high feasibility). The response in step 3 of the example translates to the Priority Matrix in the following way (see figure 6.68):

		FEASIBILITY H	FEASIBILITY M	FEASIBILITY L
IMPORTANCE	H	Choice C Choice D		Choice A
	M	Choice E	Choice G	Choice B
	L	Choice F		Choice H

Figure 6.68. Priority Matrix: Procedural 2. ***Author created (1st edition)***

5. Number each cell in order of priority as shown in figure 6.69.

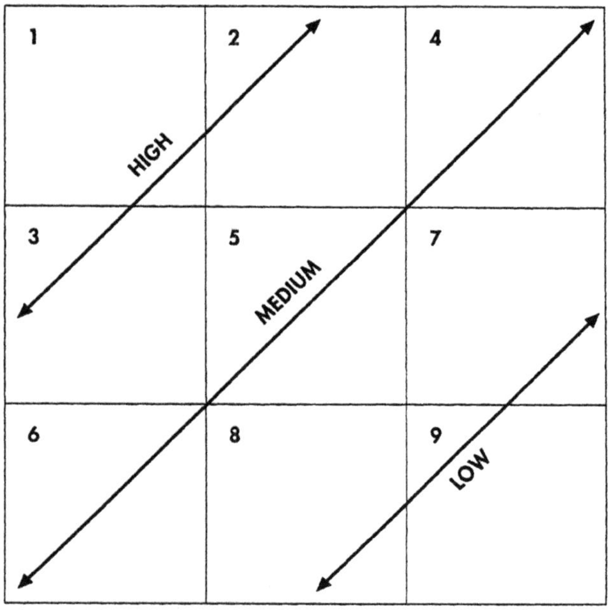

Figure 6.69. Priority Matrix: Procedural 3. ***Author created (1st edition)***

6. Use the numbers in each cell as the order of priority and write the list sequentially (see figure 6.70).

	Choice C	C=1
High Priority {	Choice D	D=1
Cells 1, 2, 3	Choice E	E=3
	Choice A	A=4
Medium Priority {	Choice G	G=5
Cells 4, 5, 6	Choice F	F=6
Low Priority {	Choice B	B=7
Cells, 7, 8, 9	Choice H	H=9

Figure 6.70. Priority Matrix: Procedural 4. ***Author created (1st edition)***

Variations

- You can change dimensions to such dimensions as "cost" (high, medium, or low) or "time" (near term, mid-term, or for term) or "priority" (high, medium, or low).
- You can have each participant do an individual priority matrix and compare results.

Cautions

- Be sure to allow enough time for processing and discussion.
- Participants must understand and define "programs" or "projects."

Example

We completed the following priority matrix in our university department. Our department needed to set priorities among seven possible activities we might pursue. The results were as follows (see figures 6.71 and 6.72):

- High Priority
  - Hire student recruiter
  - Improve access to technology
  - Do alumni follow-up study
- Medium Priority
  - Refurbish building
  - Add two classrooms
  - Hire new faculty member
  - Expand research tapes
- Low Priority
  - Buy new furniture

IMPORTANCE				FEASIBILITY		
H	M	(L)	A. Expand Research Tapes	(H)	M	L
(H)	M	L	B. Refurbish building	H	M	(L)
H	(M)	L	C. Hire a new faculty member	H	(M)	L
(H)	M	L	D. Hire a student recruiter	(H)	M	L
(H)	M	L	E. Improve computer system	H	(M)	L
H	(M)	L	F. Do alumni follow-up study	(H)	M	L
(H)	M	L	G. Add two new classrooms	H	M	(L)
H	M	(L)	H. Buy new furniture	H	(M)	L

Figure 6.71. Priority Matrix: Example 1. ***Author created (1st edition)***

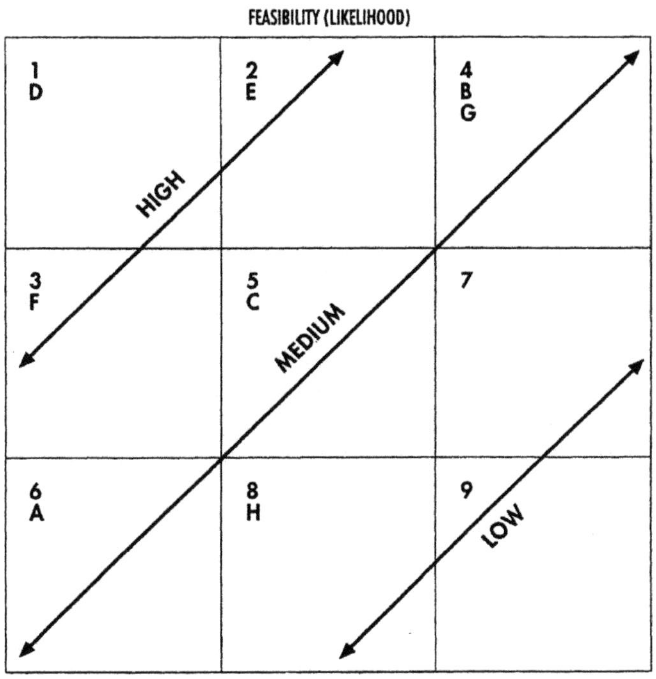

Figure 6.72. Priority Matrix: Example 2. ***Author created (1st edition)***

Priority Matrix: Worksheet

See table 6.67 for a Priority Matrix worksheet template.

Table 6.67. Priority Matrix: Worksheet. ***Author created (new for 2nd edition)***

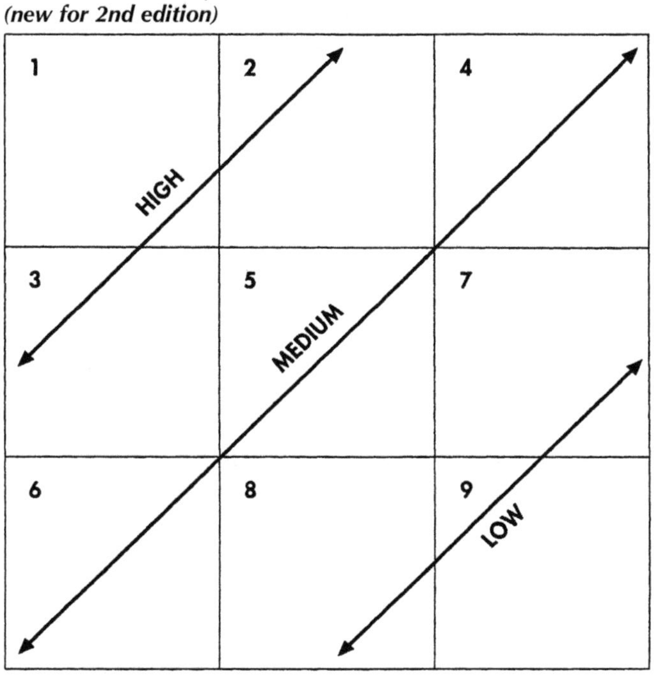

References

Brassard and Ritter (1994, 105).

RISK ANALYSIS (IF, THEN)

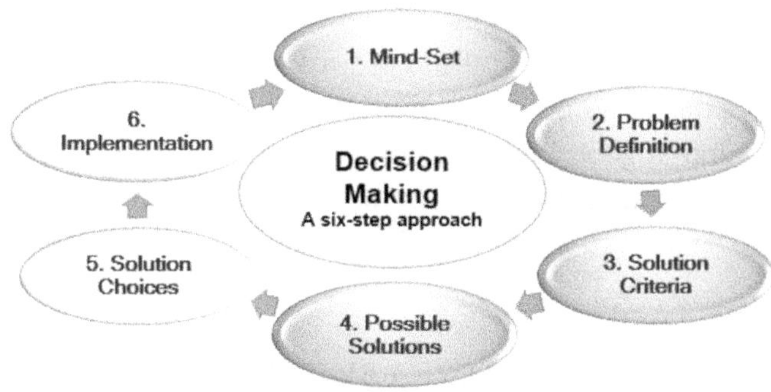

Figure 6.73. Decision Making: A Six-Step Approach: Risk Analysis (If, Then). ***Author created (updated from 1st edition)***

Description

An "If, Then" Risk Analysis allows the decision makers to look at the risks involved in selecting a choice. It also allows decision makers to identify potential blocks to success. In this way, "all the cards are out on the table," and the factors working for and against success are identified.

Application or Illustration of Use

- Use the "If, Then" Risk Analysis to understand consequences of alternatives.

Time, Materials, and Other Considerations

Time: Approximately 30–60 minutes.
Materials: See table 6.68.

Table 6.68. Tech Table: Risk Analysis (If, Then). ***Author created (new for 2nd edition)***

Nondigital	*Digital*
• Chart paper	• Collaborative Document (e.g., Microsoft Word Online, Google Docs)
• Pens, markers	• Whiteboard Collaborative Tools (e.g., Jamboard)
• Post-it notes	• Devices (e.g., Interactive LFD)

Procedural Steps

1. For each alternative, ask, "If we do ____, then
   a. will happen" *or* "We have selected ____
   b. now what can go wrong?"

2. Generate a list of words to complete the statements.
3. Record the words.
4. Clarify the meanings of the words and discuss.
5. After looking at the risks, ask "Can we take preventive, contingent action?" "How can we turn this into a good thing?" Look at the contingency.
6. After discussion is complete, the group discusses level of risk for each alternative.

SCENARIO BUILDING

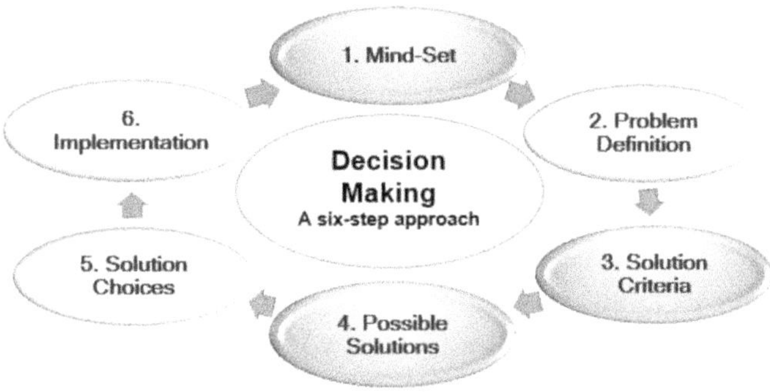

Figure 6.74. Decision Making: A Six-Step Approach: Scenario Building. *Author created (updated from 1st edition)*

Description

Scenario Building is a creative technique that requires the scenario builder to analyze information through storytelling to examine possibilities for the organization. It requires futuristic thinking on the part of the writer and the decision makers who make choices based on the information. It is a narrative description of some situation or setting.

Applications or Illustrations of Use

- Use for organizational strategic planning. Decision makers can determine what direction the organization might want to take and future areas of focus. It is useful when coupled with the SWOT analysis.
- Use Scenario Building to describe possible solutions and their consequences.
- Use this device in the mind-set step to define the context of the problem and to focus the thinking of the decision makers.

Time, Materials, and Other Considerations

Time: This technique is elastic relative to time and can take from 1–3 hours to (1) analyze data, (2) write the scenario, and (3) discuss the scenario.
Materials: See table 6.69.

Table 6.69. Tech Table: Scenario Building.
Author created (new for 2nd edition)

Nondigital	*Digital*
• Chart paper	• Collaborative Document (e.g., Google Docs, Microsoft Word Online)
• Pens, markers	• Devices (e.g., Interactive LFD)

Procedural Steps

1. Pick a particular future time and setting that is appropriate to the decision (e.g., your organization in the year 2030).
2. Ask participants to write a story for that setting.
3. Ask participants to share stories in total group or in subgroups if the group is large.
4. Have participants discuss their stories about organizational changes and needs.
5. Pick a particular solution possibility.
6. Ask participants to write a story about how it would work if it were to become a reality.
7. Have participants share what the story says about the value of the solution.
8. Have participants discuss their stories.

Variation

- Role playing could be used in conjunction with Scenario Building.

Caution

- Scenario Building is time consuming and requires participants to be creative.

Examples

On the following pages are two different scenarios. The first scenario involves a university setting. The second scenario involves a business.

Scenario 1

Crescent University
Office of the President
Dear Mr. Megadonor,

We are delighted that your son has been chosen to attend Crescent University. I'm sure that he will have a positive and rewarding experience. There are quite a few changes in the university since you graduated in 1995 and your mother graduated in 1966. Some of the highlights in which you might be interested are the following:

- The BA degree is now a three-year degree, with a required year of public service placed between the first and second years.
- Students in their second year select a professor to work with. They become their apprentice and work to master their chosen area. This is our academic artisanship program.
- While our students reside on campus, the faculty are located throughout the world. They visit the campus twice a year but interact with students through video conferencing and other web-based applications.
- Our class size is generally small (10–20 students) and are technology driven. All students must own their own MacBook Pro (or its equivalent) and be proficient in its use.
- Our degrees are guaranteed, and refresher courses are available for students throughout their lifetime.

In these ways, we think we can make for a rich and vital college experience for your son. As always, we appreciate your support and repeated donations. They are the lifeblood of this great university. If you have any questions, feel free to contact me at any of my offices.

Sincerely,
Shari L. Fox, EdD
President

Scenario 2

August 23, 2020
Los Angeles Times

Tenth Anniversary Reflects Success of Past

Yesterday, the Ajax Label Company threw a party for itself, a party it can well afford and well deserve. It was just ten years ago that Ajax was a small Ohio-based label printer with a staff of twelve and sales of $3 million. They were successful in those days, but nothing like the company today that dominates the market with a 60 percent share and an international volume of sales fifty times greater than that fateful day in August when Doug Devore suggested "the change." As a regional sales manager, Devore proposed a series of technology-driven strategic alliances with label printers in other countries. He proposed that in that way the company could grow large and still stay small and personal. These alliances have mushroomed into an Ajax network of four hundred semiautonomous entities each making local sales to local customers.

In fact, it was Ajax that coined the term the *local imperative*. The only way to maintain strong market presence is to maintain a local, small company sense of local identity and service. The "local imperative" became the hallmark of Ajax's growth and success. Devore, now the chief coordinating officer of Ajax, gives all credit to the previous president of the company. "When I proposed the alliances, Peggy Lynch was all for them. She listened and analyzed and then gave the go ahead. Without her openness, this could not have occurred. I would still be sales manager in Akron."

Yes, the party was a raging success and so has the company. By the way, all the entertainment was local!

References

Higgens (1994, 157–158).

SNOW CARD

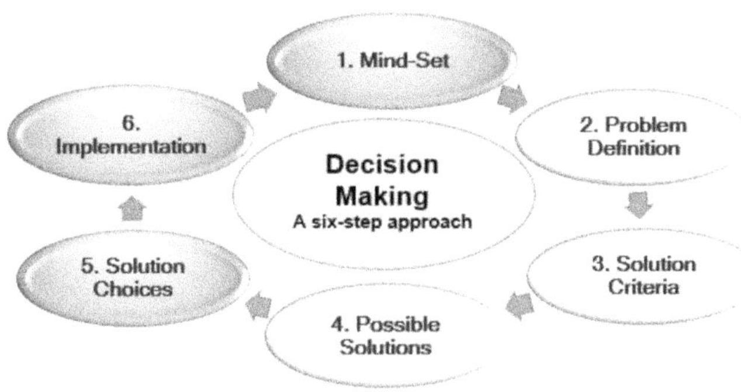

Figure 6.75. Decision Making: A Six-Step Approach: Snow Card. ***Author created (updated from 1st edition)***

Description

The Snow Card technique is a structured activity that uses cards to show visually commonalities and differences of generated ideas. The Snow Card technique is also a useful device for generating ideas and possible solutions. It is a nonthreatening technique to start discussions revolving around topics of importance within the organization.

Applications or Illustrations of Use

- Use Snow Cards to identify areas of likeness or similarities.
- Use Snow Cards to identify possible causes of a problem.
- Use during strategic planning to identify norms and tenets during the development of the vision.
- Use to identify possible solution choices.

Time, Materials, and Other Considerations

Time: Approximately 1–2 hours.
Materials: See table 6.70.

Table 6.70. Tech Table: Snow Card. ***Author created (new for 2nd edition)***

Nondigital	*Digital*
• Index cards or post-it notes	• Collaborative Document (e.g., Microsoft Word Online, Google Docs)
• Flip chart	• Whiteboard Collaborative Tools (e.g., Cardsmith)
• Pens, markers	• Devices (e.g., Interactive LFD)

Procedural Steps

1. Present the decision situation.
2. Give each participant one to three index cards (five by eight inches or larger) and instruct them to write one response per card.
3. Post the cards on the wall.
4. Read the idea on the cards and ask for clarification.
5. As similar ideas are expressed by individuals, move and group cards with similar ideas.
6. After all the cards are grouped, there will be a "snowstorm" of cards in columns posted on the wall.
7. The ideas that have the most cards can become a starting point for discussion.
8. Talk, discuss, and reach consensus to narrow down the list.

If the group is large, you might want to work in smaller groups of three. Within the smaller group, complete the following tasks:

1. Present the decision situation.
2. Give each participant one to three index cards (five by eight inches or larger) and instruct them to write one response per card.
3. Within the small group, have each participant share out and post their cards.
4. Have the small groups discuss and reach consensus on one idea to present to the group.
5. Have a reporter from each group post their idea on the wall. Remind the reporter to group similar ideas, particularly if a similar idea has been expressed by another group.
6. After all the cards are posted and grouped, there will be a "snowstorm" on the board.
7. The ideas that have the most cards can become a starting point for discussion.
8. Discuss and reach consensus to narrow the list down.

Variation

- In smaller groups, have individuals post their cards as they go along.

Caution

- Do not assume that the column with the longest/largest list "wins"; it simply indicates a starting point.

Example

A school staff used the Snow Card to identify the core values that they believed the organization represented. What follows is a sample of the "snow cards" that show the grouping of their identified values.

Working together	Honesty	Hard work
Customer service	Change Competence Teamwork	Cooperation
Integrity	Collaboration	Promptness
Innovation	Trust	
High standards	Cooperativeness	

References

Bryson (1988, 126–128).

SPEND-A-DOT

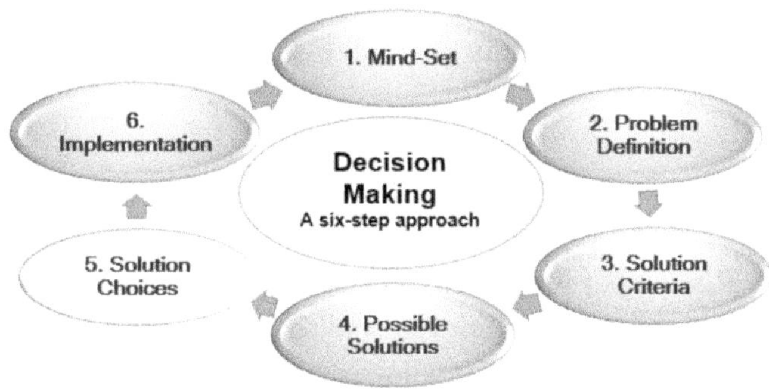

Figure 6.76. Decision Making: A Six-Step Approach: Spend-a-Dot. ***Author created (updated from 1st edition)***

Description

Spend-a-Dot is a device that is used to prioritize or winnow items on a list. This device causes people to talk and assess important items as they narrow down possibilities. Participants enjoy this process because it allows them to spend resources.

Applications or Illustrations of Use

- Use Spend-a-Dot to prioritize and rank-order a number of possible solutions.
- Use Spend-a-Dot to get people up and moving.

Time, Materials, and Other Considerations

Time: Approximately 10–45 minutes. The device is particularly useful when the group has between seven and ten people.

Materials: See table 6.71.

Table 6.71. Tech Table: Spend-a-Dot. ***Author created (new for 2nd edition)***

Nondigital	*Digital*
• Colored dots with adhesive backing. Recommendation: Consider colors (e.g., green dots = go; red dots = stop; multiple colors = teams)	• Devices (e.g., Interactive LFD)

Procedural Steps

1. Record the possible solutions or ideas on a chart or series of charts and post the chart(s) on a wall.
2. Give each participant a set number of resources (green dots). The number of dots should be approximately 20 percent or 30 percent of the total of ideas posted, not to exceed ten dots.
3. Advise each participant to place one or all of the dots next to an important item or items.
4. Count the number of dots.
5. Discuss the implications for importance of each item to the group.

Variation

- Give participants a red dot (in addition to other green dots) to designate an idea they are against.

Cautions

- Posting dots may be intimidating. In that case, have people post their dots during a break.
- Be sure to remind the group that this is simply a device that narrows down choices and is *not* voting.
- Remember that Spend-a-Dot is not an indication of consensus unless all of the dots end up on one item.

References

Brassard and Ritter (1994, 93).
Higgens (1994, 190).
Klubnik and Greenwood (1994, 177).
Scholtes et al. (1994, 2–43).
Van Gundy (1988, 248).
Viability Corporate HR, Performance Development Division (1994, 7).

STACK THE DECK

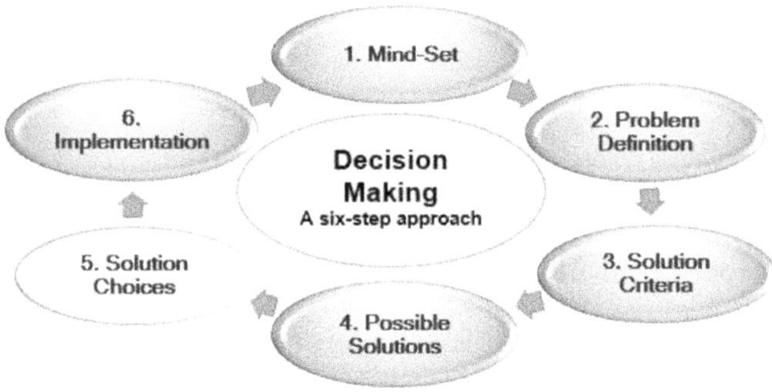

Figure 6.77. Decision Making: A Six-Step Approach: Stack the Deck. ***Author created (updated from 1st edition)***

Description

Stack the Deck is a method of prioritizing, winnowing, or rank-ordering a number of possible solutions. By "stacking a deck" of cards, the decision makers are forced to choose by condensing alternatives.

Application or Illustration of Use

- Use this device to narrow the focus of the options. For example, this device is useful during budget development to quickly identify which budget cuts to make or which capital outlay purchases to make.

Time, Materials, and Other Considerations

Time: Approximately 15–30 minutes.
Materials: See table 6.72.

Table 6.72. Tech Table: Stack the Deck. ***Author created (new for 2nd edition)***

Nondigital	*Digital*
• Index cards	• Whiteboard Collaborative Tools (e.g., Cardsmith)
• Pens, markers	• Devices (e.g., Interactive LFD)

Procedural Steps

1. Instruct each participant to select their most important possible solutions. Choose the appropriate number not to exceed ten.
2. Each participant writes one idea per card.
3. Lay the cards out on a table.
4. Each person stacks their deck by putting the most important card on top, followed by the next most important, and so on until every card has a place in the deck.
5. Share out each person's top items. We suggest two or three and record these.
6. Discuss.

Variation

This can be used in groups:

1. Have each individual in each group proceed through the steps. Then have the group select the top three cards.
2. Have the groups prioritize their top selections together.

Caution

- Remember that Stack the Deck is simply a prioritizing or winnowing device and should not be used for the final selection or choice.

STAKEHOLDER ANALYSIS

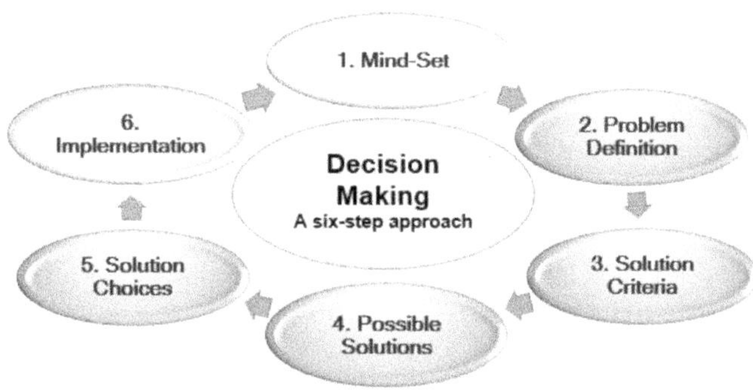

Figure 6.78. Decision Making: A Six-Step Approach: Stakeholder Analysis. ***Author created (updated from 1st edition)***

Description

In the mind-set stage, it is important to understand the stakeholder—those for whom the decision holds import, those who are in some way affected by the decision. This device helps group members to identify stakeholders and their degree of "stakeholding."

Applications or Illustrations of Use

- Use the Stakeholder Analysis to specify stakeholders.
- Use this device in complex situations where multiple stakeholders might be involved.

Time, Materials, and Other Considerations

Time: Approximately 30–60 minutes.
Materials: See table 6.73.

Table 6.73. Tech Table: Stakeholder Analysis. ***Author created (new for 2nd edition)***

Nondigital	*Digital*
• Stakeholder Analysis worksheet	• Collaborative Document (e.g., Microsoft Word Online, Google Docs)
• Flip paper	• Whiteboard Collaborative Tools (e.g., Cardsmith)
• Pens, markers	• Other application (e.g., Poll)
	• Devices (e.g., Interactive LFD)

Example

See table 6.74 for an example of Stakeholder Analysis.

Table 6.74. Stakeholder Analysis: Example. ***Author created (1st edition)***

Decision Issue

Internal Stakeholder	*DOS*	*External Stakeholders*	*DOS*

Procedural Steps

1. Use the Stakeholder Analysis worksheet (table 6.75) or copy it onto chart paper.
2. Explain that stakeholders are people for whom the decision holds importance; the decision affects them.
3. Ask participants to identify potential internal stakeholders—people inside the organization who have stake in the decision.
4. Ask participants to identify potential external stakeholders—people outside the organization who have stake in the decision.
5. Rate the "degree of stakeholding" (DOS) of each group/individual using a scale of 1 to 10 with 1 meaning little import and 10 meaning very high import.
6. Lead the group in discussion of which stakeholders should be involved in the decision. Those with a DOS of 7 or above should be involved. Those with 2 or less should probably not be involved. Those between 3 and 6 may or may not be involved, depending on group desires. Remember the Accordion Process for varying degrees of involvement.

DOS # (Degree of Stakeholding): how important are the results of this decision issue to this individual/group; 1 to 10 scale with 1 = little import and 10 = very high import.

Stakeholder Analysis: Worksheet

See table 6.75 for a Stakeholder Analysis worksheet template.

Table 6.75. Stakeholder Analysis: Worksheet. ***Author created (new for 2nd edition)***

Decision Issue

Internal Stakeholder	*DOS*	*External Stakeholders*	*DOS*

STRAW POLLING

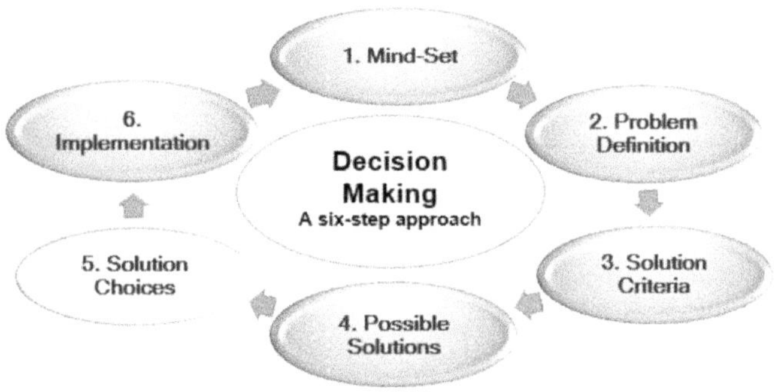

Figure 6.79. Decision Making: A Six-Step Approach: Straw Polling. ***Author created (updated from 1st edition)***

Description

Straw Polling is a device that serves as a consensus gauge by "checking the feelings" of the team members. Unlike voting, straw polling is not a final decision but a way of checking where the team is as they work toward consensus. Straw Polling can be used to narrow down lists or ideas. Instead of a show of hands, the team uses a show of thumbs.

Applications or Illustrations of Use

- Use Straw Polling if the process seems "bogged down" or an idea seems to be "caught" in a lot of discussion.
- Use when conflict is present.

Time, Materials, and Other Considerations

Time: Approximately 3–5 minutes.
Materials: See table 6.76.

Table 6.76. Tech Table: Straw Polling. ***Author created (new for 2nd edition)***

Nondigital	*Digital*
• None	• Collaborative Document (e.g., Microsoft Word Online, Google Docs) • Devices (e.g., Responder)

Procedural Steps

1. Ask the group members if they are open to a straw poll.
2. State what the vote concerns and be sure to clarify so that there is agreement in understanding.
3. Ask for a show of thumbs.
   a. Thumbs up means that the item stays on the list or the discussion continues.
   b. Thumbs down means that the item is eliminated or discussion stops.
   c. Sideways thumb indicates no opinion.
4. If the team is evenly split, move to another device that allows for further discussion. On the other hand, if there is a majority poll, allow those who disagree an opportunity to share their concern and solicit for consensus.
5. Repeat the straw poll if needed.

Variations

Here are three variations to vary Straw Polling step 3:

1. Gas gauge: Use a show of thumbs to indicate if their "tank" is empty (thumbs down), full (thumbs up), or anywhere in between such as two-thirds full.
2. Survey 1–10: Instead of a show of thumbs, ask the participants to give a show of fingers to indicate how they feel about the possible solution. Ask, "On a scale of 1 to 10, show how you feel. 1 = totally opposed, 10 = positively for.
3. Fist to five fingers: Have the participants show how they are feeling about the solution by showing a fist to represent the least support for and five fingers to show a high degree of support for a possible solution.

Cautions

- Be cautious not to use this as the final vote.
- Straw Polling should not be used to force people to change their opinion.

SWOT: STRENGTHS, WEAKNESSES, OPPORTUNITIES, THREATS

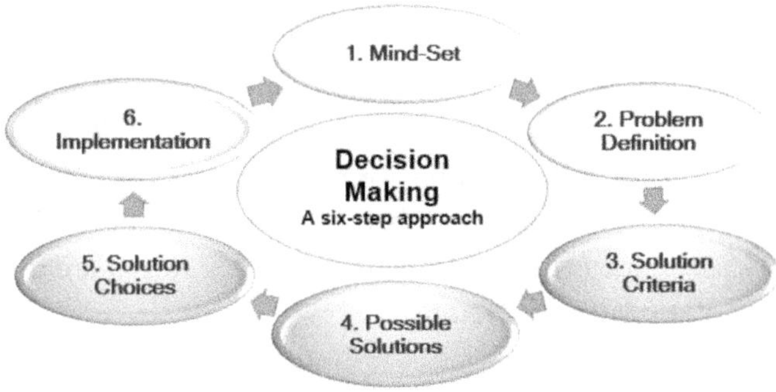

Figure 6.80. Decision Making: A Six-Step Approach: SWOT.
Author created (updated from 1st edition)

Description

The SWOT is a device used to bring to light opportunities and threats and for ongoing assessment of strengths and weaknesses. In this device, one is asked to assess four elements about the organization: strengths, weaknesses, opportunities, and threats.

Applications or Illustrations of Use

- Use the SWOT at the beginning of strategic planning to focus the group on the strengths, weaknesses, opportunities, and threats facing the organization.
- Use as a needs assessment to update or determine the organization's direction.

Time, Materials, and Other Considerations

Time: Approximately 20–60 minutes.
Materials: See table 6.77.

Table 6.77. Tech Table: SWOT.
Author created (new for 2nd edition)

Nondigital	*Digital*
• Chart paper	• Collaborative Document (e.g., Google Docs, Microsoft Word Online)
• Pens, markers	• Whiteboard Collaborative Tools (e.g., Jamboard)
• Tape	• Other application (e.g., Padlet)
	• Devices (e.g., Interactive LFD)

Procedural Steps

1. Post four charts on the wall. Label each chart with one of the following words: *Strengths*, *Weaknesses*, *Opportunities*, and *Threats*.
2. Divide the group of participants into four subgroups.
3. Assign each of the subgroups to a chart. Review and post rules of brainstorming.
4. Request that the members of the subgroup brainstorm ideas that address the label (e.g., what are the organization's strengths?)
5. Participants in each of the groups discuss each topic and record their ideas.
6. After a limited time (or when that list is complete), the subgroup participants rotate to the next chart. (Review the Carousel Brainstorming process.) Begin the first chart with 10 minutes; lessen time at each cycle.
7. Carousel through each chart until each group cycles through each chart.
8. Discuss implication for organization.

References

Bryson (1988, 128).

T CHART

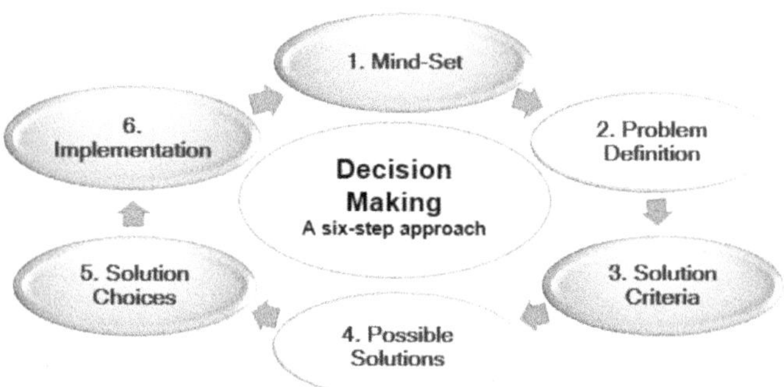

Figure 6.81. Decision Making: A Six-Step Approach: T Chart. ***Author created (updated from 1st edition)***

Description

The T Chart is a device that looks at any dichotomous possibilities such as pros and cons. This device allows the decision makers to be more objective by looking at the factors working for (the positives) and against (the negatives) a possible solution. The decision makers can visually compare the pros and cons.

Applications or Illustrations of Use

- Use the T Chart to understand consequences of alternatives.
- Use to define a problem.
- Use in any situation involving dichotomous possibilities (e.g., personnel selection).

Time, Materials, and Other Considerations

Time: Approximately 15–30 minutes.
Materials: See table 6.78.

Table 6.78. Tech Table: T Chart. ***Author created (new for 2nd edition)***

Nondigital	*Digital*
• Chart paper	• Collaborative Document (e.g., Google Docs, Microsoft Word Online)
• Pens, markers	• Whiteboard Collaborative Tools (e.g., Cardsmith)
• Tape	• Presentation (e.g., Google Slides)
	• Other application (e.g., Poll)
	• Devices (e.g., Interactive LFD)

Procedural Steps

1. On a sheet of paper, draw a horizontal line across the top of the page.
2. Draw a vertical line from the center of the horizontal line.
3. Write the words *Positives* or *Pros* on one side and *Negatives* or *Cons* on the other side. See table 6.79.

Table 6.79. T Chart: Procedure. ***Author created (1st edition)***

Positives	*Negatives*

4. Generate ideas for (pros) or against (cons) under the appropriate column for each solution possibility.
5. Discuss how they balance out and what they mean for the solution choice.

Variation

- A different way to use a T Chart is to label one column *Facts* and the other *Rumors*. This is useful to clarify what we know from what we assume. The T Chart can be used for any opposites, pluses or minuses, and so on.

TRADE-OFF ANALYSIS

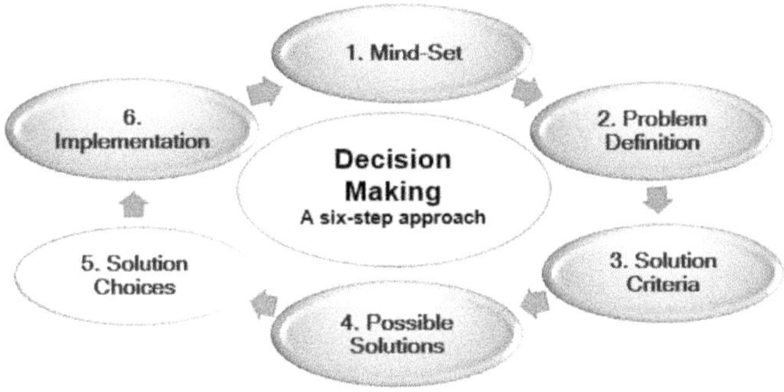

Figure 6.82. Decision Making: A Six-Step Approach: Trade-Off Analysis. ***Author created (updated from 1st edition)***

Description

Trade-Off Analysis is a device that allows the decision makers to systematically analyze data to determine the value of various alternatives. It builds on the previously generated solution criteria and compares solution possibilities against the solution criteria. This approach does not divide criteria into needs and wants.

Applications or Illustrations of Use

- Use the Trade-Off Analysis when you want to decide the relative merits of adopting a new program.
- Use the Trade-Off Analysis during the solution choice step of DM.

Time, Materials, and Other Considerations

Time: Approximately 45–90 minutes.
Materials: See table 6.80.

Table 6.80. Tech Table: Trade-Off Analysis. ***Author created (new for 2nd edition)***

Nondigital	*Digital*
• Flip chart	• Collaborative Spreadsheet (e.g., Google Sheets)
• Pens, markers	• Whiteboard Collaborative Tools (e.g., Limnu)
• Tape	• Collaborative Presentation (e.g., Prezi)
	• Other application (e.g., Poll)
	• Devices (e.g., Responders, Smartboard)

Procedural Steps

1. List the solution possibilities (or alternatives).
2. Form a matrix where the possible solutions represent one dimension and the solution criteria the other dimension (see table 6.81).
3. Determine the weight of each criterion. The weights are numerical descriptions of the importance of each criterion. The weights may be unequal. We suggest a scale of 1 to 10.
4. Determine the values of each cell using a Likert scale of 1 to 5 (1 = high negative, 5 = high positive). The value in the cell represents the degree to which the alternative meets the criterion.
5. After all the cell values are identified, calculate weighted totals. (Multiply cell values by weights for each cell and then add across criteria.)
6. If step 4 is done as consensus, make a choice, showing both the totals and the weighted cell values. If done individually, have each person share his/her individual matrix.

Table 6.81. Trade-Off Analysis: Procedure. ***Author created (updated from 1st edition)***

General Trade-Off Matrix				
Criteria	*Weighting*	*Alternative 1*	*Alternative 2*	*Alternative 3*
Criterion 1 Criterion 2 Criterion 3 Criterion 4				

Caution

- The two dimensions of the matrix can be reversed. It makes no difference.

Example

In this example, you are being called on to choose a graduate program. Five criteria are being used to judge three alternatives. Practicality and convenience are the most important criteria (as determined by the group making the choice). Institution A has been given a rating of 1 on cost—it is expensive—while Institution C has received a 5—it is inexpensive. Institution B got a rating of 5 on practicality—meaning it is very practical—while Institution A got a rating of 2—fairly theoretical or at least not practical. Overall, in this example, Institution B has the highest weighted value of 45. The criteria of practicality and convenience are the strongest in favor of Institution B. The numbers in ( ) are derived by multiplying weightings times ratings. See figure 6.83 for an example.

CHOOSING A GRADUATE PROGRAM				
CRITERIA	WEIGHTING	INSTITUTION A	INSTITUTION B	INSTITUTION C
Cost	2	1 (2)	3 (6)	5 (10)
Practicality	3	2 (6)	5 (15)	2 (6)
Convenience	3	2 (6)	4 (12)	2 (6)
Prestige	1	3 (3)	4 (4)	4 (4)
Job Access	2	3 (6)	4 (8)	2 (4)
Weighted Total		23	45	30

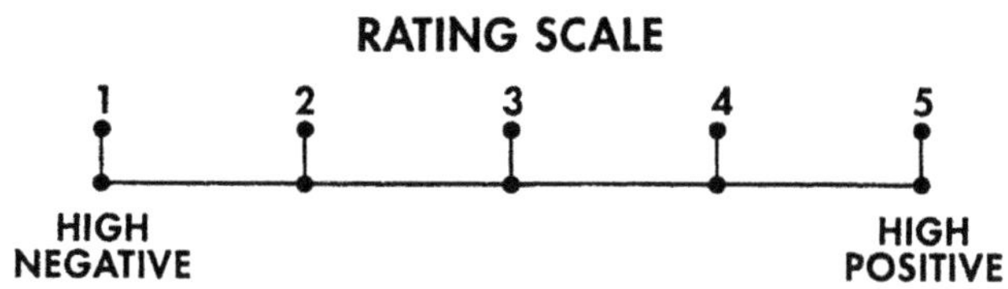

Figure 6.83. Trade-Off Analysis: Example. *Author created (1st edition)*

Trade-Off Analysis: Worksheet

See table 6.82 for a Trade-Off Analysis worksheet template.

Table 6.82. Trade-Off Analysis: Worksheet. ***Author created (1st edition)***

Criteria	*Weighting*	*Alternatives*					
Weighted Total							

TREE DIAGRAM

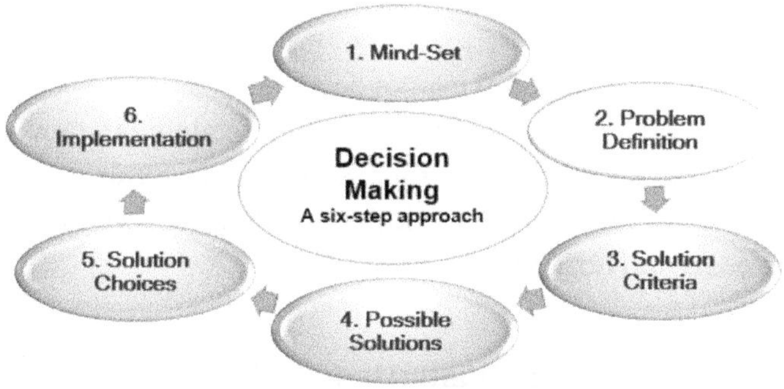

Figure 6.84. Decision Making: A Six-Step Approach: Tree Diagram. ***Author created (updated from 1st edition)***

Description

The Tree Diagram is similar to the Cause/Effect Diagram. The Tree Diagram is a visual display of the relationships between factors that influence problems. This device helps the decision makers sort information. The Tree Diagram can be used to identify causes of a problem.

Application or Illustration of Use

- Use the Tree Diagram to help define and clarify the causes of the problem.

Time, Materials, and Other Considerations

Time: Approximately 30–90 minutes.
Materials: See table 6.83.

Table 6.83. Tech Table: Tree Diagram. ***Author created (new for 2nd edition)***

Nondigital	*Digital*
• Chart paper (recommend drawing the "tree trunk" prior)	• Collaborative Document (e.g., Microsoft Word Online, Google Docs)
• Pens, markers	• Whiteboard Collaborative Tools (e.g., Jamboard)
• Post-it notes	• Collaborative Presentation (e.g., Prezi)
	• Other application (e.g., Padlet)
	• Devices (e.g., Interactive LFD)

Procedural Steps

1. On a large sheet of chart paper, draw a "tree trunk."
2. Distribute one pad of post-it notes to each participant.
3. Ask the participants to individually write what they see as causes of the problem on post-it notes during a specified time (5 minutes).
4. Tell the participants to stick their ideas on the trunk.
5. Once all of the ideas are on the trunk, number each one; then organize and categorize causes (e.g., through Snow Cards or Affinity Diagram).
6. Organize and line up the causes in order of sequence and determine main causes.
7. Transfer the "Main" causes to the "tree" (as if they were limbs extending from the trunk). Note the numbers of individual items that comprise the category.
8. For each main cause, ask "Why is this happening?" These become sub-causes.
9. Post the sub-causes under the main cause as smaller "limbs."
10. Review and discuss each major cause category.
11. Ask, "Why (is this a cause)?" and record responses.
12. Use the Why Cycle to get to the root cause and repeatedly ask "Why?"
13. Agree on causes.
14. When completed, reflect on visual display and decide next steps.

Example

Problem: Poor internal communication. See figure 6.85.

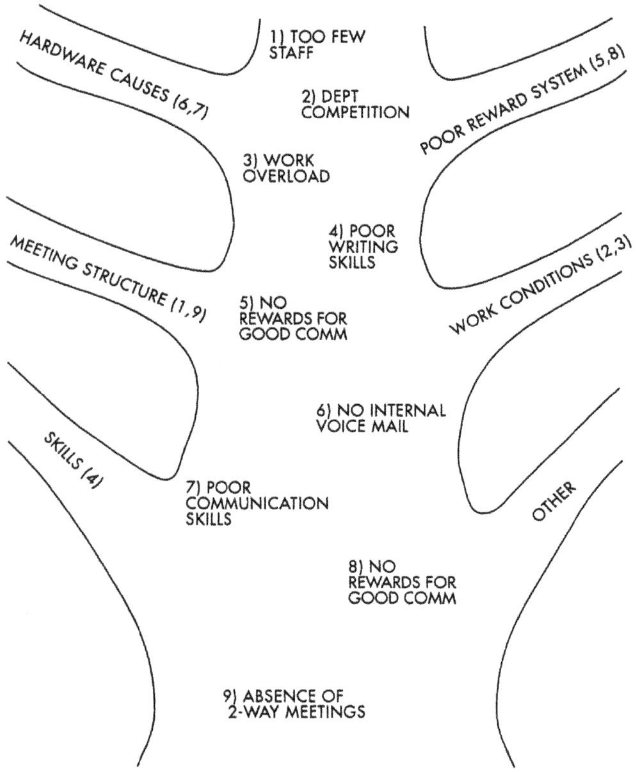

Figure 6.85. Tree Diagram: Example. ***Author created (1st edition)***

The "trunk" messages indicate individual estimates of causes. The limbs represent the grouped causes. For example, work condition is the overall category for items 2 and 3 on the trunk-department competition and work overload.

VISION SETTING

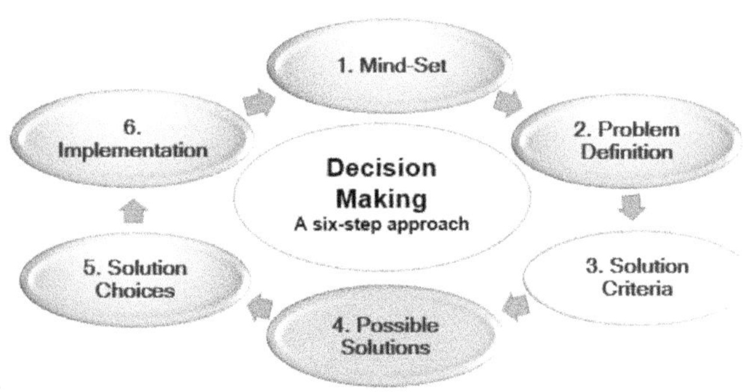

Figure 6.86. Decision Making: A Six-Step Approach: Vision Setting. ***Author created (updated from 1st edition)***

Description

When a decision involves organizational planning, Vision Setting becomes an important part of problem definition. The group cannot adequately decide or plan goals and direction without a vision statement. A vision statement includes four elements: 1) future state, 2) clients served, 3) services provided, and 4) strategies to deliver services.

Applications or Illustrations of Use

- Use to plan decisions.
- Use to define planning goals.

Time, Materials, and Other Considerations

Time: Approximately 1–3 hours.
Materials: See table 6.84.

Table 6.84. Tech Table: Vision Setting. ***Author created (new for 2nd edition)***

Nondigital	*Digital*
• Four flip charts	• Collaborative Document (e.g., Google Docs, Microsoft Word Online)
• Pens, markers	• Whiteboard Collaborative Tools (e.g., Deskle)
• Tape	• Collaborative Presentation (e.g., Google Slides)
• Sheet of paper labeled *Time* and *Context* (see storytelling in chapter 9)	• Other application (e.g., Padlet)
	• Devices (e.g., Interactive LFD)

Procedural Steps

1. Put four flip charts at the front of the room; write a different heading on each flip chart:
   a. Chart 1: Future state
   b. Chart 2: Clients served
   c. Chart 3: Services provided
   d. Chart 4: Strategies to deliver services
   e. Turn pages on flip chart so that participants cannot see heading.
2. Have the group discuss the role of vision in an organization.
3. Ask each participant to write a future letter. An example of this is to write a letter to a potential customer explaining why your company is the best in

the field. This letter is dated five years in the future. Alternatively, have them write a letter to the editor describing why your school is the best in the area. Again, the letter is dated five years in the future. We usually provide a form with the organization's name at the top and the year on the side. Refer to the example shown in table 6.85.

Table 6.85. Start of Letter Example. ***Author created (updated from 1st edition)***

Crescent University	May 10, 2027
Dear ______________________ ,	

4. Have volunteers read their letters.
5. As letters are read, you and your helpers record on each flip chart appropriate descriptions from the letters. For example, if a letter describes a certain kind of clientele, record it on chart 2 or a particular future state on chart 1, and so on.
6. When all letters are read (or at least as many as want to be shared), review the contents of each chart and see what it says about the future.
7. Write a potential vision statement like the examples in the section that follows.
8. Review and edit.

Examples

VISION STATEMENT

Averbeck Company will be the leading risk-management and employee-benefit consulting firm in the Inland Empire and Southern California region. With a $200 million client base, two hundred employees, and offices placed strategically throughout the area, the Averbeck Company will provide services and risk-management products to medium-to-large companies throughout the region.

Founded in 1931, Averbeck Company has a long heritage of successful relationships with clients and a commitment to assisting those clients in identifying their needs and matching these with a wide array of traditional and nontraditional risk-management solutions. Averbeck Company is committed to using a team approach to diagnose and meet client needs.

Averbeck Company works in partnership with its clients by providing consultation and competitively priced insurance products in the following five areas: 1) Commercial Property Casualty, 2) Employee Benefits, 3) Bonds, 4) Personal Lines, and 5) Financial Planning.

Averbeck Company is also committed to public service and believes in contributing to the betterment of people and organizations in its communities.

VISION STATEMENT

The La Puente Valley Regional Occupational Program (LVROP) will be the leading regional occupational program in the state of California. This cooperative effort of the four school districts of Walnut Valley, Rowland, Bassett, and Hacienda–La Puente will be known for its regional collaboration and client centeredness. The LVROP will be seen as a lighthouse for innovation and a beacon for new technologies. In order to serve the diverse student body of the 2020s, there will be vocational offerings and programs for very different student populations—such groups as college-bound students, job-bound students, special education students, multicultural groups, and gender groups. There will be programs for students sixteen years and older, both traditional and nontraditional, and for those previously served and those underserved.

The LVROP will provide preservice and in-service vocational programs in all major vocational and technical areas, including but not limited to computer technology and service, retail sales, animation, hospitality services, animal care, cosmetology, robotics, energy services, automotive care, and the like. In providing knowledge, and job skills in these areas, it will also prepare students to be adaptive and resourceful in a fast-changing vocational/technological world. To aid students in their successful transition to job placement and/or advanced vocational training, the LVROP will provide significant career guidance, placement services, business partnerships, and cooperative (2 + 2) programs with other educational institutions.

The vision for the LVROP will be one of excitement, excellence, and respect. Fully integrated into the educational life of the member districts, vocational education will be seen as one of the hallmarks and prides of the Walnut Valley, Rowland, Bassett, and Hacienda–La Puente school districts.

References

Bryson (1988, 192–195).

WHY CYCLE

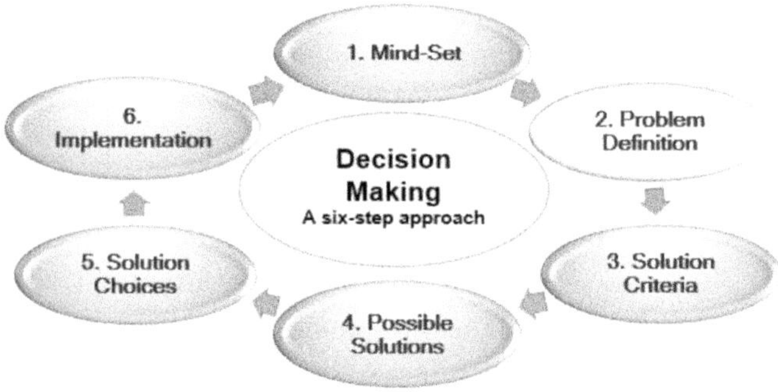

Figure 6.87. Decision Making: A Six-Step Approach: Why Cycle. ***Author created (updated from 1st edition)***

Description

The Why Cycle is a device that is used to clarify problems and causes. By repeatedly asking "Why?," the decision makers deeply analyze the causes of problems. This device digs into the layers of the real problem and separates root causes from the symptoms.

Application or Illustration of Use

- Use the Why Cycle to help slow down the clarifying process and analyze what is happening.

Time, Materials, and Other Considerations

Time: Approximately 15 minutes to 2 hours, depending on the complexity of the problem or decision.
Materials: See table 6.86.

Table 6.86. Tech Table: Why Cycle. ***Author created (new for 2nd edition)***

Nondigital	*Digital*
• Flip chart	• Collaborative Document (e.g., Microsoft Word Online, Google Docs)
• Pens, markers	• Whiteboard Collaborative Tools (e.g., Jamboard)
• Tape	• Other application (e.g., Padlet)
	• Devices (e.g., Interactive LFD)

Procedural Steps

1. Establish problem or decision; then identify causes (use whatever structuring devices are appropriate).
2. As a primary cause is identified, ask, "Why is this the cause?"
3. Record responses to the question "Why?"
4. Repeat the question "Why is this the cause?" With this newest response (cause), ask again, "Why is this the cause?" Record the response.
5. Repeat this questioning, ("Why is this the cause?") until the group has answered the question "why" as often as it can or as needed. Asking "why" repeatedly will help identify the root cause; the last response is generally the root cause.

Cautions

- Use a positive format (focus on what you want to happen).
- The quality movement argues that "why" should be asked at least five times.

Chapter Seven

Core Steps in Four Illustrative Cases

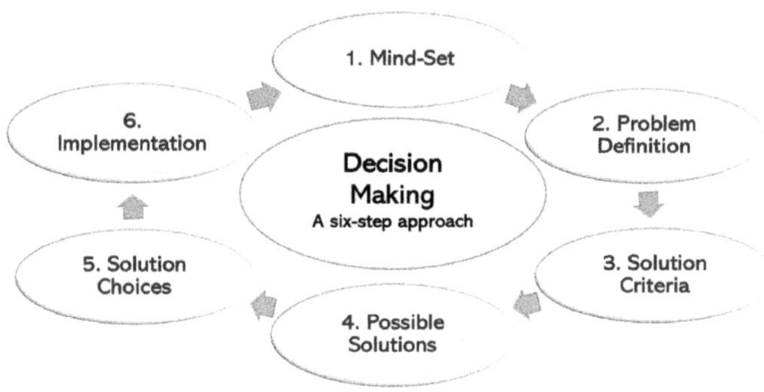

Figure 7.0. Decision Making: A Six-Step Approach.
Author created (updated from 1st edition)

Remember in the introduction, in which we agreed that decision making (DM) is as easy as 1-2-3? It simply involves the following:

1. Knowing the six core steps of DM
2. Answering eight basic questions of adaptation
3. Applying appropriate structuring devices

In this chapter, we want to demonstrate this assertion by describing four real-life case examples and then laying out the decision-making process for each. By the time you finish reading these case studies, we hope that you will agree with us that DM is truly as easy as 1-2-3.

CASE 1—CRESCENT HOSPITAL: A SHORTFALL SITNA

Crescent Hospital is a 240-bed private facility in a suburban town on the East Coast. It has had a series of complaints from emergency room (ER) nurses and interns who believe that the ER is badly managed. The director is a generally liked physician but does not seem to be an effective leader. The same holds true for the assistant directors. The hospital administrator is worried about employee turnover and morale. The ER is one of the better profit centers for the hospital, and it cannot afford to have this area erode in profitability. Poor management seems also to have affected a number of ER patients, and the administrator fears that the hospital's reputation may suffer.

Some employees propose changing the leadership; others argue that the ER administrator simply needs better training. There is also a small group, particularly one of the assistant administrators, that feels the ER cannot be run as a "democracy" and that employees need to accept a more "demanding" kind of atmosphere. The hospital administrator has put together a team to solve this problem. How can the decision-making model be used to address these problems?

Decision Process 1-2-3

The six-step process consists of mind-set, problem definition, solution criteria, possible solutions, solution choice, and implementation. Now you have to answer the eight questions outlined in chapter 3.

1. Is there a history of toxicity in the organization?
   Answer: Not before this year
2. Have the members of the problem-solving team worked together before?
   Answer: Yes
3. What type of problem are you dealing with?
   Answer: Short-term situation that needs attention (SiTNA)
4. Is the problem clear, and do we already have high agreement on the problem definition and desirable outcomes?
   Answer: Clear: No
   Agreement: No

5. Does the organizational or problem context require that the solution criteria be quantified?
   Answer: No
6. Is there prior experience with this problem?
   Answer: No
7. Is there a need to prioritize the possible choices rather than choose from among them?
   Answer: No need to prioritize
8. Is there a time crunch, or is there high risk due to the consequences or cost?
   Answer: Yes

Given these answers, we recommend the following steps be followed and provide recommended structuring devices that will assist each step of the way (see table 7.1).

Table 7.1. Case #1. *Author created (1st edition)*

Process	*Device*
Mind-Set • Because stakeholders may be edgy, you need to set positive context. Discuss what is to be achieved for all (win-win)	Positive Context
Problem Definition • Short-term SiTNA • Not much agreement	Discrepancy Analysis Cause/Effect Diagram
Solution Criteria • No need for quantification or complexity	Criterial Development
Solution Possibility • Because personalities are involved, sharing may be awkward • Looking at other hospitals might help	Nominal Group Technique Competitor Mapping
Solution Choice • Physicians are analytical	Trade-Off Analysis
Implementation	Action Plan
Probable Time • Five meetings (two hours each), plus visitation time	

Summary

To deal with this problem, you would get your team together and establish its positive context first, then you would analyze the problem using a Discrepancy Analysis and a Cause/Effect Diagram. These two approaches together would act to clarify and focus the problem. This is a key stumbling block for this group. After this was completed, they would need to develop solution criteria and then start the solution search process. First, it is recommended that they try the nominal group technique; then they would need to visit some bellwether ERs to see what they could learn from them and then come back and review/expand their possible solutions. After generating several possibilities, they would need to do a Trade-Off Analysis to see what would work best. Finally, they would need to convert their choice into an incremental Action Plan. Throughout this process, the intent would be to remove blame from the problem and find a win-win solution.

CASE 2—CRESCENT CORPORATION: A BUSINESS OPPORTUNITY

Crescent Corporation is a small printing company in New Mexico. It has been approached by another printing company in Canada to form a strategic alliance so that each can go global. The effectiveness of the alliance will depend on the purchase of new technology and linking information systems. This is an intriguing opportunity, but it also could be costly. On top of this, there is the concern that the company will lose its focus in the "mad-cap" effort to go global. In fact, resistance from the employees is very high. The owner wants this to be a collaborative decision because most of the employees have been with the company for its full twenty-two-year history. How can the decision-making model be used to address these issues?

Decision Process 1-2-3

You already know the six steps; so what are the answers to the eight questions?

1. Is there a history of toxicity in the organization?
   Answer: No
2. Have the members of the problem-solving team worked together before?
   Answer: Yes
3. What type of problem are you dealing with?
   Answer: Opportunity

4. Is the problem clear, and do we already have high agreement on the problem definition and desirable outcomes?
   Answer: Clear: Yes
   Agreement: No
5. Does the organizational or problem context require that the solution criteria be quantified?
   Answer: Yes
6. Is there prior experience with this problem?
   Answer: No
7. Is there a need to prioritize the possible choices rather than choose from among them?
   Answer: No
8. Is there a time crunch, or is there high risk due to the consequences or cost?
   Answer: Yes

Given these answers, you have a decision process and structuring device that appear as follows (see table 7.2):

Table 7.2. Case #2. *Author created (1st edition)*

Process	*Device*
Mind-Set • Little work needed here; just need to allay fears, review how they'll work together, and describe clear process • What to involve all	Accordion Process
Problem Definition • Opportunity issue • Need to deal with resistance • Cost issue	Vision Setting Goal Setting Cost Iceberg
Solution Criteria • Want quantification	Criteria Development Criteria Standards
Solution Possibility • Essentially a go-no decision	No device
Solution Choice • Want quantification • Need to know consequences	Needs/Wants Matrix Payoff Matrix Decision Tree Analysis
Implementation • Consequences important	Action Plans Gantt Chart
Probable Time • Three meetings of three hours each	

Summary

To deal with this opportunity (this go-no go decision), you would need to include everyone through the Accordion Process and make them understand that they will have a say in the decision. You will need to spend time focusing on the future vision and goals of the company and what costs/revenues look like. Establishing specific, measurable criteria will be the next step. You will then need to compare alternatives against criteria. If neither alternative meets needs, then you may want to expand the solution possibilities. If either alternative works, then implement but with an understanding of workflow.

CASE 3—CRESCENT VISUAL AND PERFORMING ARTS MAGNET SCHOOL: AN ISSUE OF IMPROVEMENT

Crescent Unified School District is a large comprehensive school district in southern California. Its Crescent School of Visual and Performing Arts magnet school has been suffering an enrollment decline in the number of students as well as quality of students. In the past, the school assumed that good students would be attracted to the school without a need to market. Therefore, minimal marketing had been done. Due to the recent changes the school is experiencing, there is agreement that marketing needs to be improved somehow. How this is to be done is unknown and has created a lot of finger pointing and blaming. The school has been toxic for a long time, and faculty genuinely do not trust each other.

They like to operate as independent silos and do not want to be involved in DM outside their disciplines. The principal has put together a faculty task force to improve marketing for the Crescent School of Visual and Performing Arts. How can the decision-making model be used to address these issues?

Decision Process 1-2-3

You already know the six steps; so, again, what are the answers to the eight questions of adaptation?

1. Is there a history of toxicity in the organization?
   Answer: Yes
2. Have the members of the problem-solving team worked together before?
   Answer: No

3. What type of problem are you dealing with?
   Answer: Improvement
4. Is the problem clear, and do we already have high agreement on the problem definition and desirable outcomes?
   Answer: Clear: Yes
   Agreement: No
5. Does the organizational or problem context require that the solution criteria be quantified?
   Answer: No; quite the opposite. The faculty generally distrust quantification.
6. Is there prior experience with this problem?
   Answer: No
7. Is there a need to prioritize the possible choices rather than choose from among them?
   Answer: Yes
8. Is there a time crunch, or is there high risk due to the consequences or cost?
   Answer: No

Given these answers, we recommend the following steps be followed and provide recommended structuring devices that will assist each step of the way (see table 7.3):

Table 7.3. Case #3. ***Author created (1st edition)***

Process	*Device*
Mind-Set • You need to make this group operate as a team • Much work here because of toxicity and arrogance • Group likes creativity	Boundary Setting Mission Setting Anecdote Positive Context
Problem Definition • Improvement issue • Need focusing	Why Cycle Tree Diagram
Solution Criteria • Need creative approaches • Need focusing	Brainstorming Snow Cards
Solution Possibility • Humanities faculty like creative approaches	Brainstorming Analogies Affinity Diagram
Solution Choice • Participants prefer little quantification • More than one solution may be chosen	Spend-a-Dot Priority Matrix
Implementation • Scenarios	Action Plans
Probable Time • Four meetings of two hours each	

Summary

The emphasis here is on creativity and nonquantitative approaches. You need devices to move the group forward, or it will argue forever. You must spend more time up front in the mind-set step with the three techniques to get the group focused on the need to work as a team and make the school stronger. After that, you must use various creative approaches to generate and focus the problem, criteria, and solution possibilities.

At the choice step, you need to remember that more than one solution may be chosen, as many will work given the resource constraints. Action Plans will be important to make decisions concrete. Scenarios provide a story approach to understanding Action Plans.

CASE 4—CRESCENT UNIFIED SCHOOL DISTRICT: A NEW VENTURE

Crescent Unified School District (CUSD) is a large-sized K–12 school district in southern California. In response to the effects of COVID-19 along with the economic recession in full force, families are leaving the community or doubling up with relatives in other cities. CUSD is faced with declining enrollment as well as massive state budget cuts. In response to the ongoing federal call for charter schools, CUSD is proposing to do so for the first time and has created a task force to begin the planning. The task force may add other members as needed. There is both strong support and opposition to the idea. The board and superintendent want consensus with the decision, but they also strongly want the charter school. They have experience with magnet schools in this district and believe they work well, but this will be their first foray into a charter school. How can the decision-making model be used to address these issues?

Decision Process 1-2-3

As in the other three cases, the six steps remain consistent, but the process varies according to conditions and the answers to the eight questions.

1. Is there a history of toxicity in the organization?
   Answer: No

2. Have the members of the problem-solving team worked together before?
   Answer: No
3. What type of problem are you dealing with?
   Answer: New Venture
4. Is the problem clear, and do we already have high agreement on the problem definition and desirable outcomes?
   Answer: Clear: Yes
   Agreement: Yes
5. Does the organizational or problem context require that the solution criteria be quantified?
   Answer: No
6. Is there prior experience with this problem?
   Answer: No
7. Is there a need to prioritize the possible choices rather than choose from among them?
   Answer: Yes, prioritize
8. Is there a time crunch, or is there high risk due to the consequences or cost?
   Answer: No

Given these answers, we recommend the following steps be followed and provide recommended structuring devices that will assist each step of the way (see table 7.4):

Table 7.4. Case #4. *Author created (1st edition)*

Process	*Device*
Mind-Set • New venture needs planning and new possibilities • Group hasn't worked together before • Need to involve public	Personal Power Grid Positive Context Accordion Process Stakeholder Analysis
Problem Definition • Planning effort Solution Criteria	Vision Setting Goal Setting Competitor Mapping Brainstorming Snow Cards
Solution Possibility • Want to generate many possibilities	Morphological Analysis
Solution Choice • Need to progressively winnow down possibilities	Bean Count Advocacy Teams Multi-Attribute Analysis Precedent Chart
Implementation	Action Plans Flow Chart Scenarios
Probable Time • Twenty meetings of two hours each, plus visitation time	

Summary

This is clearly a planning issue that will take time up front. We propose nine structuring devices in the first two steps. These are needed to focus vision and intent for the charter school. There is also a need to let the public be heard and be involved.

It is also important in the possible solutions step to expand the number of possibilities, to get participants "outside the box." That is why we have used Morphological Analysis. At the choice step, we have used Bean Count to winnow the list of possible school types, and then Advocacy Teams and Multi-Attribute Analysis to clarify the alternatives and their consequences. Finally, we would use a Precedence Chart to choose any possibilities, particularly where budget and capital decisions are involved. We would encourage implementation through Action Plans and a Flowchart followed by Scenarios to get a sense of "feel" for the new school.

CONCLUDING NOTE

All four of these cases illustrate that DM is as easy as 1-2-3. You simply need to follow the six steps involved in this decision-making model and adjust them to your conditions. This does not mean that there is not an art to carrying out these devices and leading DM. There is a real need to have sensitivity to how people work best together and how to facilitate that consensus. But what is not complex is defining the decision-making process. It is as easy as 1-2-3.

Chapter Eight

Team Facilitation Tips and Techniques

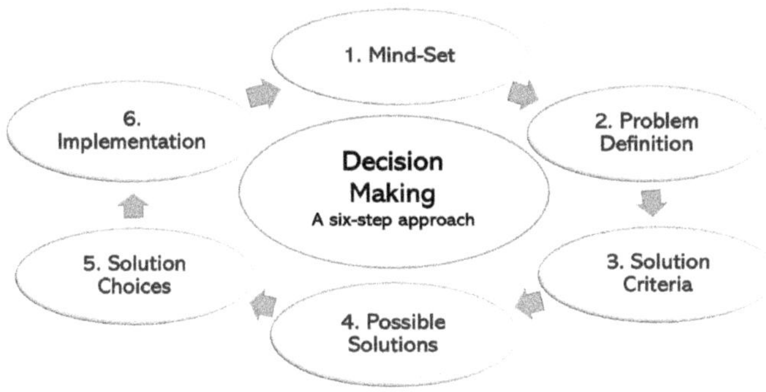

Figure 8.0. Decision Making: A Six-Step Approach.
Author created (updated from 1st edition)

Much of decision making (DM) relies on the use of groups. The earlier chapters in this book have presented approaches to problem solving and DM. This chapter provides some tips and techniques to help the facilitator or leader work with the team. The chapter begins with group formation, the role of the facilitator, and how teams develop to become effective and efficient at problem solving.

Next, we present some ideas to help you prime the pump of creativity and ways to maintain the neutral role of the facilitator through the use of questions. The chapter concludes with some general processes and some ways to maintain the positive state of the team.

TEAM FORMATION

When you convene a group of people to make a decision, or to deal with a situation that needs attention (SiTNA), it is important that the individuals come together in a way that makes them a productive team. The mind-set step of the problem-solving approach is designed to formalize that process once the team is together; however, the leader who selects the members of the team needs to be aware of how to put together people who have the potential to become an effective and efficient decision-making group.

There is broad consensus in the literature about what defines a team. Katzenbach and Smith (2015) define a team as "a small number of people with complementary skills who are committed to a common purpose, performance goals, and approach for which they hold themselves mutually accountable" (p. 41). Brannick and Prince (1997) identify regular communication, defining roles, interdependency, and shared norms as important elements of teams. Reilly and Jones (1974) suggest four necessary conditions for "teamness":

1. The group must have a clear objective for working together. In the case of a SiTNA, this condition is dealing with the situation. Having said that, the leader must be prepared to provide the team with a clear understanding of their objective and any constraints that may affect their deliberations.
2. Members of the team must be interdependent—that is, they must believe that they need one another's experiences, abilities, and commitments in order to make the decision and deal with the SiTNA. A leader must keep this in mind as she selects the members. The mind-set step helps the members of the team understand and agree on this condition.
3. Team members must be committed to the principle that working together as a group leads to more effective decisions than does working in isolation. As the leader selects team members, he can talk to them about the importance of a team commitment to resolving the SiTNA. Additionally, having norms holds the team accountable to each other for behaviors while working within the team. Again, the mind-set step helps the team understand and commit to working together.

4. The group must be held accountable as a functioning unit within the larger organizational context. The leader must be prepared to set clear guidelines for the team and to hold the members accountable as the process proceeds. These guidelines must include time lines for completion, expected outcomes (not decisions), and the role of the team in the process (consultation vs. consensus).

When selecting people for the team, the leader should not just choose friends or select people just because they are members of a stakeholder group. Harvey (1995) suggests that the leader selects stakeholders who represent key decision-making categories. These categories are the following:

- Either a key decision maker or someone who represents the key decision maker. This may be the leader herself or a representative.
- Stakeholders who have a vested interest, in that they must either implement the decision or they will be directly affected by the decision.
- If the SiTNA involves a technical area or one where there is expert knowledge, it is important to include an expert on the team.
- A supporter who is already committed to resolving the problem and has given some thought to how to deal with the SiTNA.
- Decisions require change, and there are usually those in the organization who prefer the status quo. A resister can serve a useful role on the team to help question assumptions and to provide a different point of view.
- A facilitator who has no strong vested interest in the SiTNA. This person should possess the attributes discussed in the following section on the role of the facilitator. Sometimes this role can be filled by the leader herself; however, due to the perceived power of the leader, it is often best left to some other person who is perceived by the members of the team as being more neutral.

In forming the team, one person might fit in more than one category; however, you should consider representation from all categories. As discussed in chapter 2, it is imperative that those selected culminate in a diverse team: diverse in age, gender, cultural background, thinking styles, and perspectives. Diverse teams tend to focus on facts and remain objective, they tend to process facts more carefully, and they dodge the pitfalls of conformity in their decision-making processes. Finally, the decision-making team must be kept to a manageable size. Our experience is that six to fifteen members is productive. If the problem involves many stakeholders, use the Accordion Process presented in chapter 1 to involve them, but keep the size of the core problem-solving team to around fifteen or less.

THE ROLE OF THE FACILITATOR

A decision-making team is usually focused on solving the problem and not on how the team is functioning. The role of the facilitator is to concentrate on the processes of the group, not on the "content" of solving the problem. Doyle and Straus (1993) suggest that there are four distinct roles that exist in most decision-making teams: leader, group member, facilitator, and recorder. The first two roles focus on the task of solving the problem, while the last two focus on the processes and functioning of the group. In their approach to managing meetings, these roles are carried out by different people. For the purpose of this book, we will reflect only on the role of the facilitator. Doyle and Straus indicate that the facilitator

- is a neutral servant of the team,
- does not evaluate or contribute ideas related to the SiTNA,
- focuses the energy of the group on the task at hand,
- suggests possible methods and procedures for dealing with the SiTNA,
- protects individuals and their ideas from attack,
- encourages everyone to participate,
- helps the group find win-win solutions, and
- coordinates pre- and post-meeting logistics.

In general, it is the responsibility of the facilitator to move the team through the stages of development and the steps in DM as well as assist them in maintaining their productivity in dealing with the SiTNA. The facilitator suggests and facilitates the process, keeping the communication and interaction open and flowing. He or she does not get involved in the content of the problem itself; instead, the facilitator plays an active and assertive role in the processes of the team.

In self-managed teams that have a long history of working together, the role of the facilitator may flow within the group. For ad hoc teams that come together to deal with a specific decision, it is often better to include a neutral person to carry out the role of the facilitator. This person must be people centered and task focused.

The facilitator should understand the decision-making steps described in this book and know how to use structuring devices to aid the team in reaching a decision. This person must understand how teams develop to become productive at problem solving and have skills in facilitating meetings, managing collaboration, and bringing groups to consensus.

In situations involving hostile participants, controversial problems, or large groups of stakeholders, you may want to consider using co-facilitators. This way they can provide feedback to each other and can tag-team during difficult sessions.

TEAM DEVELOPMENT

While this book provides specific steps that will assist you in DM, when working with a team in the decision-making process, you must concern yourself with development of the team so that they become efficient and effective in dealing with the SiTNA. There are two concerns when working with teams: first, how they deal with the task of DM, and, second, how they relate and work together as people. Teams move through distinct phases in each of these areas as they become productive at working together to accomplish the goals of the team.

In their model of group development, shown in figure 8.1, Jones and Bearley (1998) describe four primary stages on the two dimensions of task behaviors and process behavior, through which teams must move to become effective. On the task dimension, teams move through orientation, organization, open data flow, and finally to problem solving. On the process (people) dimension, teams move through dependency, conflict, cohesion, and then to interdependence. The movement on these two dimensions together makes up the stages of team development of the immature, fractionated, sharing, and effective team.

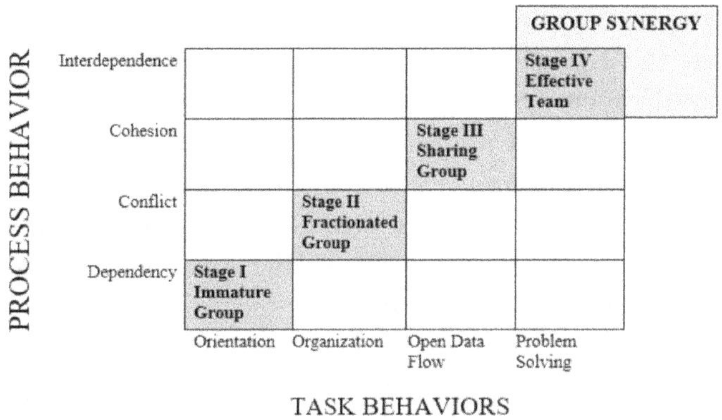

Figure 8.1. Process Behavior vs. Task Behaviors. ***Author created (1st edition)***

To be productive at problem solving, the team must consistently function in stages III and IV, depending on the expected outcome at the time. The facilitator must focus on assessing the current state of the team, then choose strategies and techniques to move or maintain the team to the appropriate stage.

The mind-set step of the decision-making approach presented earlier in this book is clearly designed for moving the team through the immature and fractionated group stages. Each time the team comes together, the facilitator must revisit these stages to ensure progress toward problem solving. Also, if the makeup of the group changes, or the task of a meeting changes, these early stages must be quickly revisited. Many of the structuring devices in this book are designed to give the facilitator tools to aid the team at different stages. Processes such as agenda building, norm setting, and establishing clear agreements aid in moving quickly through stages I and II.

The best preparation for the future productivity of the team is to use the problem-solving approach within the mind-set step to build the attitudes, beliefs, behaviors, and agreements required to support the team in stages I and II of their development. The facilitator then conscientiously moves the team through these initial stages at each meeting.

Team Development and the Problem-Solving Steps

Mind-set is the most important step in terms of initial team development, especially in stages I and II. When the team first forms, there are many concerns and questions related to the first two stages, for example, Why are we here? Who's here and why? What are the expectations of the team? How are we to proceed? What are our constraints? How will we work together? What are our expectations of each other? Also, it is during these initial stages that the facilitator must set the expectations, norms, and agreements that the team will live by for the remainder of the decision-making steps. It is here that you set the tone for the future success of the team. In addition, the facilitator must move the team through all four stages to complete this step.

In order to successfully share needs and ideas during the mind-set step, the facilitator must move the group to stage III, open data flow. This has to be a safe space where there is trust enough to share and structures in place to prevent the session from turning into a debate session. Finally, the team needs to move to stage IV so that they can come to consensus on how the group will relate and work together.

During the problem-definition step, the team ought to be in stage III, open data flow, and cohesive to share ideas and information about the SiTNA. The group then needs to move to stage IV to come to an agreement on the actual definition of the problem. The facilitator should continue to move the group through the early stages at each meeting to get members reoriented, clear any personal or interpersonal issues, and agree on the tasks and reengage the predetermined group norms.

Developing solution criteria requires that the team function at stages III and IV. Open data flow is necessary for people to identify, share, and carry on a dialogue about possible criteria. The team needs to progress toward the problem-solving stage to come to consensus on the final solution criteria for the SiTNA. As usual, the facilitator must pay attention to the first stages at each meeting in case there is any possibility for disagreement and conflict concerning the solution criteria.

The most successful sessions at generating possible solutions require the team to function in stage III where they have open communications and feel free to be creative. It is especially important that the facilitator deal with any personal or interpersonal issues at the beginning of these meetings and set the stage for individual and group spontaneity. The team may spend brief periods in stage IV winnowing the possibilities to a manageable list.

Solution choice requires concentrated effort in stage IV, and the facilitator again may need to focus on possible conflicts, working the team to a win-win choice. There may be some time spent in stage III identifying benefits, consequences, and risks, as well as collecting more information on some of the possibilities.

Implementation often requires the highest level of interdependence. It is in this step that members of the team are functioning interdependently carrying out the implementation plan. This step requires that the team function at a high task level as it plans the implementation. The facilitator may need to spend more time in stages I and II, especially if new members are brought onto the implementation team.

Intentional planning for team development can serve as a powerful assessment and diagnostic tool for the facilitator, resulting in group productivity. Additionally, it can serve as a tool to help the facilitator select the appropriate structuring device or intervention for the team.

RUNNING PRODUCTIVE MEETINGS

When you are meeting with a team, it is important to realize people can bring baggage to any organizational situation. With that in mind, it is important to do a kind of preventative maintenance first. The PITS model (Personal, Interpersonal, Task, and Summary) was developed to deal with this phenomenon (Jones and Bearley, 1994). The four steps in the PITS approach are the following:

P: Personal. Sharing what is going on with you these days.
I: Interpersonal. Clearing perceptions of each other.
T: Task. Getting on with the job of clarifying the situation and developing a plan.
S: Summary. Summarizing decisions, next steps, and responsibilities, etc.

The use of the PITS model requires that all participants open themselves up to each other, forming a working relationship, before they concentrate on the task.

Often, members of decision-making teams seldom discuss who they are or "where they're at" with each other, and their lack of openness results in poor plans, inadequate buy-in, and lack of implementation. This model not only can be used in decision-making teams but also can serve as a model for other gatherings such as staff meetings.

PRIMING CREATIVITY

Coming to win-win decisions and resolutions to problems often requires new ways of thinking about the situation. The members of the team are often called on to move outside of their comfort zone and into new arenas. To accomplish this, the facilitator must often "prime the pump" of creativity so that new ideas can flow within the team. To do this, the facilitator moves the group from their current, concrete ways of thinking about the situation, to the abstract, then back to the concrete, but with a new orientation drawn from the abstract. We suggest two ways to initiate this paradigm shift in the way the team approaches the decision-making situation: storytelling and imagery.

While storytelling is often done through writing, it may be done verbally or through techniques such as role plays. For now, we will focus on writing since it is the easiest to orchestrate and requires less risk on the part of the team members. Although there are many ways to release creativity through writing, here are five ways that we have used successfully.

1. Have each member write a letter, for example, when setting the vision of the team, have them write a letter to someone in the future describing the outcomes of the vision.
2. Have each member write a newspaper article, for example, the article might describe the implementation of a new plan that resolves the situation, or an editorial might describe the requirements of a solution.
3. For a quick "burst" of creativity, have each member come up with words, such as adjectives, that describe the current and future state of the team or decision situation. For example, if the team seems "stuck," have each member write several adjectives that describe how they are feeling "right now" about the state of the process. Then, have them write several words that describe what would be better for them.
4. Writing scenarios is a useful way to look at a variety of conditions in depth. For example, you might use scenarios to develop an implementation plan or to identify possible outcomes of various solutions.
5. Have the group watch a film or video clip, then have them write on how this clip might be a metaphor for the problem at hand. What does the fictionalized story tell us about the real SiTNA?

A facilitator can use writing at any step to uncover how the group is feeling about where they are. It is especially useful in priming creativity in the problem definition, generating possible solutions, and planning for implementation.

Imagery is used to get the team to dream so that they can create. A facilitator can use mental approaches such as guided imagery, fantasy, and quick word association, or they can use a combination of physical and mental strategies such as collages, building artifacts, or creating metaphors. These techniques are especially useful during problem definition and for developing possible solutions; however, the facilitator can use them any time they feel that the team needs to free their thinking.

The advantage of all of these approaches is that they free individuals from the ties of current assumptions and forces them to deal in the creative domain. Creativity unleashes possibilities that many of us do not realize are within. Creativity induces possibilities.

QUESTIONS

The use of questions is one of the most valuable tools for a facilitator. They can be used to clarify, probe, generate dialogue, and help us cull information. They can also prevent the facilitator from getting hooked into the task of the group. In his book *The Fifth Discipline*, Senge (2006) distinguishes between dialogue and discussion. The quality movement supports the need for dialogue with customers, vendors, and employees rather than adversarial approaches. Questions provide a mechanism for focusing the decision-making team on dialogue rather than discussion and debate.

Questions to Encourage Dialogue

The idea of using questions to encourage dialogue is not new. The Socratic approach, used as a primary method of teaching and learning, is designed to develop a dialogue. Elder and Paul (1998) suggest six types of questions that the facilitator can use:

1. Questions of clarification:

   What do you mean by . . . ?
   Could you put it another way?
   What do you think the SiTNA is here?
   Could you give me an example?
   Why do you think that?

2. Questions that probe assumptions:

   What are you assuming?
   What might be some different assumptions?
   Is this always true?
   Why is it true for this SiTNA?

3. Questions that probe reasons, evidence, and causes:

   Why do you say that?
   How do you know?
   What is your evidence of that? What do you suppose causes that?
   Are those adequate reasons?
   Where can we go to find the causes?

4. Questions about viewpoints and perspectives:

   How would your constituents respond?
   How are your ideas different than . . . ?
   How do you suppose . . . would respond?
   Why do you see it that way?
   What would someone who disagrees with you say?

5. Questions that probe implications and consequences:

   What are the consequences of that?
   What effect would that have on . . . ?
   If that is the case, then what else must be true?
   If we did this, what might happen?
   What is the worst/best case?

6. Questions about questions:

   How can we find out?
   Does everyone understand the question?
   Do we all agree that this is the question/situation?
   Why is this question important?
   Do we need more information to answer this question?

Several of the structuring devices presented in this book, for example, the Why Cycle and the Cause/Effect Diagram, are based on the use of questions. In addition, the facilitator can use questions to keep the group in dialogue rather than digressing to discussion, debating, or arguing. Also, questions are powerful tools to move toward group consensus.

If the facilitator is feeling they are getting pulled into the task, the question is a good way to maintain neutrality and to stay apart from the decision. For example, it is not uncommon for a member of the team to ask the facilitator "What do you think the problem is?" or "What do you think the decision should be?" If the facilitator "takes the bait" and gives an opinion, neutrality is lost with the group and becomes part of the problem. In this case, use a question to deflect or boomerang the question back to the team.

Questions and the Decision-Making Steps

Questions are useful in all six of the decision-making steps. The following are a few examples of some questions that a facilitator might use in each step. Use these to trigger your thinking as a facilitator about questions you can use with your team and in your environment.

1. Mind-Set

   What are your needs?
   What would you like to see as a possible outcome?
   What's going on between/among groups that can help/hinder?
   Who's involved?
   What are our current attitudes/beliefs? What would we like them to be?
   How do we want to work with each other?
   What are your personal constraints?

2. Problem Definition

   What is the problem?
   Is this the real problem? How do we know?
   How do we see the problem "playing out" in this organization?

What are the causes of this problem?
What would happen if we didn't do anything about this situation?

3. Solution Criteria

How will we know we have a good solution?
What would make a bad decision?
How are our solution needs alike/different?
What are the measures for that?

4. Solution Possibilities

What are some possible solutions?
What might we do about the situation?
What are others doing?
Are there some other ways?

5. Solution Choice

Which of the possible solutions works best for us?
What are the benefits/consequences of each possible solution?
Can we combine some of the possibilities to make a better/more workable/more accepted solution?
Are we ready to choose?

6. Implementation

How do we get there?
Who's going to do what, when . . . ?
Who's going to monitor? How will they do this?
How are we going to manage this?
How will we know when we did it right?
How much can we do at one time?

Questions are important in the decision-making process, both in conjunction and independent of structuring devices. A good facilitator is a good questioner.

KEEPING THE TEAM PRODUCTIVE

Sometimes teams get bogged down, and start thinking and acting in unproductive ways. If this phase persists, it can sap the energy from the team and lead to mediocre decisions. The facilitator must stay in touch with the current state of the team and be prepared to intervene when needed. For example, if the team is stuck in thinking "this is terrible" about the problem, switch them to a positive way of looking at the situation. Remember, the mind-set step is intended to set a positive focus on the situation and to establish productive ways for the team to relate to each other and to think about the situation.

There are two primary ways to change the state of the group: physical and emotional. Physical involves actual movement, which increases the flow of blood and changes the body chemistry. It causes the brain to make chemicals that stimulate the body, increasing energy and creativity, and generates positive emotions. Emotional changes involve changing the way we think, talk, and feel about a situation or event. Imagery and questions are tools that the facilitator can use to change the emotional state. The strongest approach is to use both together, thus changing the physical conditions of the body while changing the way people are thinking about the situation. At first, this may seem uncomfortable and unorthodox to the group; however, once members do it a few times, they come to appreciate the renewal and focus it brings to the decision-making effort.

CONCLUDING NOTE

The main thrust of this book is around defining DM and articulating appropriate structuring devices to aid the decision process. This is not a book about group facilitation or the leadership of group process; however, we felt that we would be remiss if we failed to couple strong process considerations with appropriate decision-making applications. Forming problem-solving teams, facilitating, and developing those teams, priming their creativity, and keeping them productive all become crucial parts of the success of DM. You cannot do one without the other.

Further, another important aspect is the use of thoughtful questions to probe and to spur the substantive decision process. The questions we have provided are not sufficient themselves but, rather, suggestions as a starting point for decision-making inquiry (see table 8.1). Use of the decision steps and structures defined earlier are most effective when used with well-conceived facilitation techniques.

Table 8.1. Questions to Encourage Dialogue. ***Author created (updated from 1st edition)***

Questions to Encourage Dialogue	Questions of clarification: What do you mean by . . . ? Could you put it another way? What do you think the SiTNA is here? Could you give me an example? Why do you think that? Questions that probe assumptions: What are you assuming? What might be some different assumptions? Is this always true? Why is it true for this SiTNA? Questions that probe reasons, evidence, and causes: Why do you say that? How do you know? What is your evidence of that? What do you suppose causes that? Are those adequate reasons? Where can we go to find the causes? Questions about viewpoints and perspectives: How would your constituents respond? How are your ideas different than . . . ? How do you suppose . . . would respond? Why do you see it that way? What would someone who disagrees with you say? Questions that probe implications and consequences: What are the consequences of that? What effect would that have on . . . ? If that is the case, then what else must be true? If we did this, what might happen? What is the worst/best case? Questions about questions: How can we find out? Does everyone understand the question? Do we all agree that this is the question/situation? Why is this question important? Do we need more information to answer this question?

Chapter Nine

Warning Signs on the Road to Decision Making

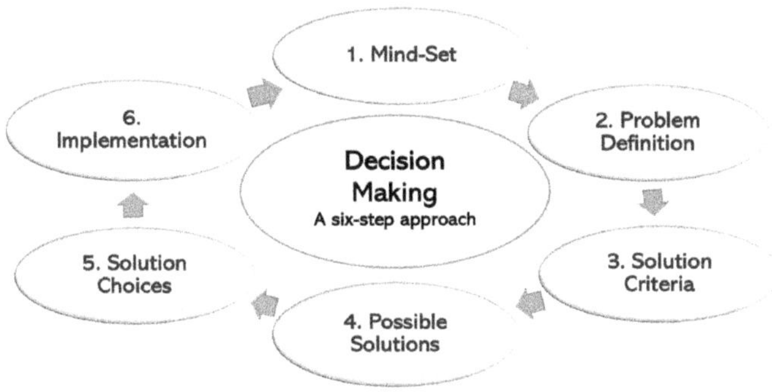

Figure 9.0. Decision Making: A Six-Step Approach.
Author created (updated from 1st edition)

For every journey on the road to effective decision making (DM), there are at least one or two potholes. This chapter will describe some warning signs of the more common or egregious problems confronted by decision makers, in the hope that you will minimize their effect on your process. This chapter is built on two assumptions:

1. There is no perfect process. Compromises and mistakes will occur with any attempt to lead human groups toward the future. The hope is that you will keep the imperfections to a minimum and that they will have little impact on the quality of your decision.
2. Potholes can occur at any step. There is no "safe" stage where the process is guaranteed. It takes skill and concentration from the decision-process leader to make sure that DM goes well.

With these assumptions in mind, we would like to suggest the following warning signs to you. These are our caution signs to you on your road to DM.

IGNORE TOXICITY AT YOUR OWN RISK

Figure 9.1. Poison.
Author created (1st edition)

One of the temptations in the mind-set stage is to ignore the toxicity in the organization and jump into the problem-definition stage. "Let's get on with the job at hand" often seems more important than the process. The dilemma is that the more toxic the organization (that is, the more it is rife with distrust, hopelessness, and anger), the more guerrilla warfare you will incur throughout the process. Participants will sabotage and undercut the process, and little will result. In order for the process of DM to work, you have to take time to address and highlight the pools of toxicity. This is not to say that all organizations are toxic, but those that need to be confronted and scrubbed a bit cleaner. Remember, you cannot change the past, but you can confront the past in a way that it does not intrude on the future. As historians have long told us, not knowing our past dooms us to repeat it. Ignore toxicity and ensure that it will be repeated. Confront it, get healthier, and then move toward DM.

GO SLOW TO GO FAST

Figure 9.2. Slow. *Author created (updated from 1st edition)*

Paralleling the Pareto principle, we argue that 80 percent of your time should be spent in the planning phases of DM and 20 percent in the solution phase. The opposite is more typically true in practice. We rush through steps 1–4 to get to step 5, solution choice. We take one meeting to plan and four meetings to fight over the solution and defend our position.

I had a meeting group that actually met twice a month for one year to decide on some relatively minor changes. The first meeting they did the planning; the second meeting they set the decision schedule, and the other eighteen meetings they argued for each of their vested interests. It was the most frustrating process I ever experienced. When it was over, no one liked the decision.

It is important to remember that you must go slow in order to go fast. By that, we mean you need to put your time in the right place, up front. When all participants have a positive and mutual mind-set and they all understand the problem, then solution choice goes quickly. High performance requires positive and thorough preparation.

BEWARE OF ROCKS

Figure 9.3. Falling Rocks. *Author created (updated from 1st edition)*

There are times when the decision maker really knows the answer she wants and is only using the group to come to the right answer. We describe this circumstance as "Bring me a rock; no, not that rock." We send groups out to find the right rock, the right answer. This is antithetical to group empowerment and effective DM that we have described in this book as a process where participants exercise judgment in finding a solution or set of solutions to an identified problem. If an answer is already known and predetermined, do not send a group out to find it. Make it yourself and accept the results. Otherwise, your team members will feel deflated and inept. They are being put through the motions of problem solving but not the true process. Effective DM says, "Bring me a rock, any rock that works, and I'll use it."

BEWARE OF ROCKS II

Figure 9.4. Falling Rocks II. *Author created (1st edition)*

A related form of process destruction occurs when the decision maker preempts the final decision after the process is well on its way to resolution. We have seen this occur on several occasions. Boundary committees will work long and hard to decide on intelligent school boundaries, only to have their recommendations preempted by nervous board members facing pockets of political complaints. These board members should never have initiated the boundary review process if they were not willing to face political complaints. Preempting the process only serves to debilitate future processes. The result will be people asking, "Why should we work so hard when they won't listen anyway?"

I remember working with a company president who was at a loss why his subordinates were frustrated with him. "I asked them to give me a recommendation about expenditure cuts, but I could see that they weren't going anywhere. So, I gave them my suggestions. I just wanted to set them right." When you preempt decisions of an ongoing decision group, you simply bury participants in an avalanche of despair and apathy. They give up. Avalanches are never good, particularly when you are at the bottom of them. Avoid starting them; avoid being in them.

But what if you inherit an organization with a history of avalanches and a host of people who have no faith in decision processes? What do you do?

1. Establish with the decision maker that the next process will not be preempted
2. Determine in the new situation that needs attention (SiTNA) what are unacceptable outcomes and what are the political and budgeting parameters
3. Work with the new decision team on the mind-set stage; have them meet with the decision maker
4. Meet periodically with the decision maker to review decision progress
5. Broadcast preliminary drafts of decision results; get buy-in

Even when all of this is done, there will be residual suspicion and distrust. Once you have been buried by an avalanche, it takes a long time to get over being edgy. Distrust remains, but it will eventually dissipate in the face of consistently rewarded trust.

GAPS AHEAD

Figure 9.5. Open Hole. *Author created (updated from 1st edition)*

DM takes skill. Without such skills or insights, DM is simply pooling collective ignorance. Therefore, one of the potholes you have to watch out for is skill deficiency. Do the participants have the necessary skills and insights to carry out the decision process? These skills fall into five domains:

1. Process skills to carry out the problem-solving endeavor
2. Substantive skills in understanding the nature of the SiTNA under discussion; if you are deciding about marketing and you know nothing about marketing, then you have no substantive skills to apply to the issue
3. Analytical skills in processing information
4. Political skills in working within and outside the organization
5. Practical skills in solution implementation and planning

Each individual does not need to have all skills. But someone in the group needs to have each of the above skills. These become the role of facilitator, expert, analyst, politician, and implementer. When the group lacks any or all of these roles or skills, then training or participant recruitment is necessary early on in the process.

BEWARE OF GROUP THINK

Figure 9.6. Group Thinking. *Author created (updated from 1st edition)*

Sometimes groups become so comfortable with each other, or so disinclined to disagree with each other, that they fall into group think. This is characterized by a lot of head nodding, little confrontation, quick movement to resolution, and much process satisfaction. On the surface, it appears to be an effective process, but typically it leads to low-quality decisions and limited innovation. Group think is usually the consequence of very high or very low group cohesion. Group think is ineffective because it fails to ask the hard question or to challenge existing assumptions or paradigms. It is comfortable and self-deluding. One of the things we know about strong, high-performing decision teams is that they experience open and honest conflict. They challenge and question. Beware of being seduced into seeing group think as good. It is a destructive, narcotic trap.

VOLUNTEER CROSSING AHEAD

Figure 9.7. VC. *Author created (updated from 1st edition)*

Volunteers are the blessing and the bane of all organizations. We need volunteers to add to the workforces of most nonprofit organizations. We need volunteers to fill out task forces and action committees. We need volunteers to bring fresh insights and new perspectives. But volunteers are almost never the right people to lead the decision process. How often have you been in groups and had someone ask, "Who would like to facilitate this group?" Unerringly, the last person you would choose quickly raises his hand, and everyone goes along with the choice. They are too afraid to offend. Always choose the process leader; never leave it to the first volunteer. The role of facilitation is too important to leave to just anyone to do. An unskilled facilitator will undoubtedly ignore much of the process and push for undue closure or personal gratification. When it comes to the key skills needed for the group, choose or appoint members who will bring effective resolution to the current SiTNA.

DON'T YIELD

Figure 9.8. No Yield. *Author created (updated from 1st edition)*

One of the potholes we often see is the instinct of decision-making participants to yield to the presumed preferences of upper-level decision makers. I had a quality circle group that spent much of its time trying to guess what the "suits" upstairs really wanted. They spent most of their energy trying to please, rather than seriously confronting the needs at hand. In other cases, I've seen this occur when the group has been dispirited by previous avalanches and is simply conditioned to give the right answer, the politically correct answer, or the career-advancing answer. In these cases, this was not DM but collective kowtowing. It is important to clarify givens, but then independence is called for. Decide to the best of your ability; do not yield to presumed preferences.

CURVY ROAD NEXT FEW MILES

Figure 9.9. Curvy Road. *Author created (1st edition)*

If people were only objective. If decisions were only rational. If only we had all the information we needed to decide. These are the cries of the rational decision maker who believes in data and analysis. But, alas, rationality is but a small part of DM and change. Rationality believes in linearity and straight pathways toward the future. Reality, however, dictates that the road is full of curves with few straightaways.

There are instead personal needs, political constraints, budgetary demands, and changing circumstances. DM is full of curves, and we simply need to drive accordingly. It is not the curves that destroy us but how we respond to them. Acknowledge the political realities all around; respond to personal needs and aspirations; live with budgetary constraints; and measure and react accordingly to changing environmental controls. In these very difficult times, take the curves smoothly and begin to enjoy the road ahead. It would be easier if the road were straighter; it would take less care and concentration, but in a world beyond the J curve, this is not likely to happen. You are not likely to optimize. Be content with satisficing.

STOP THE JARGON

Figure 9.10. Stop. *Author created (1st edition)*

Too many of us hide behind the jargon. We need to redefine the Continuous Quality Improvement (CQI) process to promote TQM teams. Our Special Education Local Plan Area (SELPA) is looking for a new individualized education program (IEP) process. We are lacking subsystem articulation. These are all real problem statements we have recently run into. To some, these statements are remarkably clear; to others they're nothing but a jumble of letters and words. The first and third of these groups do not bother us as much as the middle group; those presumably clear. These are the people who proceed as if they understand the problem, but they really don't. They allow jargon and vagueness to obscure the real problem. It is important to state problems in simple English. The question I ask myself is, "Will my eighth-grade son understand the issue?" If not, then it is not stated clearly enough. Remember, it is much easier to go from the simple to the complex than to go from the complex to the simple.

PASS TIME CAREFULLY

Figure 9.11. Pass with Care. ***Author created (1st edition)***

There is an old dictum that goes "Time is money." In the world of increasing demands, the adage may need to be rewritten, "Time is more important than money." Time is one of the dominant issues for most grown-ups. It is a key variable in product selection. It is also a key variable in trust. When you utilize time effectively, you sow trust in those with whom you work. Because of this reality, you need to pass time carefully in the decision process. Do not waste it. In this book, we have urged you to carefully apply six steps in DM and to use structuring devices along the way.

This is not a license to waste time. In fact, one of the prime reasons for structuring devices is to save time. You need to be both thorough and efficient. Obviously, different decision situations will call for different time demands, but keeping wasted time to a minimum is essential in instilling faith and trust in participants. In chapter 7, we not only described the process but proposed time lines for each scenario. Three of the four scenarios called for time lines of ten hours or less. We believe that this is a typical time expectation for most SiTNAs. Most of you will probably take longer and waste too much time. Pass time carefully. Use it efficiently. This may be the biggest pothole of them all, so heed it well. Pass time carefully.

FINAL CAVEAT

Figure 9.12. This Way Out. ***Author created (updated from 1st edition)***

These road signs are not meant to deter you from your journey to effective DM. Rather, they are meant as cautions, as warnings to heed along the road. The fewer potholes you hit, the smoother the journey.

Chapter Ten

This Stuff Works

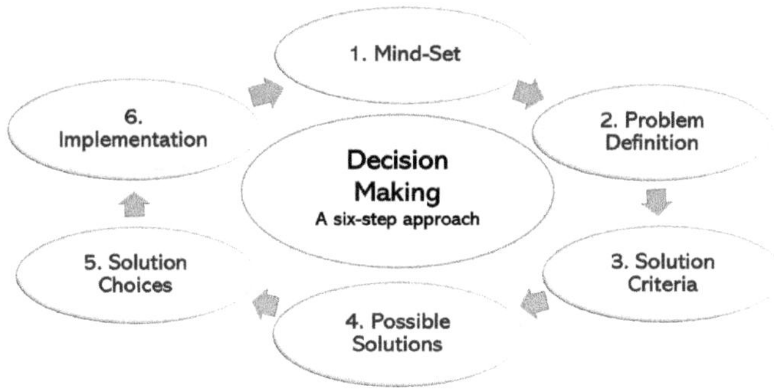

Figure 10.0. Decision Making: A Six-Step Approach.
Author created (updated from 1st edition)

In the previous nine chapters, we have taken a journey through the world of decision making (DM) and structuring devices. We have shown and described to you fifty-three structuring devices and explained how they can improve the speed and quality of your DM. In essence, we have provided a map of the decision process. Our hope is that you will use it to the fullest. Our fear is that you will ignore it.

ROAD MAP

I grew up on a farm in rural America where there were not a lot of street names or signs (this, of course, was years before GPS). In that kind of world, you just found your way on instinct and experience. As it were, whenever my family took a trip, we inevitably got lost. My father hated to consult a map or ask questions at a gas station. He knew that he would eventually "find it." As long as we stayed in a rural area, he was generally successful. But in larger cities he was lost, and he dragged all of us along with him.

That is our fear for you. A lot of you are excellent, instinctive decision makers. You know where you are going. But the world is changing, and so is the extent of information and knowledge needed to be successful. The world of DM is no longer rustic, or tame, or stable. It is demanding, fast paced, and urban. You need road maps to find your way. Otherwise, you will not only waste your own time, but also that of a lot of other people.

I always shake my head in amusement when an ex-student or client calls me and declares, with some amazement, "This stuff really works." Yes, it does. It works better with practice, and it works better with some skills in facilitation. But it does work. Road maps do give you direction. The six-step decision process and the structuring devices are your road maps to effective DM. We encourage you to take the time to use them.

KEYS TO THE MAP

We have tried to emphasize a number of precepts, or keys, to reading this map. While there are many we could mention, let us suggest ten in summary:

1. DM and problem solving are the same concept. They are not different.
2. DM is essentially the act of choosing and implementing a solution to an identifiable problem or situation.
3. In a world beyond the J curve, herding information is crucial to effective DM.
4. DM comprises six steps:

   Mind-set
   Problem definition
   Solution criteria

Possible solutions
Solution choice
Implementation

5. There are four categories of problems:

   Shortfall
   Opportunity
   Improvement
   New venture

6. To adapt the decision process, there are eight essential questions:

   a. Is there a history of toxicity in the organization?
   b. Have the members of the problem-solving team worked together before?
   c. What type of problem are you dealing with?
   d. Is the problem clear, and do we already have high agreement about problem definition and desirable outcomes?
   e. Does the organizational or problem context require that the solution criteria be quantified?
   f. Is there prior experience with this problem?
   g. Is there a need to prioritize the possible choices rather than choose from among them?
   h. Is there a time crunch, or is there high risk due to the consequences or cost?

7. There are fifty-three structuring devices that can be useful in facilitating DM.
8. Structuring devices need to fit the decision needs and steps.
9. DM needs to be accompanied with effective use of stories, questions, and facilitation techniques.
10. DM is rife with potential potholes that need to be avoided. Be savvy to the road signs.

We hope these keys help you understand the jumble of highways and byways that make up DM and problem solving.

EASY JOURNEY WHEN YOU STAY ALERT

When we began this book, we argued that DM is as easy as 1-2-3. But there is a caveat. It is easy as long as you stay alert. Driving from one coast to the other is not a difficult journey, and it is replete with beautiful sights and glorious vistas. But if you are not alert, if you fail to maintain your vehicle, if you ignore the road signs, or if you ignore your personal human needs, you will surely make the journey difficult and, perhaps, disastrous. DM is as easy as 1-2-3 if you

1. identify the steps in DM,
2. answer eight adaptive questions and adjust the core process accordingly, and
3. use structuring devices for the right needs.

But only if you stay alert. You need to build an effective decision-making team; you need to use effective facilitation techniques; you need to ask the right questions; and you need to use the right structuring devices. When you are alert, the journey is easy.

THIS STUFF WORKS

Remember, this stuff works. Experiment with it. Use it in a lot of small ways so that you are skilled when the big needs arise. Play with the devices. Do not be fearful of the unknown, and do not shy away from these devices that are quantitative. Be adventuresome and joyful and effective. Follow the map (see figure 10.2).

Now go forth and do good!

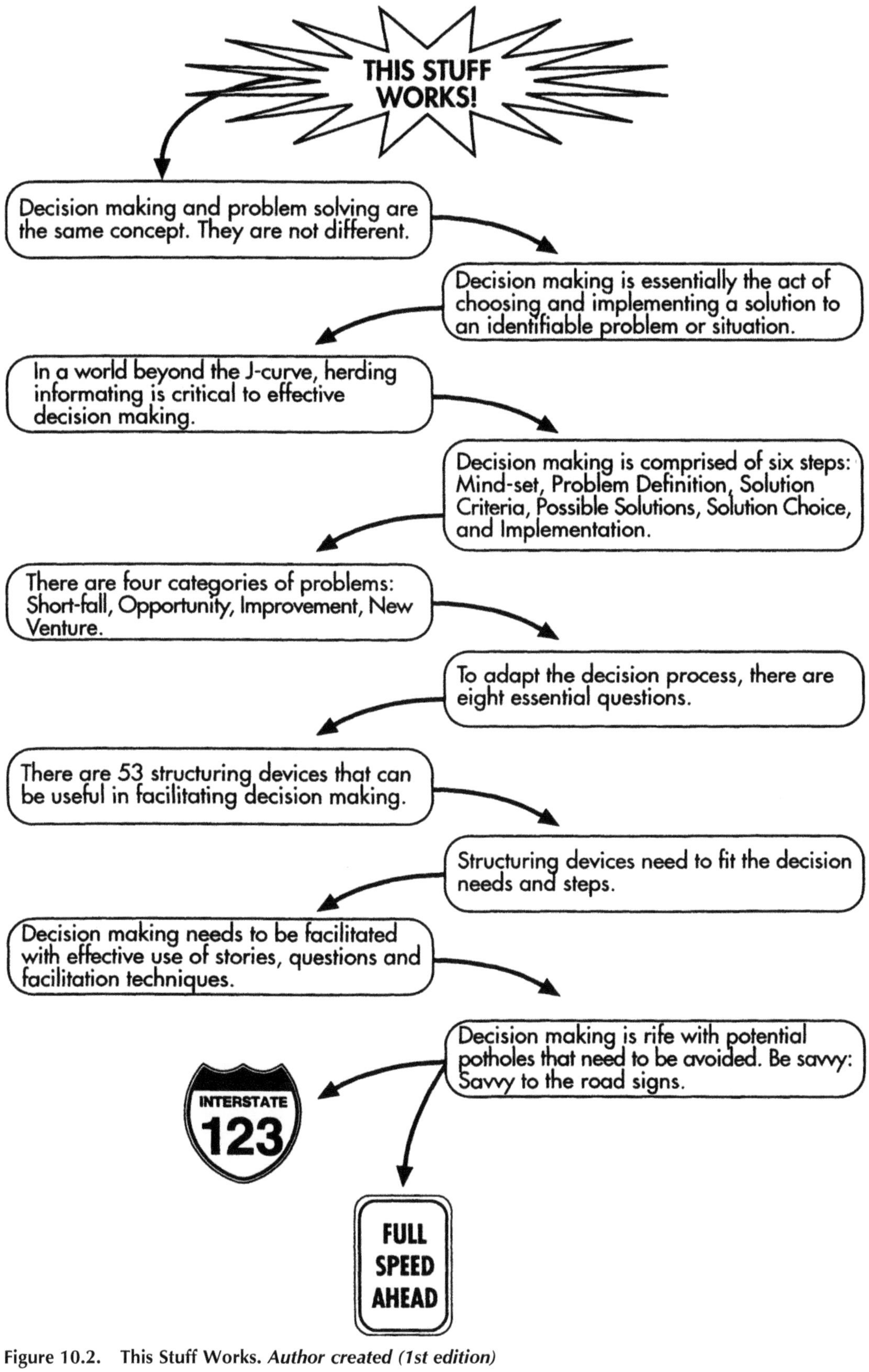

Figure 10.2. **This Stuff Works.** ***Author created (1st edition)***

References

Allen, B. J. (2011). *Difference matters: Communicating social identity* (2nd ed.). Waveland.

Brannick, M. T., & Prince, C. (1997). *An overview of team performance measurement.* Erlbaum.

Brassard, M., & Ritter, D. (1994). *The memory jogger.* GOAL/QPC.

Brassard, M., & Ritter, D. (2018). *The memory jogger 2: Tools for continuous improvement and effective planning* (2nd ed.). GOAL/QPC.

Bryson, J. M. (1988). *Strategic planning for public and nonprofit organizations: A guide to strengthening and sustaining organizational achievement.* Jossey-Bass.

Chang, R. Y., & Kelly, P. K. (1993). *Step-by-step problem solving.* Richard Chang Associates.

Chang, R. Y., & Kelly, P. K. (1999). *Step-by-step problem solving: A practical guide to ensure problems get (and stay) solved.* Pfeiffer.

Chang, R. Y., & Niedzwiecki, M. (1994). *Continuous improvement tools: Vol. 1. A Practical Guide to Achieve Quality Results*. Richard Chang Associates.

Cohen, M. D., March, J. G., & Olsen, J. P. (1972). A garbage can model of organizational choice. *Administrative Science Quarterly, 17*, 1–25.

Doyle, M., & Straus, D. (1986). *How to make meetings work.* Berkley.

Doyle, M., & Straus, D. (1993). *How to make meetings work.* Berkley.

Elder, L., & Paul, R. (1998). The role of Socratic questioning in thinking, teaching, and learning. *Clearing House: A Journal of Educational Strategies, Issues, and Ideas, 71*(5), 297–301. https://doi.org/10.1080/00098659809602729

Filley, A. C. (1975). *Interpersonal conflict resolution.* Scott, Foresman.

Fisher, R, Ury, W., & Patton, B. (1991). *Getting to yes: Negotiating agreement without giving in* (2nd ed.). Penguin.

Harvey, T. R. (1995). *Checklist for change* (2nd ed.). Scarecrow Press.

Harvey, T., & Drolet, B. (1994). *Building teams, building people*. Technomic.

Higgens, J. (1994). *101 creative problem-solving techniques*. New Management.

Hill, P. H. (1986). *Making decisions: A multidisciplinary introduction.* Benjamin Cummings.

Hill, P. H., Bedau, H. A., Chechile, R. A., Crochetiere, W. J., Kellerman, B. L., Ounjian, D., Pauker, S. G., Pauker, S. P., & Rubin, J. Z. (1979). *Making decisions: A multidisciplinary introduction.* Addison Wesley.

Jones, J. E., & Bearley, W. L. (1986). *Participative management profile*. HRDQ.

Jones, J. E., & Bearley, W. L. (1994). *Participative management profile*. HRDQ.

Jones, J. E., & Bearley, W. L. (1998). *Teambook: 27 exercises for enhancing work groups.* Organizational Universe Systems.

Jones, J. E., & Bearley, W. L. (2002). *High-performance problem solving*. Organizational Universe Systems.

Jones, J. E., & Pfeiffer, W. (1974). *The 1974 annual handbook for group facilitators.* University Associates.

Katzenbach, J. R., & Smith, D. K. (2015). *The wisdom of teams: Creating the high-performance organization.* Harper Business Review.

Klein, G. A., Orasanu, J., Calderwood, R., & Zsambok, C. (Eds.). (1993). *Decision making in action: Models and methods.* Ablex.

Klubnik, J. P., & Greenwood, P. F. (1994). *The team-based problem solver*. Irwin Professional.

Koberg, D., & Bagnall, J. (1981). *The all new universal traveler: A soft-systems guide to creativity, problem solving and the process of reaching goals*. Kauffman.

Koberg, D., & Bagnall, J. (1991). *The universal traveler.* Crisp.

Larson, Erik. (2017, September 21). New research: Diversity + inclusion = better decision making at work. *Forbes.* https://www.forbes.com/sites/eriklarson/2017/09/21/new-research-diversity-inclusion-better-decision-making-at-work/?sh=1c0e978a4cbf

Lewin, K. (1951). *Field theory in social science.* Harper & Row.

McGowan, M. (2016, August 31). *Conflict resolution through clarifying perceptions*. Business 2 Community. https://www.business2community.com/leadership/conflict-resolution-clarifying-perceptions-01642780

Moody, P. E. (1983). *Decision making: Proven methods for better decisions*. McGraw-Hill.

Murray, M. A. (1986). *Decisions: A comparative critique*. Pittman.

Nutt, P. C. (1989). *Making tough decisions: Tactics for improving managerial decision making*. Jossey-Bass.

Nutt, P. C. (1990). *Making tough decisions: Tactics for improving managerial decision making*. Jossey-Bass. Reprint.

Nutt, P. C., & Wilson, D. C. (2010). *Handbook of decision making*. Wiley-Blackwell.

Peters, T., & Waterman, R. H. (2006). *In search of excellence: Lessons from America's best-run companies*. Harper Business Review.

Quinlivan-Hall, D., & Renner, P. (1990). *In search of solutions*. PFR.

Quinlivan-Hall, D., & Renner, P. (1994). *In search of solutions: Sixty ways to guide your problem solving group*. Training Associates.

Reilly, A., & Jones, J. E. (1974). Team building. In J. W. Pfeiffer & J. E. Jones (Eds.), *The 1974 annual handbook for group facilitators*. University Associates.

Sakpal, M. (2019, September 20). *Diversity and inclusion build high-performance teams*. Gartner. https://www.gartner.com/smarterwithgartner/diversity-and-inclusion-build-high-performance-teams/

Scholtes, P. R., et al. (1994). *The team handbook for educators: How to use teams to improve quality*. Joiner Associates.

Seeds for Change. (2018, April 11). *How to make consensus genuinely democratic* [Video]. YouTube. https://www.youtube.com/watch?v=5Kns1LTtWEo

Senge, P. M. (2006). *The fifth discipline: The art and practice of the learning organization*. Crown.

Simon, H. A. (2012). *The new science of managerial decisions*. Prentice Hall.

SpaceX. (2021, February 2). *Human spaceflight*. https://www.spacex.com/human-spaceflight/

Stark, P. (2013, April 29). *Attitude is king in conflict resolution*. https://peterstark.com/attitude-conflict-resolution/

Stevens, S. S. (1956). The direct estimation of sensory magnitudes: Loudness. *American Journal of Psychology, 69*(1), 1–25.

Thomas, D. C. (1999). Cultural diversity and work group effectiveness: An experimental study. *Journal of Cross-Cultural Psychology, 30*(2). https://doi.org/10.1177/0022022199030002006

Thompson, J. (2017). *Organizations in action: Social science bases of administrative action*. McGraw-Hill.

Thompson, J., & Tudor, A. (1959). *"Strategies, structures, and processes of organizational decision" in comparative studies administration*. University of Pittsburgh Press.

Tosi, H. L., Mero, N. P., & Rizzo, J. R. (2000). *Managing organizational behavior* (4th ed.). Wiley-Blackwell.

Van Gundy, A. B. (1988). *Techniques of structured problem solving*. Van Nostrand Reinhold.

Viability. (1994). *Team works tool kit for team leaders and sponsors*. Corporate HR Performance Development Division, Corporate Training and Development.

Vroom, V. H., & Jago, A. G. (1988). *The new leadership: Managing participation in organizations*. Pearson.

Vroom, V. H., & Yetton, P. W. (2010). *Leadership and decision making*. University of Pittsburgh Press.

Weeks, D. (1994). *The eight essential steps to conflict resolution*. Tarcher Perigee.

Xerox Corp. (n.d.). *Problem solving user's manual*. Xerox Corp.

Yukl, G. (2012). *Leadership in organizations* (8th ed.). Prentice Hall.

About the Authors

Sharon M. Corkrum is a retired school district assistant superintendent. The first edition of this book evolved from her dissertation while at the University of La Verne. She is thrilled that this initial work has served so many leaders throughout the years. Corkrum recently relocated to the Seattle area, where she is enjoying time with her husband and extended family.

Shari L. Fox spent forty years as a K–12 educator, serving as a teacher, site and district administrator, and superintendent. She continues to serve K–12 educators as an executive coach to site and district administrators. In addition, Fox is an instructor in the doctoral program at the University of La Verne.

David C. Gustafson has spent the past two decades as a practitioner and leader in K–12 education at both the site and district levels. In addition, he has presented his research on virtual leadership and virtual learning both nationally and internationally. Gustafson continues to research and publish in academic journals and practitioner publications.

Thomas R. Harvey is professor emeritus in the organizational leadership doctoral program at the University of La Verne. He served as dean of the School of Organizational Management and chairman of the Department of Educational Management for fourteen years. He is the proud author of more than thirteen books dealing with change, politics, decision making, and building teams.

Deanna K. Keuilian has been a practitioner in the field of education for more than twenty years. She has extensive experience leading a variety of educational initiatives at the K–12 level. Additionally, she is an adjunct professor in the doctoral program at the University of La Verne and serves as a committee member for dissertations. She is most proud of both of her children's recent college graduation.

www.ingramcontent.com/pod-product-compliance
Ingram Content Group UK Ltd.
Pitfield, Milton Keynes, MK11 3LW, UK
UKHW051419150926
475561UK00005B/243

9 781475 863185